"Nolo's home page is worth bookmarking."
—WALL STREET JOURNAL

LEGAL INFORMATION ONLINE ANYTIME

24 hours a day

www.nolo.com

AT THE NOLO.COM SELF-HELP LAW CENTER ON THE WEB, YOU'LL FIND

- Nolo's comprehensive Legal Encyclopedia, with links to other online resources
- SharkTalk: Everybody's Legal Dictionary
- Auntie Nolo—if you've got questions, Auntie's got answers
- Update information on Nolo books and software
- The Law Store—over 250 self-help legal products including:
    Downloadable Software, Books, Form Kits and E-Guides
- Discounts and other good deals, plus our hilarious Shark Talk game
- Our ever-popular lawyer jokes
- NoloBriefs.com, our monthly email newsletter

Quality LAW BOOKS & SOFTWARE FOR NON-LAWYERS

Nolo.com legal books and software are consistently first-rate because:

- A dozen in-house Nolo legal editors, working with highly skilled authors, ensure that our products are accurate, up-to-date and easy to use.
- We know our books get better when we listen to what our customers tell us. (Yes, we really do want to hear from you—please fill out and return the card at the back of this book.)
- We are maniacal about updating every book and software program to keep up with changes in the law.
- Our commitment to a more democratic legal system informs all of our work.

OUR "NO-HASSLE" GUARANTEE

Return anything you buy directly from Nolo for any reason and we'll cheerfully refund your purchase price. No ifs, ands or buts.

AN IMPORTANT MESSAGE TO OUR READERS

This product provides information and general advice about the law. But laws and procedures change frequently, and they can be interpreted differently by different people. For specific advice geared to your specific situation, consult an expert. No book, software or other published material is a substitute for personalized advice from a knowledgeable lawyer licensed to practice law in your state.

FIRST EDITION

Surviving an IRS Tax Audit

by
Frederick W. Daily

KEEPING UP TO DATE

To keep its books up to date, Nolo issues new printings and new editions periodically. New printings reflect minor legal changes and technical corrections. New editions contain major legal changes, major text additions or major reorganizations. To find out if a later printing or edition of any Nolo book is available, call Nolo at 510-549-1976 or check our website: www.nolo.com.

To stay current, follow the "Update" service at our website: www.nolo.com. In another effort to help you use Nolo's latest materials, we offer a 35% discount off the purchase of the new edition of your Nolo book when you turn in the cover of an earlier edition. (See the "Special Upgrade Offer" in the back of the book.) This book was last revised in: OCTOBER 1999.

FIRST EDITION	October 1999
PRODUCTION	Lori Pacheco
EDITOR	Robin Leonard
PROOFREADER	Joe Sadusky
INDEX	Jane Meyerhofer
PRINTING	Consolidated Printers, Inc.
COVER	Toni Ihara

Daily, Frederick W., 1942-.
    Surviving an IRS tax audit / by Frederick W. Daily.
        p. cm.
    Includes index.
    ISBN 0-87337-537-8
    1. Tax auditing--United States--Popular works.
  KF6314.Z9 D277 1999
  346.7304--dc21   99-029725

CONTENTS

CHAPTER 5

HOW AN AUDITOR PREPARES FOR AN OFFICE OR FIELD AUDIT

CHAPTER 6

ATTENDING AN OFFICE OR FIELD AUDIT

CHAPTER 7

ENDING AN OFFICE OR FIELD AUDIT

CHAPTER 8

APPEALING YOUR AUDIT

CHAPTER 9

GOING TO COURT

CHAPTER 10

HELP BEYOND THIS BOOK

APPENDIX

INDEX

Audit Overview

Billy Bob and Peggy Sue Valley consider themselves the average American family. They have two kids, Bart and Lisa, and a ranch home. They are the proud owners of "Valley's Old Tyme Grub House," a Western theme restaurant and souvenir shop.

Billy Bob sings in a semi-professional country and western group whenever anyone asks. Peggy Sue operates a ScamWay dealership, a part-time home-based side business, selling propane cooking accessories. Bart, age 12, helps out at the restaurant to earn his allowance. Lisa, age 14, does some baby-sitting in the neighborhood. Life has its ups and downs, but basically all is good. That is, until a letter arrives at the Valley house with the return address identifying the sender as the Internal Revenue Service. Billy Bob opens the letter late one night after closing down the restaurant. He yells to Peggy Sue who is in the kitchen, "Hon, better come on in here. We need to talk about something. And, bring me a beer, please?"

We call them *audits*; the IRS prefers *examinations*. Whatever term you use, it describes one of life's most dreaded experiences—the IRS probing into your financial affairs.

A. What's an Audit?

An audit is the process by which the IRS determines whether you properly reported all of your income—the money you made—and took the correct deductions, exemptions and credits. If the IRS determines that you erred somewhere, you will be assessed additional taxes, interest and, usually, penalties. An assessment is the formal entry of a tax liability in your records at the IRS Service Center.

⚠️ **Owing without an audit.** Sometimes, the IRS reviews your tax return and determines you made errors in reporting your income or claiming deductions, exemptions or credits, but does not audit you. Instead, you simply get a billing notice (called an adjustment) for the additional amount the IRS believes you owe. If you've received such a bill from the IRS, see Chapter 2, Section B.

To determine if you've properly reported your income and claimed your deductions, exemptions and credits, Congress has given the IRS wide powers to examine your financial papers and records. IRS auditors can even ask other people about your financial affairs to determine if you are playing it straight with the IRS.

📖 IRS Publication 17, Your Federal Income Tax, explains the audit process—from the IRS' point of view. A copy of Publication 17 is in the Appendix. It's also available on the IRS' website at http://www.irs.ustreas.gov/forms_pubs/pubs.html.

The vast majority of tax returns are accepted by the IRS without question. Then why, you are no doubt wondering, did you get audited? While your chance of being formally audited in any one year is only about 1%, the odds *in your taxpaying lifetime* are closer to 50%. As your income increases, so does your audit likelihood. If you earn over $100,000 per year, you may endure any number of audits. Similarly, your likelihood of audit rises if you are self-employed. (See Section D, below, for more details on how audit victims are selected.)

In addition, the reality is that you can expect your audit to cost you money—five out of seven people who are audited owe additional taxes. A few people come out of an audit entitled to a tax refund, but don't count on it. The amount of money the IRS assesses in audits is 32 times greater than the amount the IRS gives back.

Furthermore, contrary to what you might have read, the burden of proving that you correctly reported your income and claimed your deductions, exemptions and credits is on you, not the IRS. With your audit notice, the IRS may have provided a checklist of items—typically deductions from your income—that the auditor will be investigating. You must demonstrate that the information on your tax return related to those items—and anything else the auditor raises—is correct. Think of the IRS as the "Show Me" state of Missouri. Critics have said that this means you are guilty until proven innocent.

Proving the correctness of your tax return is not always easy. The IRS wins well over 80% of all audits—mostly because people cannot verify what is on their tax returns. IRS auditors even admit that the biggest reason for this is poor recordkeeping, not dishonesty.

Once you've gotten over the shock of receiving an audit notice, various thoughts may be running through your head:

Why was I picked for an audit?

Did I make an enemy somewhere?

Does the IRS suspect me of doing something wrong?

Is the IRS going to put me in jail if they find out I've been cheating?

Will the auditor discover the money I made from playing the organ at weddings?

I lost my records in a move last year—what am I going to do?

Was I entitled to claim my mother as an exemption?

Will the IRS question my home office deductions?

Did I figure my business deductions correctly?

How will I ever pay the bill if I lose?

Should I hire a tax professional?

After reading this book, you should have answers to all of these questions. You will know why you were picked, how to prepare, what to do when you meet the auditor and what to do if the audit goes wrong. This chapter explains how the IRS selects taxpayers to be audited, what your goals should be and the rights every taxpayer has in dealing with the IRS. Chapters 2, 3 and 4 cover the different kinds of audits. Chapter 5 gives you a look at how an auditor prepares for an audit. Chapter 6 tells you what to do, and what not to do, when you meet an IRS auditor. Chapter 7 tells how audits are wrapped up and when to declare victory or throw in the towel. Chapters 8 and 9 guide you through appealing—and even taking the IRS to court. Chapter 10 provides resources beyond the book.

B. Do You Have to Know Tax Law to Win an Audit?

The audit process is a child of the Internal Revenue Code, or Tax Code, which contains thousands of pages of Congress at its worst—complex, contradictory and confusing language reflecting various economic, social and political goals of the past 15 decades. In addition, tax law is found in another 100,000 pages of IRS Regulations, Revenue Rulings, Letter Rulings, Manuals and Official Publications. Finally, thousands of federal court decisions tell us how the tax laws should be applied in individual cases.

You will never understand the tax laws. Few people do. Only tax professionals—tax lawyers, accountants and enrolled agents, with their years of special training and experience—come close. Even they tend to know specific areas of tax law, not the entire body of legal material.

But not knowing the tax laws may not be as much of a disadvantage as you might think. Tax law is so voluminous and complex, most auditors don't know it well either. Moreover, the training and experience level of IRS personnel is declining, while the law is getting more complex. So, auditors normally stick to predictable audit issues we cover in this book.

A minority of taxpayers with highly complex taxes will face specially trained auditors. Examples include investors in so-called tax shelters, real estate partnerships, family trusts and beneficiaries of charitable foundations. Even so—if you're prepared and grounded in the audit basics, you'll come out okay most of the time, experiencing the minimum damage. And if you don't like the outcome of your audit, you have several options for appealing. The auditor does not have the last word. (See Chapters 8 and 9.)

In a few hours, you can learn the tax law fundamentals you will need for your particular audit issues. Or you can call on a tax professional for help. Specific information on various tax issues is available in Chapter 10.

You can succeed in an audit without knowing any tax law. Many audit issues are factual, not legal. A factual issue is whether or not you incurred a business-related expense, such as "advertising." A legal issue is whether or not you were legally entitled to deduct that business expense.

C. Timing of Audits

The IRS is powerful, but not without limit. After getting over the shock of reading "we have selected your federal income tax return for examination," look carefully at the year or years on the audit notice. In general, after you file a tax return, the IRS has only three years to begin and end an audit of that return. If you filed it before the due date, April 15, the three years start running from April 15. If you filed on extension, August 15 or October 15, the three start running from that date.

If you were audited within the last two years and the IRS made no more than a thousand dollars or so in adjustments or issued a "no change" report, you should not be audited again. If you are, call the IRS and ask that the audit be canceled. Explain that you've already been audited recently and that the outcome was no or minimal tax owing. If the IRS employee is not aware of the IRS policy against repeat audits, ask to speak to a manager. This might not work, but it's worth a try.

1. Audit Notices for Years More Than Three Years Past

If any year on the audit notice is more than three years past, the IRS may have goofed. To check if it's a mistake, call the IRS and ask that the audit be canceled because of the three-year rule. If you're told that the audit is no mistake, head for a tax pro's office pronto.

In three situations, the IRS has more than three years to complete an audit of your tax return. So keep reading if you're being audited for a return filed more than three years past or are worried about an audit expanding into years gone by.

- If the IRS believes that you understated your income by 25% or more, the IRS has six years to complete an audit of your return.

- If the IRS believes that you filed a fraudulent return, there is no time limit for auditing that return. Tax fraud is conduct meant to deceive the IRS, such as using a false Social Security number. A really big mistake—even a stupid one—isn't fraud if it wasn't deliberate. Because the burden of proving fraud is always on the IRS, the IRS seldom audits returns after three years, even if the IRS believes that fraud is evident. So if the IRS just caught you doing something questionable, the IRS may expand the audit to returns filed within the last three years, but isn't likely to go back further.

- If you did not file a tax return, the IRS has forever to audit you. That's because the audit time-limit period, called the *statute of limitations*, starts running only if you file a tax return. As a practical matter, however, if you didn't file a return for a specific year and the IRS hasn't audited you within six years of the return's due date, you may have escaped the audit net. So if it's 2001 and you received an audit notice for your 1999 tax return, you probably don't need to worry about the IRS expanding your audit to cover 1988, when you never got around to filing.

2. Audit Notices Sent Toward the End of the Three-Year Period

Most likely, your audit notice is dated somewhere between 12 and 18 months after you filed your return, assuming the IRS isn't accusing you of understating your income by 25% or more or of fraud.

Remember that the IRS not only has three years to *begin* an audit of your return, but must *complete* the audit within three years of the filing date. On top of that, the Internal Revenue Manual directs auditors to complete audits within 28 months of when you filed your tax return. This allows the IRS an additional eight months to process any appeal.

Essentially, this means the IRS system is set up to allow auditors between ten and 16 months to open and close an audit. Sometimes, it is in your interest to slow down the process, and this book provides you with tips on how to do so. By delaying an audit, the auditor may face the 28-month deadline without having delved too far into your financial affairs.

D. Why You Were Selected for Audit

Like you, the Valleys want to know why they are being audited. Are they merely unlucky, or are more sinister forces at work?

There are nearly ten reasons why any one tax return is selected for further examination. This section explains each one. Knowing why you were chosen will help you prepare for the task ahead.

You'll never know for certain why the IRS got you. Still, there may be some clues. If you know what the IRS suspects, you can better prepare—or get professional help early on. An experienced tax pro can spot probable audit issues.

1. You Didn't File a Tax Return

As mentioned, the IRS has forever to audit if you didn't file a tax return, although you are likely to hear within three years of when the return was due. Still, it may seem odd that the IRS can check your correct income and exemptions, deductions and credits if you never filed a return. In reality, the IRS cares only about your income—the IRS doesn't grant you more than a single exemption and the standard deduction if you didn't file a tax return. You may be entitled to much more by filing a return, of course.

The IRS knows at least some of your income from data reports—1099 and W-2 forms—filed by those who paid you money. If the IRS' records show that you earned at least $6,000, the IRS computer looks to see if you have filed a tax return reporting the income. If there isn't one on file, the IRS can calculate your tax liability—in effect, file a tax return for you. The IRS handbook called the Internal Revenue Manual directs the auditor to write up a "reasonable and substantially correct" tax return, which is a license for IRS invention and creativity.

Individuals. In addition to W-2 and 1099 forms, IRS auditors rely on tables from the Bureau of Labor Statistics (BLS). They use BLS data to estimate your income and living expenses, particularly if the W-2 and 1099 forms on file show an impossibly small income for where you live, such as on Park Avenue in Manhattan. BLS tables show minimum funds necessary by ZIP code for living a simple lifestyle, taking into account the geographic area, family size and standard of living. If your income is below what the BLS tables say you need to earn to live where you do and support your family, the IRS will assume you earned enough to make up the difference.

Self-employed. IRS auditors may rely on published industry information to estimate a business owner's income. For instance, trade publications for U.S. auto parts retailers show average gross sales and profit margin. If Simon neglected to file a tax return, the IRS can ballpark how much Simon's Auto Parts World made based on the published information.

After an auditor guesstimates your income and minimum deductions for the year and your tax liability, the IRS mails an examination (audit) report to your last known address. In other words, if you didn't file a tax return, you are probably looking at an audit report, not an audit notice. Essentially, the IRS has selected income and deduction figures for you, completed a return, audited it without your participation and sent you the report.

If you receive the report, you can either sign it or contact the auditor and refute it with your own figures. Alternatively, you can file an original tax return with the auditor, which is probably your best bet. The IRS may not accept the return without seeing support for your numbers, in effect auditing the return.

If you don't sign the audit report or file your own return, the IRS must issue a Notice of Deficiency. This gives you 90 days to contest the IRS report in Tax Court. (See Chapter 9.) You do not have the right to appeal this IRS decision within the IRS, as you normally are allowed following an audit. (See Chapter 8.)

2. Computer Selection

The IRS' computer is to blame for two-thirds of all audits. Each year, your tax return data is sent to the IRS National Computer Center. There it is analyzed by a computer program called the Discriminant Function (DIF). Every tax return receives a numerical DIF rating—the higher the score, the more audit potential the return has. The DIF formula is super secret—few people even in the IRS know how it works or why a return gets a particular score. Outsiders guess that hundreds of variables on a tax return are compared to statistical models by this software program. Here is my take on what goes into the DIF scoring.

Ratios: Are you claiming more deductions than most similarly situated taxpayers? The chief component of IRS DIF scoring is likely to be how close your tax return is to the norm of others with similar deductions. According to Professor Amir Aczel (author of *How to Beat the IRS at Its Own Game*, $10.95, Four Walls Eight Windows Press), the IRS is most likely to audit returns with a high ratio of certain types of deductions to income. Three tax return schedules are critical to this process:

- Schedule A, itemized deductions such as medical expenses, unreimbursed employee expenses, state taxes, mortgage interest and charitable contributions

- Schedule C, profit and loss for unincorporated small businesses, and

- Schedule F, profit and loss for farms.

Aczel claims that as deductions exceed 50% of income, your audit likelihood rises. He lists precise ratios based on a study of 1,200 audit cases. For instance, self-employed people filing Schedule C are seldom audited when deductions are below 52% of their gross receipts. But, they are often audited when they claim expenses of more than 63% of their gross receipts. If you include a Schedule A with your tax return, Aczel claims you are most audit-safe when deductions are less than 44% of your gross income.

While Mr. Aczel's book is interesting, don't use it as a manual to avoid a tax audit. If you are entitled to a deduction, take it, no matter what the chances of audit. Just be sure to keep good records backing up why you took the deduction.

Other factors. According to the IRS Manual, only significant items are to be reviewed at an audit. What's significant depends on the IRS' overall view of the return as well as particular questionable items. Factors likely to figure into the audit scoring process—and most likely to be looked at in your audit—include the following:

- *Comparative size of an item to the rest of the return.* For example, a $5,000 deduction for medical expenses on a tax return reporting $25,000 in income would be significant, but not on a $100,000 return. Other red flags would be $19,000 of mortgage interest deduction on a return showing $18,000 of income or $32,000 of unreimbursed employee expenses on a return with income of only $17,500. These kinds of expense-income discrepancies offend common sense and stand out, although there may be a perfectly reasonable explanation for each.

- *An item on the return that is out of character for the taxpayer.* For instance, a plumber claiming expenses relating to a business airplane would cause suspicion. So would a taxpayer over age 65 who claims four minor dependent children.

- *An item that is reported in an inappropriate place on the return.* For example, $2,000 of credit card interest deducted along with business expenses is suspect. The IRS is concerned that you have improperly deducted your personal VISA interest charge as a business expense. Similarly, self-employment income simply listed as "miscellaneous" income without another form or schedule. Here, the IRS is watching out for someone who is trying to avoid paying self-employment (Social Security and Medicare) tax.

- *Evidence of intent to mislead the IRS on the face of the return.* Tax returns with missing schedules or forms not completely filled in raises an IRS audit picker's eyebrows. So does the "occupation" box left blank, or a stated occupation that does not match what the IRS has on record.

- *Your gross income.* The IRS goes after higher earners. The more your annual income exceeds $100,000, the more your likelihood of audit increases. The IRS simply believes that when you move into a high income bracket, you are more likely to cheat than when you are in a low income bracket.

• *Self-employment income.* The IRS targets people who are in business for themselves. Self-employed people are four times more often audited than are wage earners. Primarily, the IRS is scrutinizing Schedule C of sole proprietors.

• *Losses from businesses and investments claimed on your tax return.* The IRS may want to know how you paid your bills while losing money. Most likely to be audited are taxpayers reporting a business loss of more than a few thousand dollars. Losses from stock investments in privately held small companies also raise IRS eyebrows.

One in ten tax returns—those with the highest DIF scores—are initially computer-selected for audit consideration. IRS classifiers (human beings) then look at this batch and screen out nearly 90% of them. Sloppiness catches a classifier's attention. A messy return, especially if handwritten, stands out. A classifier may think you don't take your recordkeeping and tax reporting responsibilities very seriously. Round numbers—claiming $5,000 for business advertising, $2,000 for transportation and $1,500 for insurance—is a dead giveaway that you are estimating, not reporting from records. If you estimated on your return, you still may be able to prove your deductions are close to the estimated figures; just be aware that the round numbers will cause the auditor to look closely at your work.

The final say-so on who gets audited is made at local IRS District Offices by Examination Group Managers. These people supervise and assign auditors to specific cases, often according to the auditors' experience and expertise. Examination Group Managers also decide whether you'll be audited at the IRS office (see Chapter 3), or elsewhere by a more rigorous field audit (see Chapter 4). The same manager may decide on just a correspondence audit, but that decision is usually made at the IRS Service Center where you filed your return.

Examination Group Managers effectively establish their own mini-DIF scoring process. They consider income and spending patterns of their communities—for instance, more people have business car expenses in L.A. than in Manhattan. People in Kansas have more tornadoes—and casualty losses—than people in Idaho. Income in the Alaska fishing industry can fluctuate significantly season to season. Michigan workers strike more often than do workers in Texas. Examination Group Managers screen out 90% of returns received from the Service Center. The net result is that only about 1% of all tax returns are selected for audit.

3. Market Segment Specialization Program

According to IRS insiders, the Market Segment Specialization Program (MSSP) is the wave of the future. Each MSSP audit focuses on a specific industry or group of taxpayers believed to be not fully complying with the tax laws. The IRS provides specialized training to its agents and publishes an MSSP audit guide for each group. As we come to the end of the 20th century, the IRS has issued about 60 MSSP Guides and has another 60 or so in the works.

These guides are public. If you fall into one of the targeted categories, you can assume that your return was selected for audit for this reason. Assume that the auditor is familiar with the MSSP Guide for your occupation or group.

The MSSP Guides thus published cover different occupations and businesses, including architects, attorneys, entertainers, health care workers, ministers, real estate brokers and agents, retailers, taxicab drivers, tour bus operators, truckers and workers in the music industry, and owners of air charter companies, auto body shops, auto dealerships, bars and restaurants, beauty and barber shops, bed and breakfasts, commercial fisheries, garment manufacturing companies, gas stations, grocery stores, high tech businesses, laundromats, mortuaries, pizza parlors and wineries.

 MSSP Guides are available from many different sources, includ ing the following:

- Law libraries and some large public libraries

- Tax professionals, if they do significant audit representation work

- IRS offices (only for reading on the premises)

- IRS website (http://www.irs.ustreas.gov) for downloadable versions of some guides

- IRS Taxpayer Services, 800-829-1040, to order by mail.

4. Other Methods of Audit Selection

Besides being selected by the IRS computer scoring program or as part of the MSSP, there are seven possible ways to get into the audit soup.

Local projects. The IRS encourages local IRS District Offices to initiate special audit projects. Selections are based on IRS personnel perceptions of who in the community plays fast and loose on their taxes. Recent local projects have targeted real estate investors claiming passive type losses, roofing contractors, agricultural co-ops, professional gamblers, spouses who deduct or receive alimony and people whose mortgage loan appli-cations show different income than reported on their tax returns. (Under information sharing programs, mortgage lenders report certain informa-tion on mortgage applications to the IRS.)

National projects. Periodically, the IRS national office decides that certain occupations merit audit attention. Past targets include airline pilots, attorneys, car dealers, morticians and physicians. Perennial audit targets are operators of cash business, such as bars and laundromats, and owners and employees of gambling establishments. This program is being phased into the MSSP audit, described above.

The IRS has several clues to your occupation. Forms W-2 and 1099 filed by others in prior years might indicate it. Also, you must state your occupation and sources of your income at one or more locations on your tax return. And, if self-employed, you must include a four-digit business identification code on your tax return; these codes are listed in the IRS instructions for preparing Form 1040 tax returns. Some people have shown creativity here, such as Pam the prostitute who wrote she was in "public relations." Pam was audited and fined by the IRS, which was upheld in court when Pam challenged the IRS' action. Misstating the source of your income is illegal, even if you report all of it. Presumably the reason is that it makes it impossible for the IRS computer to score your tax return for audit consideration. But even if you left this information blank, the IRS obviously found a way to audit you.

Prior and related audits. Audit lightning can strike twice. One IRS examination can lead to another—if the first produced a tax bill of at least several thousand dollars. Happily, a repeat is not a sure thing. I've seen people get hit with an enormous audit bill and never hear from the IRS again. Sometimes the IRS is looking at the same issue, and sometimes the IRS is looking at a new one.

In addition, you might be audited if you're a partner, limited liability company member or shareholder in a business that is audited or if some of your co-owners are audited. If the IRS found problems during your co-owners' audits, the IRS likely to look into the same issues with you.

Criminal activity. Like grapes, trouble with the U.S. government often comes in bunches. If you are investigated for drugs or financial crimes, the IRS may be called by another law enforcement agency. The Tax Code requires that you report all income—legal or otherwise. The Tax Code is morally neutral—it doesn't care if you earned your riches as a Mafia hit man, prostitute or drug dealer or through any other illegal employment, as long as you declare it.

If you don't want to disclose the source of your income, you can file something called a Fifth Amendment tax return. At the top of the first page of the Form 1040 return, write, "I am claiming my Constitutional right against self-incrimination." Where you must list your income, do so, but the write the words "Fifth Amendment" where the return requests the source of your income and where it asks for your occupation.

Filing a Fifth Amendment tax return may keep you out of the Criminal Investigation Division of the IRS, but it undoubtedly increases your audit potential. If you filed a Fifth Amendment tax return and that's the return under audit, see a tax attorney.

Amended tax returns. Most people file amended tax returns to get money back. You may file an amended tax return within either three years of the date you filed the original return or two years of the date you paid the tax. The IRS has the discretion to reject an amended return if you would be entitled to a refund. Before sending the refund, the IRS may audit you. And here's the catch: Everything on the return—not just the items amended—is fair game for the audit.

Amending a tax return doesn't extend the time the IRS has to audit. The IRS normally has three years from the original filing date to audit a return. If you're considering filing an amended return, you might logically conclude that you should wait until close to the end of the three-year period from when you filed the original return so that the IRS has little time to audit you. In that situation, however, the IRS may accept the amended return only if you agree to extend the three-year audit limit period. Normally, you should agree to an extension of around one year.

Informants' tips. Most paranoid people feel that the world is ganging up on them. If you just received an audit notice, you might be worried that a disgruntled ex-spouse, business associate or former employee turned you in to the IRS. Worried about a tattletale you may be, but your worries should be short-lived. Fewer than 2% of audits result from people finking on others. The IRS rarely spends any serious time following up most tips, particularly anonymous ones. The IRS has found that many leads aren't provable and are motivated by spite. Reports of major cheats are most likely referred to the IRS Criminal Investigation Division, not the audit department. So if your ex-bookkeeper is the only one who knows about your questionable business travel deductions, you might be heading down the wrong road if that's the issue you think will be the focus of your audit. Instead, focus on the common business concerns discussed in Chapter 3, Section B.2 and Chapter 4, Section B.2.

Geography. Kansas gets tornadoes, Florida gets hurricanes and California gets earthquakes. Similarly, some state residents get more than their fair share of audits. The examination rate is 150% higher than the national average in Nevada, but 150% lower than that average in Wisconsin. Other high-audit states are Alaska, California and Colorado. Low-audit states include Illinois, Indiana, Iowa, Maryland, Massachusetts, Michigan, New York (excluding Manhattan), Ohio, Pennsylvania and West Virginia. Oddly, the second lowest audit rate locale is the District of Columbia, the seat of the federal government.

What's more, how you come out of an audit depends on where you call home, too. Your chances of getting away without owing a nickel are twice as good in Las Vegas (32%) as in Manhattan (15%).

Although moving now won't change the fact that you already have received an audit notice, if you have the choice, you could relocate after the audit to lower your chances of future audits.

E. Audit Goals

As mentioned at the beginning of the chapter, you have two goals in every audit. Always keep them in mind.

(1) To minimize financial damage. Accept the eight-to-one odds that your audit will end with a tax bill. Aim for damage control—keeping your tab as low as possible. I'm not saying to go in with a defeatist attitude, but at the same time don't have unrealistic expectations. In a recent year, audits resulted in additional taxes and penalties of $19 billion owed to the IRS, and only about $600 million in refunds—a ratio of 32 to 1 against taxpayers. In fact, if the IRS bills you for less than $1,000 after an audit, consider it a victory.

(2) To prevent expansion. One way to minimize the financial damage (your first goal) is to prevent an expansion of the audit. An auditor can examine any open tax year if such an examination is likely to be fruitful—that is, result in more money owed. Open tax years are those for tax returns filed within the past three years. The limit is extended to six years if the IRS believes you are guilty of underreporting your income by 25% or more, or forever if you are suspected of outright fraud.

Expansion most frequently occurs when during the audit, the auditor sees something such as an improper deduction that might be present on tax returns other than the one under audit. You might hang yourself by showing the auditor something related to an open tax year. For example, in November 2000, Noreen is audited for 1998. The auditor asks to see Noreen's business check register for 1998. Noreen cooperatively hands it over, failing to edit out the portions that relate to other years. The auditor nonchalantly rummages through the information for 1997 and 1999, the other open tax years. The auditor finds a few things she believes are questionable, and expands the audit into those years.

⚠ **Never show the auditor anything related to a year other than the tax year being audited.** This is the one rule to follow to minimize expansion of the audit. In the example above, Noreen could have photocopied the check register for 1998 before the audit, or offered to send it to the auditor after the audit meeting. The best way to avoid showing unrelated documents to the auditor is simply not to bring the unrelated documents with you to an office audit or not to have them on your premises during a field audit.

DON'T FILE A TAX RETURN WHILE UNDER AUDIT

Here's one way to minimize expansion of your audit: Don't file a tax return while an office (Chapter 3) or field (Chapter 4) audit is in progress. This rule does not apply if the IRS is conducting a correspondence audit (Chapter 2). If you file your return during an office or field audit, the audit is likely to be expanded to include that return.

When April 15 rolls around, file a request for an extension to August 15. If the audit is still going on on August 15, file a request for another extension until October 15. If the audit is still alive on October 15, consider not filing your tax return until the audit is completed. If you've paid all taxes due, you won't incur any penalties or interest for not meeting the extension deadline. If you owe money, send in your payment before October 15 with a letter requesting the payment be applied to that year's tax account. If you didn't read this in time and already filed your tax return, politely decline to give a copy to the auditor if she asks. But do not lie and say you haven't filed the return.

F. Your Rights During an Audit

IRS Publication 1, Your Rights as a Taxpayer, should have been included with your audit notice. (If you didn't receive a copy or misplaced it, you can find a copy in the Appendix or on the IRS' website at http://www.irs.ustreas.gov/forms_pubs/pubs.html.)

The following are the most important provisions related to audits:

- *You have the right to be treated fairly by IRS personnel.* If an IRS employee is not professional, prompt and courteous, you have a right to speak to a supervisor.

- *You have the right to have a representative handle your audit.* The representative must be designated to practice before the IRS—such as a tax attorney, accountant or enrolled agent—and have a written power of attorney from you. With a few exceptions, auditors (or collectors) can't force you to appear or even speak to you after you hire a representative.

- *You have the right to sound record the audit.* Taping would most likely cause the auditor to work even harder. For this reason, tax professionals don't do it and neither should you.

- *You have the right to avoid repeat audits in certain circumstances.* If you were audited within the last two years and the IRS made adjustments of $1,000 or less, you can't be audited again for the same items. If you are audited a second time, complain to the IRS appointment clerk or the auditor. There is one exception: The IRS can audit again for self-employment and small business items, such as vehicle and entertainment expenses, equipment purchases and employee benefits.

- *You have the right to have proposed adjustments explained.* The audit report you receive after your examination is typically vague and written in IRS-ese. If you don't understand something, ask for detailed explanations by phone or in person. If the auditor doesn't explain things to your satisfaction, insist on talking to her manager.

- *You have the right not to be forced to incriminate yourself.* This Constitutionally guaranteed right applies whenever you deal with a government agency, including the IRS. For example, if your income comes from kiting checks, the IRS can't demand details on the source, as long as you report the money on your tax return. But you can't lie to the IRS. If you don't want to list your occupation as "bad check artist," file a Fifth Amendment return. (See Section D.4, above.)

- *You may appeal your audit in most cases, but this is not an absolute right.* (See Chapter 8.) ■

Correspondence Audits and Other IRS Notices

IRS audits come in three flavors: correspondence, office and field. About 20% are called correspondence—that is, by mail—yielding the IRS an average of over $4,000 per audit in additional tax and penalties. Office audits are covered in Chapter 3; field audits are covered in Chapter 4.

In addition to correspondence audits, IRS Service Center computers generate tax return adjustment notices that, while technically not audit letters, are similar. And the result of getting an adjustment notice—owing more money—is the same as if you had been audited. Both correspondence audits and Service Center adjustments are covered in this chapter.

A. Correspondence Audits

Correspondence audits are not widely utilized by the IRS anymore. Occasionally, they are used to verify straightforward issues. For instance, the IRS may send you a correspondence audit notice requesting that you send in routine purchase and sale documentation to verify gains or losses on listed securities, or closing statements for real estate sales. Also, amended tax returns are often audited by mail.

Welcome a correspondence audit and be thankful that you weren't chosen for an office or intensive field audit. Read the notice carefully so that you understand exactly what the IRS is asking you to verify. Comb your records and find documentation to justify your credit, deduction or exemption. Make photocopies of the documents and promptly send them back. Do not send originals—the IRS may misplace the papers, and in any case, you won't get them back. Use certified mail, return receipt requested, to send in your documents.

If you've lost your papers or don't have any to justify a specific credit, deduction or exemption, follow the suggestions in Chapter 3, Section B.3 on proving deductions. If you want to, you can call the correspondence auditor to discuss your case. Or you can write to the IRS and ask someone to call you. The notice from the IRS should list the name and telephone number of the correspondence auditor. If you write and ask for someone to call you, send your letter certified mail, return receipt requested.

If you have a problem with the correspondence auditor—perhaps he won't accept your supporting documentation—you can request a transfer for a face-to-face meeting at your local IRS District Office. This may give the correspondence auditor a reason to rethink your case. When correspondence audits are forwarded to local IRS District Offices, those audits are often closed with no adjustments—sometimes without further contacts.

B. Service Center Automated Adjustment Notices (Not Real Audits)

Congress allows the IRS to "correct" errors on tax returns without audits, by sending computer-generated notices called Service Center automated adjustments (Internal Revenue Code § 6213(g)(2)). To add insult to injury, because these are not formal audits, your tax return is still at risk of being audited.

The IRS has four categories of automated adjustment notices. The headings differ and often change, but careful reading of the notice should make it clear what the IRS is after.

Error correction notices. If you've received an error correction notice, it is because the IRS believes it has found a math error or a similar problem on your tax return. For example, you may have stated that you have four dependents, but listed the names of only three. The IRS assumes that your mistake was in the math, not that you simply omitted the name of one of your dependents, and recomputes your tax liability with only three dependents. Or you might have claimed the standard deduction amount for head of household but failed to list dependents; the IRS assumes you get the standard deduction for a single person. This notice includes a corrected computation and a bill for the amount the IRS claims you owe.

Penalty assessment notices. If you've received a penalty assessment notice, it means that the IRS believes you did not meet a filing deadline or tax payment deadline. The notice may be wrong for any number of reasons. For example, you may have sent the payment to the IRS, but the IRS did not properly credit it to your account. Or you may have filed the form on time, but the IRS took six months to process it. Or, you may have missed a deadline, but for a reason beyond your control—perhaps a blizzard delayed your mail to the IRS—and you are entitled to have the penalty to be abated (canceled). Penalty abatements are beyond the scope of this book.

 For more information on penalty abatements, see *Stand Up to the IRS*, by Frederick W. Daily (Nolo).

Interest assessment notices. An interest assessment notice means that the IRS believes you did not pay a tax bill on time. By law, the IRS must charge interest if, in fact, you owed the bill and did not pay it on time. In a few cases, you can get interest waived even if it is correct, such as when the IRS delays in sending an audit bill by more than 30 days. Usually, however, the IRS is correct, and if you challenge the notice you may not get anywhere. Still, it doesn't hurt to ask.

Underreporter notices. An underreporter notice means that the IRS has found a mismatch between two data sources. The most common example is when your tax return doesn't list all income that others have reported to the IRS on 1099 or W-2 forms. Here's how to respond to the most common underreporter notices:

- *Unreported IRA distributions.* The IRS may generate an underreporter notice if you rolled over an IRA account into another IRA, but did not list the investment in the right blank on your tax return. This is a common mistake given the near incomprehensibility of income tax forms. Notify the IRS that you want to correct the error on your tax return.

- *Income listed on your return, such as receipts you received as an independent contractor, don't match a 1099 on file.* You may have reported the income somewhere on the tax return other than where the computer looked for it.

- *Mortgage interest deduction doesn't match your lender's report on a 1098 form.* You may have made an extra mortgage payment at the end of the year, but the lender didn't report it to the IRS until the following year.

- *Wages or withholding reported on your tax return doesn't match your employer's W-2 form.* Your employer may have made a reporting error. In that case, you will have to ask your employer to issue an amended W-2.

No matter which kind of notice you receive, it will ask you to explain the discrepancy or it will propose additional tax, penalties and interest based on the discrepancy. In either case, you'll be given 30 days to respond.

1. Reviewing the Automated Adjustment Notice

Money magazine estimates that between 25% and 50% of automated adjustment notices are erroneous. A common IRS mistake is not finding an income item that was reported elsewhere on the tax return.

Example: *Hilary reported $457 of money market fund income as interest. The financial institution labeled it as dividends in its report to the IRS. While dividends are listed right after interest on the IRS form, the computer concluded that Hilary did not report the money. Hilary was billed for tax, penalties and interest of $194.*

2. Responding to an Automated Adjustment Notice

If so many automated adjustment notices are wrong, why does the IRS send them? *Money* magazine found that most people billed for $589 or less paid without questioning. Consequently, the IRS collects $7 billion a year to which it is not entitled.

You don't have to be such a victim. You can easily fight an automated adjustment notice. Here are the steps to take.

Contesting delays the final tax bill, even if you are wrong. This gives six months or longer to get the payment together—but interest is running.

1. *Call the IRS.* If the telephone number isn't on the notice, call 800-829-1040. Ask the IRS representative for a full explanation of the automated adjustment, even if you suspect the IRS may be right. If you are prepared, state why you believe the notice is wrong—for example, if the IRS claims you didn't report something, point out where on your tax return it is. If you don't clear up the matter on the phone, ask the IRS to note on its records that you disagree with

the notice. Write down the time and date of the call, and ask the IRS representative for his name and badge number. Just asking may cause him to take extra care.

2. *Contest in writing.* If you don't object in writing within 60 days of the date on the notice, the adjustment becomes final. So don't rely on a telephone call alone to straighten out an IRS problem. Object in writing in all cases, even if the IRS representative agreed over the phone to correct the automated adjustment.

To contest automated adjustment notices, simply send a letter to the address on the notice. Follow the sample letter below. Be brief and to the point. IRS correspondence clerks have short attention spans. They won't struggle through long-winded explanations or bad handwriting. Staple a photocopy, not the original, of the IRS notice to the front of your letter. Mail it certified, return receipt requested, if you can. Include any documentation, such as a copy of the tax return highlighting where the income has been listed, or a birth certificate for the omitted dependent. The IRS bar-coded return envelope included with your notice speeds up processing.

SAMPLE LETTER TO DISPUTE A SERVICE CENTER ADJUSTMENT

(Married couples–use the first spouse's number on your tax return)

Hamilton and Jill O'Brien
SSN: 123-45-6789
123 Elm St.
Ukiah, CA 90000

June 16, 20XX

IRS ADJUSTMENTS/CORRESPONDENCE
IRS Service Center
Fresno, CA 93888

REQUEST FOR ADJUSTMENT

Re: IRS Notice Dated 6/2/XX

(Choose 1, 2 or 3 below followed by your explanation. If none fits your situation, explain in your own words.)

To Whom It May Concern:

I am responding to your notice of 6/2/XX, a copy of which is attached.

1. Math errors.

The notice is wrong. I did not make any math errors in my tax return. Here is how I made the calculations: $10,432 – $3,190 = $7,242.

2. Matching error (CP-2000 Notice).

a. The 1099 form filed by <u>Apex Industries</u> was wrong and the company has prepared a letter stating the correct amount, which is attached to this letter.

b. The W-2 form filed by my former employer is incorrect in that I made $ 42,815 in 1991, not $ 49,815.

3. Partially corrected errors.

a. I responded to your notice of 5/2/XX but you did not fully correct your error. Enclosed is a copy of my letter of 5/9/XX with a full explanation.

b. In your letter to me of 5/2/XX you said that the tax bill of $666 was corrected to $222 (copy enclosed), but I just got a notice dated 6/2/XX for the $666 again.

Please abate the taxes, penalties and interest in the amount of $ 1,612.

We can be reached at 707-555-0562 anytime.

Sincerely,

Hamilton O'Brien

Jill O'Brien

Hamilton and Jill O'Brien

Enclosed: Copies of IRS notices, prior correspondence

Keep copies! Whenever writing the IRS, always make several photocopies of whatever you send. If the IRS misplaces your first correspondence, you can send it again—and again, if necessary.

3. *If all else fails, go to court.* If you don't respond to an automated adjustment notice or the IRS rejects your explanation, it will send you by certified mail something called a Notice of Deficiency (informally called a 90-Day Letter). If you receive this notice and want to contest it, you must file a Petition in U.S. Tax Court within 90 days of the date on the letter. Filing a Petition in Tax Court is not difficult and costs only $60. (See Chapter 9.)

Consider calling a tax pro. Although it is seldom cost-effective to hire a tax professional for small IRS problems—under a thousand dollars—many tax professionals will chat with you for a few minutes on the phone free of charge. If the erroneous IRS bill is in the thousands, it may be worth your time and money to consult a tax pro for an hour—or even to have the tax pro contact the IRS for you. In most cases, a tax pro's fee is tax deductible if you itemize your tax deductions or you are self-employed.

3. Waiting to Hear From the IRS

After sending your letter contesting the automated adjustment notice, you may keep getting bills. Don't panic or feel neglected. It can take the IRS a month or longer to enter your dispute in the computer system in order to stop the notice cycle. Nevertheless, don't ignore the subsequent adjustment notices. Simply send the IRS a photocopy of your first letter.

If notices still keep coming after 90 days, call the number on the notice or 800-829-1040. If you don't get anywhere, contact the Problems Resolution Office. (See IRS Publication 1546, a copy of which is in the Appendix.) Let the PRO representative know how much time has elapsed and that the IRS has not answered your letters. The PRO representative will take action to get it resolved one way or another.

C. If You Are Billed for an Audit You Didn't Know About

Some people receive tax bills out of the blue. I call these phantom audit notices. While the IRS must send a notice when it starts an audit, the IRS must only mail it to the last known address in its records. The IRS doesn't have to prove you actually received the notice. The IRS assumes the address on the tax return is the correct one—even if you have since moved three times.

Courts have directed the IRS to update its address files regularly. It must send notices to the address on your most recent tax return or other address that you have provided on IRS From 8822. (*Abeles v. Commissioner of the Internal Revenue,* 91 U.S.T.C. 1019 (1991).) The IRS is allowed three months to process a change of address after it receives notification.

Let the IRS know when you move. Make sure you get all IRS notices by filing IRS Form 8822, Change of Address, whenever you move. A copy is in the Appendix or available on the IRS' website at http://www.irs.ustreas.gov/forms_pubs/pubs.html. The IRS does *not* recognize a Post Office change of address form.

If you didn't answer an audit letter, the IRS probably proceeded without you. Your exemptions, deductions and credits were disallowed in whatever manner the auditor so chose.

After the audit—the one you did not participate in—the IRS probably sent an audit report with a letter outlining the appeal process. Or, the IRS sent a Notice of Deficiency stating you had 90 days to go to Tax Court. These letters were most likely sent to the same bad address.

But now, finally, the IRS has the right address. And you have a tax bill for an audit about which you knew nothing.

Here are two ways to fight a tax bill from a phantom audit.

Request an audit reconsideration. The first step after you receive a puzzling tax bill is to immediately write or call the IRS at the address or phone number indicated on the bill. State that you do not understand why you've received a tax bill. You will be told that the bill is the result of an examination notice to which you did not respond or, if you are really lucky, that the bill is the result of an IRS mistake.

You can contest the bill by writing back to the IRS, stating that you never received notice of the audit and that you want an audit reconsideration. You should hear back from the IRS within 60 days. If you don't or the IRS denies your request, call the IRS Customer Service Center at 800-829-1040. If the Customer Service Representative won't help you, ask to be called back by a Problems Resolution Officer, or PRO. (See IRS Publication 1546, a copy of which is in the Appendix.) You should hear from someone within five days. Offer to mail or fax the PRO copies of the tax bill and your letter. Ask the PRO to set up a meeting with an auditor or to help you figure out how to resolve the matter by mail and phone.

Audit reconsideration is a re-opening of your audit file. It is discretionary with the IRS, but is usually granted. The IRS should set up an audit reconsideration meeting even if you admit to having received the audit notice but having ignored it. Your chance of winning an audit reconsideration is better if you never received the audit notice in the first place, however. The IRS goes back to square one and allows you to participate this time around. It's like a regular audit, but is limited to the items adjusted in the "phantom" audit.

File a Petition in Tax Court. If audit reconsideration doesn't work, and you never received the Notice of Deficiency (90-Day Letter) sent by the IRS, you can file a Petition in U.S. Tax Court. In your Petition, you would allege that the Notice of Deficiency was not sent to your last known address. If the court agrees, it will set aside the tax assessment. Very few taxpayers win this issue in Tax Court. (See Chapter 9 for more information on Tax Court.)

JEOPARDY—NOT THE TV SHOW

While the Tax Code generally requires that the IRS give you notice and the right to contest an audit before issuing and collecting on a tax bill, there is one exception. The IRS has an extraordinary "shoot first, ask questions later" power to assess taxes without an audit under its jeopardy assessment power. Jeopardy assessments must be personally approved by the local IRS Director or Director of Foreign Operations, and you do have the right to a hearing—similar to an audit—after the fact.

Jeopardy assessments are authorized only when the IRS believes its right to collect is in danger because of one of the following reasons:

- you're planning to hide out or depart the U.S.

- you're concealing, dissipating or removing property from the U.S. or transferring it to others, or

- your financial solvency is endangered.

Jeopardy assessments are uncommon and are used mostly against foreigners operating a U.S. business. Other targets are people arrested with large amounts of cash or valuable personal property—often, narcotics traffickers. If your tax bill is from a jeopardy assessment, see a tax lawyer as soon as possible.

Office Audits

As mentioned in chapter 2, IRS audits come in three flavors: correspondence, office and field. Office audits are the most popular—about half of all audits are held at IRS offices. But an office audit is also the type in which you are likely to emerge with the least amount of damage. IRS statistics show that office audits result in additional tax and penalties owed averaging only about $2,000. Correspondence audits are covered in Chapter 2; field audits are covered in Chapter 4.

An Office Examination is announced by a computer-generated form letter. It sets a time and date for a meeting at the IRS office or requests that you call to make an appointment. The letter states the year or years being audited, and may specify types of documents you are being asked to bring—such as paid receipts, bank statements and canceled checks. Office audits are performed by Tax Auditors. To keep things simple, we'll refer to them simply as office auditors for this chapter.

SAMPLE OFFICE EXAMINATION LETTER

INTERNAL REVENUE SERVICE
Examination Group 2422
450 Golden Gate Ave., Stop 6-101
San Francisco, CA 94102
Date: 1-21- XX

Person to Contact: Appointment Clerk

Telephone Number: (415) 522-6147

Dear Taxpayer:

Your Federal income tax return for the year(s) shown below has been selected for examination. You have requested that your audit be scheduled for the date shown below.

Please note, this is a <u>firm</u> appointment and can only be rescheduled to an earlier date. Because your appointment date exceeds four weeks from the date of your audit notification letter, we have issued a report to show the current status of your examination. The report you have been issued will be revised or voided when you appear for the examination with appropriate documentation.

On your appointment date please be sure to bring all information so we will be able to conclude the examintion.

APPOINTMENT INFORMATION

TAX YEAR(S): 19 XX   DATE: March 4, 20XX

PLACE: TIME: 12:30
450 Golden Gate Ave., Sixth Floor
San Francisco, CA 94102

If you have any questions, please contact our office at the number shown in the heading of this letter. When you come in for your appointment, please bring this letter with you. Thank you for your cooperation.

Sincerely,

Jasmine Wong
JASMINE WONG
Group Manager

SAMPLE EXAMINATION LETTER (cont.)

Please bring records to support the following items reported on your tax return for _____19XX_____

☐ Alimony Payments or Income	☐ Energy Credit	☐ Sale or Exchange of Residence
☐ Automobile Expenses	☐ Exemptions (Child/Children,	☐ Taxes
☐ Bad Debts	Other)	☐ Uniform, Equipment and Tools
☐ Capital Gains and Losses	☐ Filing Status	☒ Copy of your Federal tax
☐ Casualty Losses	☐ Income	return(s) for *19XW, 19XY*
☐ Contributions	☐ Interest Expense	☐
☐ Credit for Child and	☐ Medical and Dental Expense	☐
Dependent Care Expenses	☐ Miscellaneous Deductions	☐
☐ Education Expenses	☐ Moving Expenses	☐
☐ Employee Business Expenses	☐ Rental Income and Expenses	☐

Schedule C

☐ All Business Expenses	☐ Gross Receipts	☐ Salaries and Wages
☐ Bad Debts	☐ Insurance	☐ Supplies
☐ Car and Truck Expense	☐ Interest	☐ Taxes
☐ Commissions	☒ Legal and Professional	☐ Travel and Entertainment
☐ Cost of Goods Sold	☒ Rent	☐
☐ Depreciation	☐ Repairs	☒ *Other Expenses*
☐	☐	

Schedule F

☐ All Farm Expenses	☐ Insurance	☐ Repairs and Maintenance
☐ Depreciation	☐ Inventories	☐ Supplies Purchased
☐ Feed Purchased	☐ Labor Hired	☐ Taxes
☐ Fertilizers and Lime	☐ Machine Hire	☐
☐ Gross Receipts	☐ Other Farm Income	☐
☐	☐	☐

Letter 2203(DO) (Rev. 10–3)

A. Call to Schedule the Audit

After you receive an office audit notice, call the IRS to schedule the audit or confirm your appearance. While your inclination may be to get the audit over with as soon as possible, consider taking a slow -go approach. The reason for not rushing is simple. Because the IRS must complete the entire audit process within three years of when you filed your return, the longer your audit drags on, the sooner the deadline approaches. When the auditor is under pressure to close your file, the likely result is fewer adjustments being made on your return.

Here are some scheduling suggestions.

Don't call right away. Don't call the IRS the day the notice arrives. Wait a while. Two weeks is soon enough to respond to an audit notice. The IRS does not award gold stars to early callers.

Schedule far in the distance. Make the audit appointment as far into the future as possible. Don't underestimate the time you will need to locate and get your records in order. No matter how much of an ace recordkeeper you are, you'll be unable to find something when you hunt for it. Ask for at least a month or two away for your appointment. The Taxpayers' Bill of Rights gives you a say in scheduling the appointment; don't let anyone at the IRS tell you otherwise.

Schedule late in the week and day. Ask for your office audit appointment on Friday, and if possible, late morning—just before the auditor's lunch break—or late afternoon. Friday afternoons are perfect, especially right before a three-day weekend. Auditors don't work on commission or get paid overtime, so they look forward to evenings and weekends as much as you do. An auditor may want to go home so badly that she will race through without really digging.

Schedule late in the month. Ask for an audit appointment at the end of the month. Because IRS managers are prohibited from judging auditors on tax dollars produced, they measure performance in the number of file closings per month. If the auditor is behind in clearing out the files on her desk, she may zip along to avoid a bad performance review. It's kind of like a car salesperson meeting his or her quota.

Reschedule the audit. To buy more time, call a day or two before your audit appointment and ask that the meeting be rescheduled. Despite language in the IRS confirmation notice to the contrary, the IRS usually grants one or two postponements for almost any reason. Perhaps you haven't received copies of vital documents, such as canceled checks from your bank. Or maybe your accountant is out of town, you are busy at work or there is an illness in your family.

Don't worry if you can't find all your papers. On the day of the audit, you may not have been able to find all necessary records. When the auditor asks for them, apologize that you were unable to get them and ask for a couple of more weeks. If the deadline for getting the missing documents to the auditor is approaching, call and ask for a little more time. The auditor may grumble, but will probably allow it. The auditor isn't being nice; he doesn't want you to appeal his audit reports. (See Chapter 8.)

CHANGING AN OFFICE AUDIT INTO A FIELD OR CORRESPONDENCE AUDIT

If visiting the IRS would cause you great hardship, you can ask that the office audit be held at your home or business. Hardship means that you're disabled and can't travel easily or that you can't carry large boxes of records. While in most situations you don't want the auditor coming to your home or office, if it's what you need you have the right to ask for it.

Alternatively, ask that the audit be conducted by mail—that is, turned into a correspondence audit. You'll need a good reason why you can't come to the IRS office: illness or disability, lack of transportation, long distance from the IRS office, small children at home or whatever. If your audit issues are straightforward, the IRS might agree to it, in which case read Chapter 2. But the IRS might refuse, and instead offer to send the auditor to your place.

The third option: if the IRS accepts that you cannot attend an office audit and your tax return has marginal audit potential, the IRS might quietly drop the audit. Don't count on it, however.

B. Prepare for the Audit

Thankfully, auditors don't ever have time to examine every entry on a tax return. According to the IRS training manual, auditors are supposed to examine only significant items. Office audit notices typically list specific areas the IRS wants to examine—such as rental property income, interest expenses, dependents, IRA rollovers, unreimbursed business expenses or charitable contributions. The IRS usually limits office examinations to no more than four categories.

Review IRS Form 4700 (Regular) Supplement before your audit. If you are self-employed, also look at Form 4700, Business Supplement. (Both forms are in the Appendix.) These two forms function as internal checklists for auditors. They highlight the areas of inquiry you can expect. If any item on these forms gives you real concern, see a tax pro before the audit or consider hiring a representative to attend for you.

1. Who Are Auditors?

The IRS tries to maintain a diverse workforce. Many auditors are young, and some are from different cultures, have limited English skills and typically have little experience in the business world. This may present you with a challenge, especially if you are self-employed. Office auditors are usually not the cream of the IRS Examination Division. When you are preparing for your audit, keep this in mind. If you are self-employed, be ready to describe how your enterprise functions as if you were teaching a child.

2. Top Ten Office Audit Issues

Take a look at your audit notice listing the issues the auditor will concern herself with in your audit. This section discusses the most common of those issues and provides tips on how to prepare for them. For office audits, you are required to prepare only for the listed issues. If an issue is listed on the audit notice that isn't discussed below, you will need to do further research or contact a tax professional. See Chapter 10.

a. Income

The IRS says it loses far more tax dollars from unreported income than from overstated deductions. Auditors ask point blank, "Did you report all of your income?" Don't take this question to mean the IRS has the goods on you—it is a standard question asked to everyone.

Auditors have their antennae tuned for moonlighting jobs, homeowners renting out in-law units, folks who earn tips and daycare-providing homemakers, among others. They are especially alert to certain occupations—like a handyperson or gardener—whose income is often not reported to the IRS on W-2 or 1099 forms.

If the IRS is right, then don't fight it. Acknowledge any unreported income for which the IRS has a correct W-2 or 1099. But if the IRS has erroneous data, show or offer to prove that it's wrong. Ask for time to get a corrected W-2 or 1099. Or, the problem may be a tax issue you can dispute. For example, a bank wrote off a debt of yours for $15,000 and reported it to the IRS on a 1099. You didn't list it on your return because you were insolvent at the time and the income wasn't taxable. You can provide a statement of your assets and liabilities as of the date the debt was written off showing that you were insolvent—that is, your debts exceeded your assets.

b. Living Expenses

If you reported income near poverty level, the auditor may want to know how you live. Office auditors seldom go into this, but field auditors (Chapter 4) routinely do it. Be prepared to tell the auditor about your savings, relatives, disability payments or other non-taxable sources of income.

c. Dependent Exemptions

Be ready to show that you are entitled to claim everyone listed on your tax return as a dependent. For instance, if you support your elderly parents and claim them on your return, gather together documents showing you paid their expenses and their sources of income—such as Social Security. You'll have to prove that you provide more than 50% of their support. Whether or not you bring the documents to the audit is up to you. If the auditor requests documents, you can mail them in later.

Similarly, if you are a divorced parent who claims a dependent child, you probably need to provide proof that you are entitled to the exemption. Proof may be canceled child support checks, a copy of your ex-spouse's tax return showing that he or she didn't claim the child as a dependent or your divorce agreement stating who is entitled to the exemption.

d. Theft and Casualty Losses

If you claimed theft or casualty losses, be prepared to prove the deduction. Provide a list of all of the items you lost plus other documentation of your losses. Police reports, photos, purchase receipts and insurance claim forms are good ways to prove losses. If you don't have copies of these forms, contact the police department or insurance company for copies well in advance of your audit.

e. Charitable Deductions

IRS regulations require that you document all charitable deduction items of similar nature that exceed $250 in total. For example, if you dropped $40 into the collection plate every Sunday, you will have to provide more evidence than your own statement. Evidence might be a letter from your church secretary attesting to your regular attendance combined with automatic teller withdrawal slips made on Sunday mornings. In future years, consider writing a check each week.

For smaller deductions—items of $5, $10 or $25—you don't need verification, but it can't hurt. IRS auditors have a lot of discretion in this area; generally, if your claimed charitable deduction total is less than $500, the auditor won't push for documentation. You will never have to prove that an organization is an exempt charity under Section 501(c)(3) of the Tax Code—the IRS has a book with a list of all qualified charities and can look yours up if it has a question.

f. Unreimbursed Employee Business Expenses

If you are not self-employed, but on your job you spend money for which you are not reimbursed and deduct that expense on your return, you're an audit target. Auditors are especially suspicious of car, travel, entertainment and home office costs of employees. Be sure to have a statement from your employer describing its reimbursement policy—or lack thereof. Bring pages in your calendar or business appointment book and attach receipts backing up the unreimbursed expenses.

g. Itemized Deductions

If you don't claim the standard deduction, be ready to verify your itemized deductions on Schedule A. Some items are discussed above—such as theft and casualty losses and charitable contributions. Others are your home mortgage interest, points paid for purchase, real estate taxes, your motor vehicle registration, your medical deductions and a few other items. For example, if you bought a house and the seller is carrying your mortgage note, provide a statement from the seller or escrow company and your canceled checks. Points are shown on the lender's statement or escrow papers, but are deductible in full only for the original mortgage, not for any subsequent refinancing. If you don't have a copy of the vehicle registration showing the deductible amount, contact the motor vehicle office before the audit and ask for a copy. For all expenses, get copies of bills, canceled checks, credit card slips and any other documents you can think of that support your claims.

h. Previous Audits

IRS records of your audit history are spotty. Examination reports as recent as a year or two ago probably won't be in the new auditor's file. So don't be surprised if asked if you've been audited before and how it came out. Unless you came out clean, say that you don't recall. If she really wants the old report, she can hunt for it on her own time. Unless no problems were found, you won't be rewarded by showing her a copy—which points her to issues in the new audit. If the auditor does have the old report, however, and the prior auditor found problems, be prepared to address those same issues if they are on your newly selected tax return.

i. Other Years' Tax Returns

During an audit, the auditor routinely asks to see your tax returns for the year before and after the audit year. Her reason is obvious—to see if she should make adjustments for those years. But the IRS has those returns, so why is she asking you? Even in this electronic age, the IRS doesn't yet have computer-scanned copies of tax returns. Paper tax returns are piled high in warehouses for ten years and then destroyed. Your return filed two years ago may be in box 147963a-7 in the middle of Kansas. If the auditor internally requests your old tax return, it takes months to find it—if it ever surfaces. Usually the auditor just forgets it, but even if the IRS finds the return, the IRS audit clock may have run out. And if you didn't file a return for those other years, don't assume the IRS suspects you of not filing because you were asked for those returns.

What this means is that you can safely ignore the audit notice where it says to bring other tax returns. How to deal with the same request at the audit itself is covered in Chapter 6.

j. Fraud

Tax fraud—big time tax cheating, not just fudging a few deductions—is an issue in fewer than 5% of all audits. But if you are concerned that it might arise in your audit, talk to a tax attorney before meeting the auditor. Tax fraud may be punished by a heavy fine—75% of the amount of tax found due—or by a long jail term. If you're contacted by someone identifying himself as an IRS Special Agent, it means the person is from the IRS Criminal Investigation Division. Start to worry.

 Stand Up to the IRS, by Frederick W. Daily (Nolo), contains extensive details on civil and criminal tax fraud investigations.

3. Prove Your Deductions

The IRS should be headquartered in Missouri, the "Show Me" state. Prove your tax return was prepared properly and substantiate everything on it, and you'll win your audit. It is as simple as that—but most people lose their audits because something goes wrong.

Proving that your return was prepared properly isn't generally the issue. But verifying everything on it, particularly your deductions, may be another story. You must pass two tests to be entitled to claim a deduction: you must substantiate the expense and you must show that the expense was reasonable and necessary.

Substantiation. This is usually the crux of an audit. Ideally, your proof, verification, substantiation—it doesn't matter what term you use—is in writing. But auditors have the discretion to accept oral explanations in place of documents. Of course, this destroys the great IRS myth: That if you can't prove a deduction in writing, it won't be allowed by an auditor. The fact is otherwise. Courts have told the IRS that taxpayers can't be expected to keep flawless records. Published Tax Regulations and court decisions allow taxpayers—within limits—to 1) claim substantial compliance, 2) offer oral explanations, 3) claim certain business expenses under $75 without receipts and 4) reconstruct records when the originals are missing.

Reasonable and necessary. Deductions—expenses—of running your business or working your investments so they produce income must be reasonable and necessary. So even if you can substantiate an expense, the IRS may reject it if it's unreasonable or unnecessary. For example, Elmer owns a hot dog stand with gross receipts of $40,000 per year. Elmer claims a deduction of $20,000 in entertainment expenses. The auditor would likely call this unreasonable and unnecessary, even if Elmer could prove he spent this amount on his good customers. If Elmer owned a hot dog factory and made $500,000 a year, however, a $20,000 deduction in entertainment expenses would probably fly. In reality, this is usually not a major audit issue, as long as your expenses aren't laughable in size or nature.

a. Substantial Compliance

If you can't find the paperwork to support a certain deduction, be ready to tell the auditor that you are nevertheless in substantial compliance with the tax laws and show what you do have. "Substantial compliance" mean you can show sufficient proof you obeyed the tax law, even if the evidence is incomplete.

Example: *The auditor okays Rufus' deducting a cleaning person's charges of $125 per month for his real estate offices. The cleaner insisted on payments in cash because she didn't have a bank account to cash checks. Rufus cannot find four months of handwritten receipts for cash payments, and so the auditor says "no deduction" for $500. Rufus counters that the cleaner dropped out of sight, so he can't get the receipts now. But he contends he is in substantial compliance and the auditor should average the other eight months ($1,000) to approximate the missing four ($500).*

This example shows the wisdom of preparing well ahead of the audit. If you can't find bills or canceled checks, order copies from suppliers and banks. Expect to wait a few weeks; few businesses keep old records handy. And few give priority to getting copies out unless you are an exceptional customer. If getting the records in time for the audit looks like it will be a problem, call the IRS and reschedule. (See Section A.) Businesses don't usually charge for copies of invoices or receipts, but banks gouge up to $3 per canceled check copy. You may want to order copies of major expense checks only.

b. Oral Explanations

Be ready with an oral explanation of why you can't produce a record or why you're entitled to the deduction. An auditor must give some weight to an oral excuse, as long as it's reasonable. Perhaps your records were lost along with all the rest of your worldly goods moving from Iowa to New Mexico when the moving van was totaled and exploded into flames. Credibility is the key. "Aliens with ray guns hijacked it near Area 51" won't fly, even if the auditor is an *X Files* fan.

More than anything, once the audit begins you want to establish and maintain credibility with the auditor. If you lie to the auditor once, she may not believe anything else you say. You won't get the benefit of the doubt down the road. If you must, be ready to say something like, "I'm not sure" or "I'll check on that."

c. Business Expenses

You are entitled to claim most business deductions of up to $75 each without a receipt. This rule doesn't apply to the purchase of goods for resale or travel, lodging and entertainment expenses. These expenses require receipts, no matter the amount. The receipt may be a cash register tape, credit card slip or invoice marked paid. As long as the receipt looks legitimate, you should be okay.

Not needing a receipt doesn't mean that you can throw away all traces of these expenses. Keep a record of some kind. For instance, your business calendar notation, log or diary should indicate the amount of the expense, to whom it was paid, the time and place, the business purpose and the relationship you have with the person on whom you spent the money.

d. Reconstruction of Records

Generating records from scratch is not fun, but is sometimes necessary for audit success. In addition, you may have gaps from missing documents that you need to fill in by recreating lost or destroyed records. As long as the newly minted records appear to be reasonable, the auditor can't entirely disregard them. It's a judgment call on the part of the auditor, however, and different auditors apply different standards.

Courts provide some guidance on what it takes to successfully reconstruct records. The first rule is that if you once possessed records but no longer have them—due to no fault of your own—you are entitled to reconstruct them. (IRS Regulation 1.274-5(c)(5); *Gizzi v. Commissioner of Internal Revenue,* 65 T.C. 342 (1975).) You must provide the IRS with a reasonable explanation of why the records are missing.

Example: Ted's tax records were destroyed when the Mississippi River flooded into his basement. Ted can use photos of the flooded basement, an insurance claim form or even newspaper clippings reporting the flood to provide an explanation of why he doesn't have the records.

Documenting the lost record expense is the next step. Let's say you spent $1,200 for materials in fixing up your office but lost all the paperwork. You could reconstruct the expenses with a letter from your landlord attesting to the improvements or a statement from a friend who saw you doing the work. Before-and-after photos are very persuasive. If you think hard enough about reconstructing paperwork for an expense, you can do it. Be creative.

You can even write up your own receipts. You can make up duplicate paid receipts from the hardware store with the name of the store, amount and date of purchase. Most important is to be up front with the auditor; tell her the receipt is a reconstruction. Together with your landlord and friends' letters and photos, this might carry the day.

Cohan Rule. An early court ruling has saved many an audit victim with missing records. George M. "I'm a Yankee Doodle Dandy" Cohan was nailed for not producing expense receipts in a roaring '20s IRS audit. Cohan fought the IRS, and a U.S. Court of Appeals held that Cohan could "approximate" reasonable business expense deductions, as he had shown that some amounts must have been spent through his testimony and that of other witnesses. (*Cohan v. Commissioner of the Internal Revenue,* 349 F.2d 540 (2nd Cir. 1930).) The Cohan Rule is still the law, but has two principal legal limitations:

(1) As with any reconstruction of records case, you must show why the records are not available. They may have been lost or destroyed, for very small amounts or from transactions for which receipts are not normally given.

(2) The Cohan rule can't be used to approximate travel and entertainment expenses. You must verify those actual expenses.

Be ready to use the Cohan Rule as a bargaining chip with the auditor. If she says "no deduction without documentation," cry "Cohan." Her eyebrows will likely raise in surprise, and she may become more reasonable. If she balks, ask her why it doesn't apply to your situation.

4. Don't Over-Cooperate

Reread the audit notice one last time. Look at the list the auditor plans to examine. As you are putting together the documents that relate to the items on that list, don't include anything else. An auditor can't force you to produce anything unrelated to what is in an IRS office audit notice. And remember my earlier advice—if you're asked to bring other years' returns, don't, with a few exceptions.

For example, another year's tax return may relate to the one under audit—for instance, loss carryovers or depreciation of assets reported in other years. In this case, bring to the audit only the relevant part of the other year's tax return—such as a schedule of depreciation—and not the whole return.

Field Audits

A third kind of IRS audit is called the field audit—meaning that it takes place at your home or business, or your tax professional's office. (The other kinds of audits—correspondence and office—are covered in Chapters 2 and 3 respectively.) About 25% of all audits are field audits. The average bill after a field audit is for about $18,000 in tax and penalties. For taxpayers who earn more than $100,000, field audit bills typically exceed $35,000.

You know you've been selected for a field audit because the audit notice will be signed by a person who has the title "Revenue Agent." The IRS wishes to meet you at your home or business, either suggesting a date and time for the audit or asking you to call to arrange it. You are in the IRS big leagues. Local IRS senior personnel decide who gets subjected to a field audit. Typically, self-employed taxpayers, owners of multiple real estate rental properties, earners of more than $100,000 and people with complex tax returns (such as income from limited partnership investments or multiple stock transactions) are subjected to field audits. In addition, audits of tax returns filed by corporations, partnerships and limited liability companies are always conducted in the field.

Revenue Agents are the IRS elite auditors. Revenue Agents have a college degree in accounting or 30 semester hours of college-level accounting. They are given intensive IRS audit training. They are like detectives, looking for clues. Does your tax reporting match up with your home, lifestyle, business and investments? If the agent learns that you live in a Malibu mansion, drive a Range Rover and report $20,000 income from your dental practice, he'll don his Sherlock gear and start digging. This explains why field audit tax bills are, on average, eight times higher than office audit tax bills.

The field audit notice may include a list of items the IRS wants you to produce at the audit meeting. Do not assume that this list represents everything the IRS is curious about. In a field audit, unlike an office audit, everything is fair game. The Revenue Agent can probe into any area of your tax return and your financial life.

SAMPLE FIELD EXAMINATION NOTICE

INTERNAL REVENUE SERVICE

DEPARTMENT OF THE TREASURY
450 GOLDEN GATE AVENUE
SAN FRANCISCO, CA.   94102

TO:

PERSON TO CONTACT: Lou Tack
TELEPHONE NUMBER: (415) 123-4567
REFER REPLY TO:
Lou Tack
Revenue Agent Exam Group
Mail Stop 6-1-07

DATE: 3/18/XX

DATE: Apr. 16, 20XX
TIME: 9:00 a.m.
PLACE: 190 Coleman Dr., San Diego, CA 90200

TAX FORM NUMBER: 1040
TAX YEAR(S): 20XX

Dear Taxpayer,

I have decided to exam 20XX tax return and I would like to meet with you at the time, place and date noted above. Please call if there is any problem with the appointment.

In order to make the examination as brief as possible, please have the information available that is listed on Form 4564, Information Document Request. Please include any other records that you believe are necessary to substantiate your income and expenses.

It is my desire to make the review of your records as brief and pleasant as possible. Please feel free to raise any questions that you may have during the examination.

If you wish to be represented, please complete the enclosed form 2848 and give it to your representative for submission.

Sincerely,

Lou Tack

Lou Tack
Revenue Agent

Enclosures:
Form 2848 Power of Attorney
Form 4564 Information Document Request
Notice 609 Privacy Act Notice
Publication 1 Taxpayer's Rights

⚠️ **If you get a call from someone saying he is from the IRS and is auditing you, what should you do?** Tell him to send it in writing. Refuse to discuss any audit or personal matter with him no matter what he says. Don't worry about upsetting him—you are within your rights. Don't let him pressure you into going further. These are legitimate calls from Revenue Agents, and in some parts of the country the calls take place frequently. Still, refuse to talk to the Agent until you have an audit notice in writing.

A. Call to Schedule the Audit

Before you call the Revenue Agent to set up the audit meeting, give thought to where you want the audit held. The Revenue Agent will go wherever you keep your financial records. If it's at your office, then the agent will come to your business site. If you keep the records at your home or you work at home, the agent will do the audit there.

Also, think about when to schedule the audit. (See Chapter 3, Section A, for tips on scheduling the audit.) Give yourself plenty of time to prepare by asking for at least a month—preferably two. The IRS doesn't start before 7:30 a.m. or go past 5:00 p.m., and never on week-ends.

Finally, consider whether you feel comfortable handling the audit yourself or whether you want to hire a tax pro. If you want to send your tax pro, have him call to schedule the appointment.

💼 **Tax Professionals.** If you give a qualified representative a completed IRS Form 2848, Power of Attorney, he can insist that the field audit be at his office, not yours, as long as your records are there. The representative must be your tax return preparer or an Enrolled Agent, CPA or attorney. (A copy of the form is in the Appendix or available on the IRS' website at http://www.irs.ustreas.gov/forms_pubs/pubs.html.)

KEEPING THE AUDITOR AWAY FROM YOUR HOME OR BUSINESS

My advice is to avoid having an audit at your home or office, even if you think you have nothing to hide. Maybe you earn only $30,000, but live much better because you inherited your house, rebuilt your BMW from junkyard parts and live extremely frugally. You might think you won't have any problems with the IRS once the agency knows the truth, but don't count on it. Claims of inherited property, rebuilding expensive cars and living a frugal life that would put even Scrooge to shame are just the kinds of things that may cause the auditor to dig even deeper.

Under the Taxpayers' Bill of Rights, small business owners have the right to refuse to have a field audit at the business' premises if it would virtually shut them down. Even if the audit would cause only minor disruption, request that it be at the IRS office or at your tax pro's office. If your request is denied, complain to the Revenue Agent's manager and then if necessary, to the IRS Problems Resolution Office, located at Service Centers and District Offices.

B. Prepare for the Audit

Many of the issues in a field audit are the same as those in an office audit. So before continuing on with the rest of the chapter, turn to Chapter 3, Section B, and read the material on preparing for an office audit.

1. Basic Preparation Steps

Once you review the office audit material in Chapter 3, follow these basic steps:

- *Step 1.* Review the tax return being audited. If you had your return professionally prepared, go over it with the preparer. If you prepared the return yourself and have any uncertainties, review it and your audit notice with an audit-experienced tax pro. Keep in mind that you weren't picked at random. There's a good chance that something on the face of the tax return caused you to be selected for a field audit. An experienced tax pro should be able to review your tax return and have some ideas about why you were selected. Then you can focus on those likely areas.

Whether or not you hire the tax pro to represent you at the audit is your call. It may depend on your pocketbook and IRS anxiety level. Remember, you must provide documentation to support items on your tax return. Make the decision to hire a tax pro or handle the audit yourself before the audit begins, although you are allowed to bring in a tax pro at any time.

• *Step 2. Organize all the records you or your tax preparer used to prepare the return.* Put your records into logical and clear order according to the income, deduction, exemption or claim category. Run adding machine tape totals of receipts and proof of payments for each classification, such as "rent, "travel" and "utilities." Staple the tapes to the receipt to show your work. If the tapes don't match numbers on your tax return, be ready to explain why. Well-organized records are the key to winning most audits.

• *Step 3. Review IRS Form 4700 (Regular) Supplement before your audit.* If you are self-employed, also look at Form 4700, Business Supplement. (Both forms are in the Appendix.) These two forms function as internal checklists for auditors. They highlight the areas of inquiry you can expect. If any item on these forms gives you real concern, see a tax pro before the audit or consider hiring a representative to attend for you.

• *Step 4. Research the tax law, if necessary.* Few audits involve legal issues—they tend to focus on substantiation of deductions—so it's unlikely that you will have to look up any tax law. But if you are unsure as to whether or not you were entitled to a tax benefit claimed on your tax return—for instance, whether or not you met all the requirements for a home office deduction—put on your research cap. You can hire a tax pro to research the question for you or hit the library or Internet. (See Chapter 10 for information on basic tax research techniques.)

2. Top Six Field Audit Issues

Some field audits last a couple hours and are wrapped up that day. In extreme cases, a Revenue Agent may spend hundreds of hours over a year or two conducting a field audit. The typical field audit, however, involves an interview with the Revenue Agent that lasts an hour or two, followed by the Revenue Agent spending ten to fifteen hours reviewing your records.

The vast majority of people who are subjected to a field audit are small business owners who the IRS historically suspects of having not reported all of their self-employment income and having claimed personal expenses as business deductions. For this reason, field audits focus almost exclusively on unreported business income, verification of business expenses, sales of assets, living beyond one's means, rental of real estate and classification of workers as employees or independent contractors.

a. Unreported Business Income

This is the Revenue Agent's number one concern, particularly if your business has many cash transactions. The Revenue Agent suspects owners of businesses that deal in cash of skimming cash off the gross receipts rather than reporting 100% of the income. This is why owners of restaurants, bars, liquor stores, pizza parlors, video arcades, laundromats, vending machine companies and grocery stores are perennially audited.

Unless the IRS has direct evidence of you cheating—such as your confession—the Revenue Agent will use one or more of four common methods to detect income. Your best preparation for the audit is to know how to counter these methods.

i. Net Worth Method

Using the net worth method, the IRS attributes any increase in your net worth—assets minus liabilities—during the year in question to taxable income. The Revenue Agent hunts for any financial statements prepared for your business or as part of a mortgage or other loan application. He will ask related questions of you in an interview. He'll look back at your bank records. He uses that information to establish your net worth at the beginning of the audit year and then again at the end. He values assets at their original cost and doesn't consider any appreciation. If your net worth has risen but your reported income has not, the IRS assumes you're not reporting everything. It's up to you to refute it.

Defense. There are two ways to defend against the net worth method: Show the Revenue Agent that his valuations or calculations are wrong, or show him that your net worth increased due to non-taxable factors. Maybe you inherited a substantial sum of money—inheritances and gifts are not taxable. Or, it's possible that you worked, paid taxes on the money you earned and accumulated a huge amount of cash that you kept hidden in your home. If you deposited the money during the year under audit, it will look like unreported income for that year. Once you offer a reasonable explanation of where you obtained non-taxable income, the legal burden shifts to the IRS to negate your explanation.

ii. Expenditure Method

Using the expenditure method, the Revenue Agent estimates all of your spending for the year and compares that amount to your reported income. If you spent more than you earned, the IRS attributes the difference to unreported income.

Defense. As with the net worth method, first show that the Revenue Agent didn't add or subtract correctly. More likely, you can demonstrate that the Revenue Agent overestimated your spending. Again, perhaps the money you spent came from non-taxable sources—loans, gifts, inheritances or prior accumulations.

iii. Bank Deposit Method

The bank deposit method is the IRS' favorite way of establishing unreported income because it is the easiest. The Revenue Agent simply totals up 12 months of bank account deposits and compares the total with the amount of income you reported. If you deposited more than you reported, the IRS assumes that the difference is unreported income. Keep in mind that your financial and property records are easily obtained by the IRS from banks, stock brokers and county recorders.

Defense. As with the net worth and expenditure methods, your first possible defense is to show that the Revenue Agent made math mistakes. Or, if you have several accounts, there is a very good chance that some of the deposits are actually transfers of money among accounts and the Revenue Agent is counting that income twice. Prepare to counter this double counting by listing all of your bank deposits before the audit begins. Note the source of money for each deposit, whether taxable receipts or non-taxable sources, such as a transfer. Other non-taxable sources include proceeds of a loan, redeposits of bad checks, inheritances and gifts received, sales of assets, holding money in accounts for relatives or friends and depositing cash earned in other years.

iv. Mark-Up Method

Using the mark-up method, the Revenue Agent looks at reported sales, cost of goods sold and net profit for a business that sells goods. If these numbers are much lower than the figures for similar businesses, the Revenue Agent may assume that you have not reported all income.

Example: Garth's roofing materials business sold $1,000,000 of supplies, which Garth purchased wholesale for $600,000. He had $375,000 in overhead expenses, netting him only $25,000 for the year. The IRS has data showing that the average mark-up on roofing materials for similar operations is 100%, meaning that Garth actually sold the $600,000 of materials for $1,200,000, not $1,000,000. The IRS assumes that Garth underreported the sales—and his income—by $200,000.

Defense. First, examine the source of data the Revenue Agent is using for the mark-up analysis. He may be comparing your business to one of a completely different type—for example, you wholesale computer parts and the agent has figures from home electronics retailing. If he is comparing apples to apples, then provide an explanation of why your operation underperformed similar businesses. Is your business newly established? Were you closed several months because of your ill health? Did you lose a major customer or key employee? Is your operation sensitive to extreme weather conditions? Did a competitor undercut your pricing to try to put you out of business? Were you victimized by an embezzling bookkeeper?

b. Verification of Business Expenses

Revenue Agents always ask for verification of major business expenses. For sole proprietors, this means the deductions shown on Schedule C. The agent is on the lookout for phony deductions (adding an extra "0" to a deduction—$200 instead of $20) and for business owners claiming personal expenses as business expenses (running personal errands using your business vehicle or installing the "office" stereo system in your living room).

The agent is particularly interested in auto, travel and entertainment deductions. The tax law mandates that you must keep accurate written records for these three categories. A business diary, calendar or log will be expected of you. If you lost or didn't keep one, create it for the audit—but tell the auditor it is a reconstruction. Auditors have a keen sense of freshly minted records. Honesty here builds your credibility.

c. Sales of Assets

If you sold any asset, the IRS may ask for substantiation of the "tax basis" you claimed on your tax return of the asset if it was used in your business or held for investment. The tax basis is the figure from which the IRS calculates the profit or loss you made on the sale or verifies your annual depreciation deduction. Essentially, tax basis starts with the amount you paid. To this figure, you add the cost of improvements and subtract expenses such as depreciation. If you received property as a gift or inheritance, your tax basis is the asset's tax basis at the date of the transfer, not the date of the original purchase.

Proving the tax basis can be a problem if you bought an asset many years back. Do the best you can to dig up the original purchase papers; if they are lost, you will have to recreate them. Also, you'll need receipts for real estate improvements done during your ownership. And with stock sales, you'll need to show any reinvested dividends on which you previously paid taxes.

For more details on substantiating an asset's tax basis, see *Tax Savvy for Small Business*, by Frederick W. Daily (Nolo).

d. Living Beyond One's Means

If the Revenue Agent has a strong suspicion that you have not reported all of your taxable income, he may use something called a financial status analysis to detect unreported income. He will ask himself one essential question: Does the income on your tax return support your financial condition and business transactions? Be ready to show how you acquired a Lamborghini while clerking at Futon World. While financial status inquiries were discouraged by the 1998 Tax Code changes, they were not banned altogether.

i. Standard of Living Issues

The IRS' training materials given to auditors direct them to consider the following questions:

- The standard of living of a taxpayer:
    - —What do the taxpayer and the taxpayer's dependents spend?
    - —How much does it cost to maintain this level of consumption?
    - —Is the reported net income sufficient to support this?
- The accumulated wealth of a taxpayer:
    - —How much capital/assets has the taxpayer accumulated?
    - —When and how was this wealth accumulated?
    - —Has the reported income been sufficient to pay for these items?
    - —If not, how did the taxpayer obtain and repay credit?

- The economic history of a taxpayer:
  - —What is the long-term pattern of profits and returns on investment in the reported activity?
  - —Is the business expanding or contracting?
  - —Does the reported business history match with changes in the taxpayer's standard of living and wealth accumulation?
- The business environment:
  - —What is the typical profitability and return on investment for the taxpayer's industry and locality?
  - —What are the typical patterns of non-compliance in the taxpayer's industry?
  - —What are the competitive pressures and economic health of the industry within which the taxpayer operates?
- Other non-taxable sources of funds:
  - —Do claims of non-taxable sources of support make economic sense?
  - —How creditworthy is the taxpayer—how many claimed loans?
  - —How did the sources of claimed funds' transfers obtain those funds?
- Goal:
  - —Do the taxpayer's books and records reflect the economic reality of his or her personal and business activities, or has the taxpayer omitted income in order to minimize tax liability?

ii. Lifestyle Questions

To investigate his suspicion that you are living beyond your means, the Revenue Agent is likely to ask you the following questions, which are taken from IRS training materials. Suggested answers follow. Don't say "no," but don't bite the IRS hook, either.

Question (Q). What are your home and work telephone numbers?

Suggested Answer (SA). Give your home number only and say, "Please don't call me at work," or vice versa.

Q.   What are your and your spouse's dates of birth?

SA.   I don't see how those relate to the year under audit.

Q.   Show me a copy of your tax return or extension for the past year.

SA.   I don't see how that relates to the year under audit.

Q.   What is the name of your previous employer and dates of employment?

SA.   I don't see how that relates to the year under audit.

Q.   Have you or your spouse had other occupations?

SA.   I don't see how that relates to the year under audit.

Q.   Can I see the purchase documents on your home?

SA.   I will show you these documents because *[choose all that apply:]* I claimed a casualty loss for my home, I sold my home or I claimed a home office deduction. *[If none of those apply:]* I don't see how they relate to the year under audit.

Q. What other real estate do you own?

SA. *[Answer only if you earn income from renting other real estate or you take a depreciation deduction or other tax benefit from the ownership. If that's not the case, then:]* I don't see how that relates to the year under audit.

Q. How many autos do you own, and what are your monthly payments?

SA. *[The auditor can easily check local DMV records for autos, boats and planes, so you might as well answer the question asked. If those vehicles are registered in other states, the auditor may not have this information, in which case let your conscience be your guide. Lying to the IRS is never recommended, however.]*

Q. Do you own any other valuable (over $10,000) assets?

SA. I don't see how this relates to the year under audit.

Q. Did you loan money to anyone?

SA. *[If you received interest from the loan during the year under audit, answer the question. Otherwise, say:]* I don't see how this relates to the year under audit.

Q. Did you take cash advances from your credit card or line of credit?

SA. I don't see how this relates to the year under audit.

Q. How much cash did you have on hand at your home, business, safety deposit box, buried in the back yard?

SA. *[Don't guess, even if the Revenue Agent pushes you.]* I don't see how this relates to the year under audit.

Q.   What is the largest amount of cash you had on hand?

A.   *[Again, don't guess, even if the Revenue Agent pushes you.]* I don't see how this relates to the year under audit.

Q.   Were you involved in cash transactions exceeding $10,000?

SA.   *[If you say yes, and the transaction was business-related, you may have had an obligation to file a currency transaction report with the IRS. If you didn't do this, you just confessed to a crime. If you say no, it had better be the truth, or you just broke an even more serious law. Ask a tax lawyer how to answer if you are in doubt.]*

To summarize, answer IRS economic reality questions with questions of your own—or don't answer them at all. You were selected for an audit, and shouldn't be treated like a criminal. Suggest that if the auditor wants to make an adjustment based on "economic reality," you'll appeal. More likely than not, the auditor will back off.

e. Rental Real Estate

If you claimed rental property income and expenses on Schedule E of your tax return, you will have to verify them to the Revenue Agent. As a property owner, you should keep records. If you don't, you must reconstruct records from canceled checks, deposits, receipts and notes.

f. Classification of Workers as Employees or Independent Contractors

The Revenue Agent will be keenly interested in whether you properly classified people working for your business as independent contractors or employees. For all employees, you are required to withhold and pay over taxes to the IRS and probably your state taxing authority. By contrast, you have no tax withholding responsibilities or FICA taxes for independent contractors. But you must meet strict standards to classify a worker as an independent contractor, and the IRS has a strong bias toward finding that workers are employees. If the IRS finds that you have misclassified workers, the tax bill could be enormous.

 For more information on correctly classifying your workers, see *Hiring Independent Contractors,* by Stephen Fishman (Nolo).

IF THE AUDITOR COMES TO YOUR HOME OR OFFICE

As mentioned earlier, holding a field audit at your business or home isn't recommended by most tax professionals. A Revenue Agent can't enter your home without an invitation or a court order. Of course, if you don't let him in, he may legitimately disallow a home office deduction.

If you hold the audit at your home or office, don't feel compelled to make it too comfortable for the Revenue Agent. You don't have to be cruel—such as sticking the agent in an unheated storeroom—but this could result in an abnormally brief audit. All's fair in love and dealing with the IRS.

If the audit is held away from your business, an auditor can still pay you a visit. He may want to verify a tax return item. For instance, he might spot-check for equipment that was tax deducted. Ordinarily, he will call before showing up. This gives you time to remove items that might cause suspicion, like the picture of your Chris-Craft or alpine ski cabin. If he wants a tour, schedule it when employees or customers aren't likely to be around. And don't let him wander—stay by his side. This prevents the agent from talking to people who'll then know you're under the audit microscope. An innocent remark or a vengeful employee could stab you in the back. If he asks for records during an observation visit, say that they aren't accessible, are at home or are in your tax pro's office. He won't start opening your file cabinets to verify your assertions.

CHAPTER 5

How an Auditor Prepares for an Office or Field Audit

The training manual instructs auditors on how to conduct the first audit meeting, be it an office audit or field audit. Selected portions of the manual follow. My comments are in the brackets.

(1) The initial interview is the most important part of the audit process. The first few minutes should be spent making the taxpayer comfortable and explaining the examination process ... *[Read that first sentence again; first impressions are vital.]*

(3) Sufficient information should be developed to reach informed judgments as to:

    (a) Financial history and standard of living. *[See Chapter 4, Section B.2, for a discussion of IRS lifestyle audits.]*

    (b) Nature of employment to determine relationship to other entities. *[This means the auditor may want to look at your partnership or corporation's tax returns too, and look for the possibility of any bartering.]*

    (c) Money or property received ... determined to be ... not taxable ... *[For instance, did you get loans or inheritances or sell assets during the year?]*

    (d) Potential for moonlighting income. *[For example, are you a firefighter who does odd jobs on your days off?]*

(4) If warranted ... *[If, after covering the above areas, the auditor becomes suspicious, she should question the following areas.]*

    (a) Property owned, including bank accounts, stocks and bonds, real estate, automobiles, etc., in this country and abroad. *[The IRS has records of most, if not all, of these transactions, or can get those records.]*

    (b) Purchases, sales, transfers, contributions or exchanges of ... assets. *[Did you buy or sell anything in the thousands of dollars?]*

    (c) The correctness of exemptions and dependents claimed. *[If you claimed a large number of dependents, be prepared to explain, especially if any of the dependents aren't immediate family members.]*

(5) Remember, the taxpayer is being examined and not just the return. *[This is in the back of every auditor's mind.]*

In addition, the Tax Code gives office auditors and Revenue Agents wide authority to pry into your financial affairs. The basic tools in their kit are the taxpayer interview, the information document request, the third-party summons and information requests, IRS records and other government and private agency records.

A. Taxpayer Interview

Auditors and Revenue Agents generate many of their questions for the audit from IRS Form 4700 Supplement and IRS Form 4700 Business Supplement. Both are in the Appendix, and you'll do yourself well to read these well before your audit. They highlight the areas of inquiry you can expect. If any item on these forms gives you real concern, see a tax pro before the audit or consider hiring a representative to attend for you.

B. Information Document Request

Take a look again at your initial audit notice and the materials from the IRS. Something called an Information Document Request, or IDR, may have come with it. An IDR is an IRS request that you bring to the audit certain documents or information either in your possession or accessible to you. Bank statements and canceled checks are typical IDR items. The IRS knows well the truth of the words of a Supreme Court Justice that "a person can be defined by the checks he writes."

In field audits, Revenue Agents commonly issue follow-up IDRs when they haven't seen everything at the first appointment. Ordinarily, you're given a few weeks to mail the items to the agent or you are asked to bring them to the next meeting.

SAMPLE INFORMATION DOCUMENT REQUEST

Form 4564 Rev.Jan.1984	Department of the Treasury Internal Revenue Service INFORMATION DOCUMENT REQUEST	Request Number 2A

TO: (Name of Taxpayer and Co. Div.or Branch)

	Subject 1040

SAIN No. n/a	Submitted to: 19XX

Please return with listed documents
to requester listed below.

Dates of Previous Requests
   n/a

Description of Documents Requested   Years Under Exam: 19XX

1. General ledger and all subsidiary ledgers maintained.
2. Journals: General, cash disbursements, cash receipts, sales, purchases, and any other journals maintained including depreciation schedule.
3. Working trial balance.
4. Adjusting and closing journal entries.
5. Any other books and records.
6. Retained copy of year-end and/or monthly financial statements.
7. Tax return preparer's workpapers, if they are needed in order to reconcile the tax returns figures to general ledger figures, and account groupings and/or chart of accounts, etc...
8. Bank statements, cancelled checks, and deposit tickets for the months of December, 19XW through January, 19XY (For Both Business and Personal Bank Accounts).
9. All stock and mutual fund statements for the year under exam.
10. all F1099s & F1098s issued and received.
11. Employment tax returns such as 940, 941s, and W3, W2s.
12. Rental contracts, books and records, and purchase escrow of the property.
13. Related returns (F1120)
15. All documents necessary to document and substantiate the following items:

    Items will be sampled later.

Response Date: 4/16/XX   Date Furnished:

	Name and Title of Requestor Lou Tack, Revenue Agent	Date 3/18/XX
FROM	Office Location 450 Golden Gate, San Francisco, Ca94102 Mail Stop 6107,	Telephone # 415-123-4567 Fax # 415-987-6543

Page 1

An IDR carries no legal force. If you don't provide what was asked for, the auditor cannot do anything to you, other than deny your deduction or exemption. If an item is really relevant to your audit and not likely to cause harm, you might as well turn it over. This is especially true if it's a bank record the IRS already knows exists.

If you don't understand an item's relevance to your audit, however, simply decline to provide it. For example, the IRS commonly uses IDRs to request copies of other years' tax returns—and it's rarely a good idea to supply them.

If you would rather not discuss the item requested, simply ignore the IDR and see if the auditor pursues it. If she does, ask her to justify how the item or items requested relate to the year audited. If you believe she is crossing the line, just say no. If an item being requested may severely damage or incriminate you, see a tax attorney before you have any conversation with the auditor.

C. Summons

If the Revenue Agent is not satisfied with what you have provided—by oral request during the audit interview with you or your representative or through an IDR—she may issue something called a summons. (Internal Revenue Code §§ 7602(a) and 7604(b).) An IRS summons is a legally enforceable order. It orders you to appear before the auditor to answer questions and/or to bring specified items. The summons is issued by the IRS itself, not by a court.

A summons is not to be taken lightly. If you don't comply, the IRS can force you to appear before a federal court judge in a summons enforcement proceeding. The judge can order you to provide the information requested or produce the documents listed. If you don't show up or cooperate, you might be fined or jailed.

If you get a summons and have questions about what might happen to you if you do or don't comply, contact a tax lawyer. In rare cases, you may be able to successfully oppose the summons on legal grounds, such as:

- self-incrimination—your constitutional right to withhold something from the government if it would subject you to criminal prosecution for any type of offense, not just a tax offense

- the summons is vague, overbroad or unduly burdensome—for example, you've been asked to produce an overwhelming amount of documents, or

- the items are protected by a legal privilege—such as the attorney-client privilege.

Despite the power of a summons, the IRS rarely hauls an uncooperative taxpayer into federal court for failing to comply. Instead, the IRS is likely to do one of the following if you don't give the auditor information that she has requested.

Drop it. You'd be surprised how many auditors back off or forget. Keep in mind that an auditor has a fairly large caseload. If the agent has most of the information she needs, she may let it slide.

Go further without your cooperation. Auditors can summons third parties, such as your bank, for the records you refuse to hand over. (See Section D, below.) This is a fairly common practice and is perfectly legal.

Issue an Examination Report. The auditor can issue an Examination Report based on the information she does have, by estimating missing income and disallowing unverified expenses. Receiving an unfavorable audit report is the most likely consequence of your not cooperating.

D. Third-Party Contacts

Auditors have two ways to get data about you from third parties: informally request the information or order the information by way of a summons. Most auditors avoid issuing a summons unless informal requests for information fail.

An auditor can contact third parties who have dealt with you by letter or telephone, and may very well do so to confirm information in your tax return. For example, if you claimed to make regular office supply purchases at a neighborhood stationary store, the auditor might call the store to see if the clerks know you. In most situations, you have no grounds for objecting to these contacts. Your only legitimate complaint is if the auditor reveals personal or financial information about you or your spouse to another person. It's perfectly fine for the IRS to tell the third party that you are under investigation, but it's not fine for the IRS to say more. If the auditor says too much, contact your local IRS District Director and complain that your right to privacy has been violated.

If an auditor doesn't want to rely on an informal request—or it goes unanswered—she can issue a summons for data from banks, employers, business associates and any other third party who has information about you. The auditor is most likely to do this if you (or the third party) don't voluntarily provide the information or the auditor wants to verify information you do provide. You will be sent a copy of the IRS summons so that you know the IRS is taking this action. You can rarely stop a third-party summons, but if you want to try, see a tax lawyer.

⚠ Never tell someone not to comply with an IRS summons. It's illegal if they follow your advice and could get both you and the person who received the summons into trouble. Federal judges do not think highly of taxpayers who attempt to disrupt the work of an IRS agent.

E. IRS Files

The auditor will have in her file the actual tax return you filed and a summary of the IRS' income records (W-2 and 1099 forms) for the audit year. She is very unlikely to have other tax returns, audit reports or tax account history. This information is scattered throughout the IRS' various computer systems. Much of this data is not easily accessible to the auditor, so she might first ask you for your copies of other returns or audit reports. If you don't turn them over, the auditor can request that the documents be taken out of storage. Auditors don't go to this trouble unless they feel the taxpayer is not being truthful or that a problem with the tax return for the year under audit is so severe that it permeates other returns and will lead to a big audit bill.

F. Other Government and Private Records

All federal and state (except Nevada) agencies share data with each other, to some extent. An IRS auditor can access the Treasury Enforcement Communication Systems (TECS) computer for data on you, such as your criminal record. She can also search Social Security Administration, Passport Office and Postal Service records. These records show your previous addresses, trips abroad and income history from previous jobs.

Auditors can also search local and state government records for ownership of vehicles, boats, airplanes, real estate and business entities. Auditors also tap into private databases and credit reporting agency files (Equifax, Experian and Trans Union) if they are looking for personal data on a taxpayer. All kinds of information are in these files—such as credit card accounts, mortgage loans and previous addresses—that could provide clues about your property and resources.

Office auditors seldom request information from other government or private agencies, but field agents often do. ■

CHAPTER 6

Attending an Office or Field Audit

The big day has arrived. Before leaving for the audit—or before the Revenue Agent arrives at your home office—take one last look at your documents and do an inventory of the receipts and records you have for the audit.

If you are heading to the IRS for an office audit, give yourself plenty of time to arrive punctually and start off on the right foot. Otherwise, you risk irritating the auditor and giving the general impression that you don't take the IRS very seriously. Approach the audit as your would any business meeting because to the IRS office auditor, your audit is strictly routine. If the IRS suspected you of any real wrongdoing, you would be meeting with the criminal investigators, or at least have been hit with a field audit.

Your clothes should be in keeping with your job and station in life. Anything else looks and feels odd—and an audit is uncomfortable enough already. Don't wear your Sunday best if you work at Burger World or dress like a fry cook if you are a dentist. If you are a bus driver coming from work, wear your uniform. It's simple, really—be yourself.

Office auditors keep pleasantries to a minimum due to a tight time schedule. IRS District Offices set two audits per day for small business owners or four for wage earners. Expect your audit to last from one to four hours. Auditors must write up their findings between appointments, so they keep moving. The auditor generally starts with background questions, such as, "Are you married?" or "Where do you live?" Then the auditor starts questioning in earnest.

If you're facing a field audit and the IRS auditor is coming to your place, be ready for her. (If you have a representative handling the audit for you, skip ahead to Section A, below). Have the documents out and in order. Preparation is the key to winning most audit issues, meaning that your papers should be organized beforehand. Chances are you are self-employed, so you want the Revenue Agent's first impression to be that you are a careful businessperson. Most Revenue Agents prefer that you address her or him as Ms. Lui or Mr. Hernandez, and not as Christine or Mark. Offer coffee, tea or a soft drink as you would to any business guest you are about to meet with. The Revenue Agent knows you don't want to be there, so don't put on a phony chummy front—but don't complain, either. Consider the audit another cost of doing business, like paying your rent.

A. Who Should Attend the Audit?

You can attend the audit by yourself, bring a supporting cast with you or stay at home and send a representative—a tax return preparer, enrolled agent, CPA or attorney. There are many reasons why you might send a representative. As mentioned in Chapter 5, the initial taxpayer interview is the most important phase of an audit to the IRS. You—not just your tax return—are under examination. Your behavior is being observed. Will you act guilty? Will your answers sound evasive? Will you start to shake when some items are discussed? If any of these describes you, think hard about hiring a representative to send to the audit in your place.

If you bring people along or send a representative, the auditor will require that you sign an IRS form waiving your right to privacy and allowing the other people to be present. He'll give this form to you at the audit. A tax representative must give the auditor a different form (IRS Form 2848, a copy of which is in the Appendix) to represent you. You don't have to disclose in advance that you'll send someone else or will bring people along.

If you don't send a representative in your place, consider bringing any of the following people with you:

- *Employee.* Your bookkeeper, manager, accounts payable supervisor or anyone else with knowledge of your business records can help you explain them.

- *Spouse.* If a joint return is being audited, only one spouse must attend; certainly both can. If a tax return filed by only one spouse is being audited, the other can attend to provide support and comfort.

- *Family member or friend.* You can bring along anyone who will provide you with moral support, can translate if your English isn't very good, wipe away your tears, stare at the auditor or do whatever else might help.

B. What to Bring to the Audit

As explained in Chapter 5, audit notices typically include a list of documents, called an IDR, to bring to the audit. Start by gathering these documents. You can omit any items not related to the year or years listed in the audit notice. If the auditor asks about listed items you didn't bring, ask why they are related, and then say you forgot or just shrug your shoulders. Let the auditor interpret this however he wants.

Avoid showing the auditor things overlapping into other years. Although the auditor's fishing license is restricted to the year on the notice, he'll gaze at other years' stuff—and make adjustments—if they're under his nose. For instance, checking account statements typically overlap—January's statement has checks for December. Remove checks for the year not being audited.

If the auditor asks you about non-listed items, say you didn't come prepared to discuss them. The auditor may just drop it or, at worst, set a second meeting date. And don't do anything that might lead the auditor to ask you about non-listed items. For example, leave at home canceled checks and receipts for personal expenses that weren't claimed as deductions.

You may need to bring with you items that are not on the list to justify deductions, explain cryptic documents or reconstruct missing records. You may have even left off your return some deductions for which you now have supporting documents. Bring those along, too. Remember that your job is to document your income and your deductible expenses to the auditor.

As mentioned in other chapters, don't bring tax returns for any year other than the one being audited. If the auditor asks about them, say something like, "I couldn't find them." Or, make a vague offer to supply them later. Just stall. Don't worry about making the auditor mad. Auditors know that you never have to provide a copy of a tax return to the IRS again after you file it. Only if the IRS denies having received a return should you give a copy to get it on file.

Avoid giving original documents to the IRS. If the auditor wants to keep your document, ask him to make notes from it instead. Or, if the item is harmless, allow him to make a copy. If the item isn't harmless, state that you don't see why he needs a copy. Usually, he will back down and make notes. This takes more of his time, which means less dirt-digging in other areas. Why not give the IRS any originals? Because the IRS is a black hole for paper. If the auditor insists and you give in, demand a receipt specifically describing each document left with the auditor. And demand that the auditor make you a copy of the original documents he is keeping. That way, if the auditor claims not to have something, you'll have proof that it did exist at one time.

1. Canceled Checks and Receipts

Take with you only the canceled checks and receipts related to the areas listed. Even if the audit list asks for your business expenses, don't take personal expense checks. If you don't have the canceled check, the IRS allows an account statement from a financial institution showing a check has cleared.

Don't let the auditor rummage through personal checks and receipts not related to the tax return. He might get the idea you are spending more money than you are reporting and may dig deeper.

2. Books and Records

Under the Tax Code, only certain businesses like insurance companies and banks must keep a formal set of books. If you are audited as an individual or small business owner, however, you should be ready to show records that reflect your true income and expenses. For example, a check register or a printout from financial management software, such as *Quicken,* may serve as a set of books for an individual or small business. Of course, you will need to back up your statement with canceled checks and paid receipts.

If your business has no records at all, you may be subject to a fine. Even worse, the auditor can make up records by pure guesswork. For example, he may double the gross receipts reported by estimates based on published industry or government sources. This forces you either to come up with records or accept his figures.

3. Appointment Books or Business Diaries

If you're in business for yourself, you probably claimed travel and entertainment expenses. To legitimately claim these deductions, the Tax Code requires that you keep records specifically showing:

- the dates and times the expenses were incurred
- the business purpose, and
- who you visited or entertained.

If you didn't keep a diary or calendar or you lost the one you did keep, you can write one up for the audit. Tell the auditor it is a reconstruction of travel and entertainment expenses, if he asks.

SAMPLE APPOINTMENT BOOK AND BUSINESS DIARY

4. Auto Logs

The Tax Code does not require that you keep an auto log—despite what some auditors say—but one can sure help prove your business vehicle expenses. If you didn't keep an auto log, you can create one for the audit. This is a time-consuming task, but it sure beats the disallowance of auto expense deductions. If you need help determining mileage for the year, look at your repair and maintenance receipts. They usually have the odometer reading on them. In addition, your business calendar or diary should include notations of trips and expenses, such as parking and tolls.

SAMPLE VEHICLE EXPENSE LOG

Vehicle Expense Log							
January, 19XX			**Odometer Readings**			**Expenses**	
Date	Destination (City, Town or Area)	Business Purpose	Start	Stop	Miles this trip	Type (Gas, oil, tolls, etc.)	Amount
1/18/98	Local (St. Louis)	Sales calls	8,097	8,188	91	Gas	$18.25
1/19/98	Indianapolis	Sales calls	8,211	8,486	275	Parking	2.00
1/20/98	Louisville	See Bob Smith	8,486	8,599	113	Gas/	16.50
		(Pot. Client)				Repair flat tire	
1/21/98	Return to St. Louis		8,599	8,875	276	Gas	17.25
1/22/98	Local (St. Louis)	Sales calls	8,914	9,005	91		
1/23/98	Local (St. Louis)		9,005	9,005	0	Car Wash	8.50
///	MONTHLY TOTAL	///	8,097	9,005	846	///	$62.50
TOTAL JANUARY, 19XX	Business Miles Driven				846	Expenses	$62.50

5. Real Estate Papers

To support your annual tax deduction for rental or business property depreciation, and to report the gain or loss when you sell investment real estate, you will need documents showing the purchase price and the costs of any capital improvements. Your original purchase-escrow papers should have the original cost information. Major capital improvements—such as a new roof, fire escape or electrical rewiring—should also be documented.

C. How to Behave—Playing It Cool at Your Audit

There are some definite dos and don'ts in dealing with an auditor. This section explores the dangers of over-talkativeness, what to do when you have something to hide, getting along with difficult auditors, what happens when a new auditor comes into the scene and acceptable ways to stand up to an auditor.

1. Mum's the Word

IRS encounters are inherently stressful. People under stress often talk too much. The IRS knows this, and so auditors are trained to listen and create opportunities for you to talk. They examine your records silently, hoping you'll fill the void. Some people, uncomfortable with silence, hang themselves by blurting out answers to questions that weren't even asked. During Randy's audit, he volunteered that he had always deducted clothing expenses because he had to wear nice clothing as a salesperson. Until then, the auditor hadn't noticed this deduction, which was fairly large. The auditor disallowed the deduction, and expanded the audit to cover the two open years. Randy came away owing several thousands of dollars for three years, thanks to his big mouth.

If you're really uncomfortable with prolonged periods of silence, perhaps you should not attend the audit or should bring someone along to kick you (gently) if you begin to babble on.

Eventually, you will have to talk. Every auditor asks routine interview questions. Keep in mind that every question in the auditor's script has a reason—even if it is not obvious to you. Think carefully before you answer any question. Keep your answer to a minimum. Do not deliver your best Shakespearean-like monologue. Instead, the best responses to a question posed by an auditor are:

- Yes.

- No.

- I don't recall.

- I'll have to check on that.

- What specific items do you want to see?

- Why do you want that? What does this have to do with the year being audited?

In summary: Never say more unless it is absolutely necessary. As a rule, you can't hurt yourself when your mouth is shut. For example, if the auditor asks about items that were not listed in the audit notice, say you didn't come prepared to discuss them. The auditor may just drop it or, at worst, set a second meeting date.

⚠ Never lie. Don't say "no" if the answer is "yes." If you don't want to hang yourself, say, "I don't recall," "I have to check on that" or "My tax preparer might know, but I'm not sure." Sometimes, auditors ask for information they already possess just to test your credibility. A favorite technique when you failed to declare dividend or interest income is to ask if you have any investments—when you obviously do because the IRS Form 1099 shows that you earned interest and dividends. Or, she may ask about your boats, planes or vehicles, even though she has a printout from your state motor vehicle department.

WHEN YOU HAVE SOMETHING TO HIDE

It may not be in your best interest to cooperate in an audit. Maybe your bank records show larger deposits than you reported as income and you don't want to explain. Or maybe you highly exaggerated some deductions. Here, you wisest course of action may be to skip the audit. First consult a tax attorney. If you attend the audit and nervously blurt out something, you might earn a visit from the IRS Criminal Investigation Division. Something stupid, like, "I guess you caught me, ha, ha," or "I didn't think you would find that account," can cause auditors to stop the audit and bring in the criminal investigators.

Even if you skip the audit, you can contest the outcome by going to Tax Court. (See Chapter 9.) By disregarding the audit notice, you keep the IRS away from your records—unless this auditor issues a summons. (See Chapter 5, Section C.) Once in Tax Court, you can contest only the items of your choosing and can stay away from the problem areas. This strategy has its pitfalls, however, and before trying it out, check with a tax pro.

When you ignore an audit notice, the IRS will proceed in one of three ways:

- *Do the audit without you.* The auditor may simply issue a report disallowing all items he thinks are questionable. A month or so later, you'll receive a bill from the Service Center. You may want to accept the bill and move on with your life. The danger is that if you don't cooperate and the IRS thinks you are hiding something, the auditor may expand the audit to other open years—returns due and filed within the past three years (six years if the auditor suspects serious misdeeds).

- *Call you.* The auditor or his manager may call to ask why you are not cooperating. You can ignore the call or give a vague answer, such as, "I am giving it thought," "I've had other pressing matters" or "I'm sick." Eventually, the auditor will issue a report based on what he has. As with the point just above, he may disallow many of your deductions and exemptions. A month or so later, you will receive a tax bill.

WHEN YOU HAVE SOMETHING TO HIDE (continued)

• Issue a summons. The IRS use of a summons to get information from you is covered in Chapter 5, Section C. The IRS can use that same power to order you to appear at an audit. As discussed in Chapter 5, if you ignore a summons, you could be held in contempt of court—even jailed. If you receive an IRS summons, talk to a tax attorney.

2. Don't Offer Favors to the Auditor

Auditors must report offers of favors. Some taxpayers are from countries where bribing government officials is the norm. Forget it. IRS employees are among the cleanest civil servants of all—maybe because they know the IRS has zero tolerance for bribery and that they would go to jail if caught. They can accept a cup of coffee at your place, but that's about it. If you offer a discount on merchandise and the auditor ignores you, consider yourself lucky. An outright bribe attempt will get you a visit from the criminal investigators—as well as a very thorough audit.

3. Try to Get Along With the Auditor

Don't go in to the audit with a chip on your shoulder and an anti-IRS attitude, even if you think the agency is the devil incarnate. The auditor knows you are not happy to be there, but he is just doing his job and didn't have anything to do with picking you. Remember what Grandma said about catching more flies with honey than with vinegar.

When meeting the auditor or Revenue Agent, be polite, even if it hurts. Try to chit-chat about the weather, traffic or sports to break the ice. If the office auditor seems cold and businesslike, don't take it personally. They are under time pressures and may want to get right down to business.

Field auditors, on the other hand, are encouraged to chat you up. You can be friendly without disclosing anything that might hurt you by avoiding talking about yourself. Try showing an interest in the auditor's job and life. "How long have you been with the IRS?" "How does someone get to be an auditor?" "Where did you go to school?" "Do you have children?" Everyone likes to talk about their favorite subject—themselves. At worst, it reduces the time for examining your return.

While you don't have to attend the audit with a chip on your shoulder, you also don't have to become best friends with the auditor. Some taxpayers meet great success by taking a defiant stand with an auditor—for example, asking the reason for each question. Some auditors are intimidated by this. Others are so unused to being challenged that they get flustered. A small number of taxpayers have found that certain types of obnoxious or peculiar behavior—such as attending with bad B.O. or giving a field auditor a dark, noisy, cramped space—work wonders.

HANDLING A DIFFICULT AUDITOR

The typical auditor is just doing his job. Undoubtedly though, some auditors go overboard in giving you a hard time. He may be impolite, hostile or rude. Worse, he may disallow deductions unless you can produce ironclad proof in triplicate. Why is he behaving like this? Perhaps you did something to upset him, he is having a bad day or all of his days are bad and everyone upsets him. Whatever the reason, you don't have to take guff from an auditor. Ask him politely to lighten up. If he doesn't, ask to see his manager, or say something like, "I'm too upset to continue. We must recess to another day so I can regain my composure." If he balks, say, "I want to consult a tax pro before continuing." He must grant your request under the Taxpayer's Bill of Rights. Once you leave the audit, you can change your mind and not call a pro. But the audit is finished for that day.

Threatening to walk out—or demanding a time-out—may cause the auditor to change his tune. He loses face if you call his manager. Furthermore, he really doesn't want to see you again. He already has a backlog of cases. His performance is largely judged by how many files he closes over a given period. He wants you to sign his report so he can get a top rating.

If you wind up meeting a second time, the auditor may be in a better mood. Auditors also knows that if you bring in a tax pro, she won't put up with a lack of professionalism. You might even have a new auditor. You never know what is going on in the auditor's life. His misery may have nothing to do with you. Maybe he was ill, in the process of quitting, getting fired or transferring to another IRS department.

If the auditor continues to run roughshod over you, demand to see his Group Manager. Tell the manager that you're not being treated respectfully and want a different auditor. While chances are slim that you'll get a new face, the old one should start treating you more civilly.

Have you seen this auditor before? The Internal Revenue Manual discourages, but doesn't prohibit, future examinations by the same auditor within three years. But, the first audit must have been officially closed. If you recognize the auditor—this might happen if your local office has only a few auditors—and you don't want him again, complain to his manager.

4. If a New Auditor Appears on the Scene

Field audits commonly drag on for months or even several years. Revenue Agents may be replaced midstream due to a job transfer, promotion, maternity leave, training, resignation or firing. It's even possible that you'll see a new auditor if your field audit takes more than one meeting.

If you get a new auditor, the IRS won't tell you what happened to the first one; the second one just magically appears. This could be a blessing. No two auditors document their work the same way; some people's handwriting is not easily decipherable. The newcomer may jump at a chance to close the file if you throw him a bone. Consider this case of Laura, which shows how a new auditor can be a godsend.

Example: Laura had mistakenly claimed an improper business deduction for three years running—totaling $120,000. Auditor Bob spotted this irregularity toward the end of their first meeting and asked her to explain. Laura asked for time to contact her tax pro and to address it next time around. Laura talked to Luke and found out she was dead wrong. Laura could only be saved by a miracle, and got one when Bob was replaced by Beth. Beth either couldn't read Bob's notes or didn't understand them, and completely missed the issue. She found a few small adjustments, and presented a report which Laura cheerfully signed.

A new auditor is not always a positive development. He may be determined to re-plow old ground. You—or your representative—may be asked questions you've already answered or asked to produce documents already shown. If you are asked to produce the same records a second time, become indignant. The longer the audit, the louder you should squeak. After all, the change of auditors isn't your fault, and you shouldn't be punished. Use this as an opportunity to take control of the situation. Tell the auditor what your records indicate, and show him a few items to back up your story. Consider proposing a few small adjustments, if appropriate, and an immediate closing.

If the new auditor persists in traveling over old terrain, call in the manager. He might agree or compromise to get rid of you.

But what if your complaints don't get you anywhere—that is, the manager insists that you drag out your papers again? Before you give in, ask to speak to the head audit person, called the Examination Branch Chief. Even if everyone turns you down, by squeaking your wheels you have shown yourself to be someone unlikely to meekly accept an examination report.

5. Standing Up to the Auditor

As your audit progresses, the auditor will continually make notes in his workpapers. Don't expect him to voluntarily tell you what he is writing or thinking. But, as a rule, the more he writes, the more bad news is on its way. There is one way to keep an auditor from running amok. When he finishes examining one group of items—for example, your business travel expenses—ask him if he has found any problems? If he says yes, insist that he spells out the facts or law on which he is relying before he proceeds to a new topic.

This strategy can help you in two ways: First, it identifies you as someone who is not a pushover. Second, it makes the auditor justify his actions to your face. You are perfectly within your rights to politely ask questions, and then to respond. For example, the auditor says that he is making an adjustment because your records are incomplete. Your response: "Please hold off for 15 days and I'll get the missing records to you." Or, the auditor says you have no legal right claim a certain deduction—for example, that your Beanie Baby business is a non-deductible hobby. Your response: "Please give me the specific legal authority on which you are relying. I want to research the matter or talk to my tax pro."

By repeatedly challenging the auditor to justify his decisions, he'll soon think twice. It's basic human nature to avoid conflict. This tactic can also soften the auditor up for negotiation. One feisty taxpayer once flatly refused to leave the IRS office until the auditor canceled a penalty—and he did. Auditors don't like to justify their actions, particularly if they are not 100% sure that they are correct, which is often the case. They prefer to hide behind a mailed report rather than give bad news to your face.

A minority of auditors—usually new ones straight from IRS basic training—come on strong. They look at every little thing and bark like a Marine drill instructor. When this happens, let him know that two can play this game. Drop the nice guy approach, get your back up and argue over every item. If serious problems ahead become evident—questionable items or missing documents—demand to end the audit for that day so you can consult a tax pro. He won't appreciate being slowed down, but he knows he must grant your request. At your next meeting, the auditor may take a calmer approach, if for no reason other than to get rid of you. If the auditor continues to hassle you, take a look at the sidebar in Section C.3, above.

Will standing up for yourself get you a tougher audit? No—in fact, the opposite is generally true. The auditor has absolutely no incentive to make your life hell. He doesn't get bonus or overtime pay from the IRS. Now keep in mind that standing up for yourself is *not* the same thing as being disrespectful or impolite—and you are well-advised not to be. But the more you make the auditor explain, the more he will want to close shop and go on to a timid, easier mark.

6. If You Didn't Bring Everything

It is okay not to resolve the audit in one meeting. There is a good chance the auditor will ask for something you didn't bring. That's not a problem. Reply that you need time to submit it—15 to 30 days is reasonable. Mail in a copy—never originals—with a letter to jog the auditor's memory explaining how it helps your audit. Call a week later to confirm that the auditor received your packet. If he wants voluminous records or you think he won't understand what you are sending, request another meeting.

What if you don't want the auditor to see a particular item? You can vaguely promise to send it in but conveniently forget to—he may overlook it, too. If he doesn't forget, you won't lose any more than you would have by cooperating.

D. Negotiating With an Auditor

Auditors have no power to change your tax liability without your consent. An auditor only can *propose* tax changes. He knows that if you don't go along, you can appeal or take the IRS to court. The IRS' fondest wish is to close examinations with your signature on the dotted line, keeping the workload down for the Appeals Office and courts. For this reason, an auditor's performance is judged in part on his closing ratio— that is, how many examination reports are accepted by taxpayers. This puts you in a perfect position to negotiate.

Officially, auditors aren't supposed to wheel and deal. They're told to discover the facts by asking questions and examining documents, and apply the law to those facts. In reality, however, if you can show the auditor that the facts are not black and white or that the tax law is not clearly against you, you can reach a compromise. But keep in mind this truth: You can bargain based on the facts or a disagreement with application of the law; you cannot cut a deal because you cannot afford the tax bill. Contrary to what you might think, an auditor is not a bill collector, and whether or not you ever pay the tax bill is not his concern! The auditor's only job is to determine the correct amount of tax.

1. Negotiating Common Audit Issues

Here are some examples showing how to negotiate the two most common audit issues: missing documents and legal grounds for a deduction.

*   *Missing documentation.* You deducted a storage rental expense of $200 per month for your inventory of goods for sale. You paid in cash but either lost or never bothered to get paid receipts from the business. The auditor wants to disallow the $2,400 for lack of verification. The clerk at the storage facility signs a letter attesting to your regular payments, but the company records aren't accessible. You might propose a compromise: a disallowance of 20% ($480) to get the audit over with. If the auditor agrees, you have negotiated a fairly decent settlement—and learned a lesson about keeping records.

*   *Questionable legal ground.* You spent $5,000 to replace a deck and $5,000 for a rebuilt roof on rental property you own. On your tax return, you deducted $10,000 in repairs. The auditor says these are not repairs, but are long-term improvements. As such, they can't be deducted 100% in one year. If she's right, and each improvement has a ten-year estimated life, you could deduct only 1/10 of the cost ($1,000) per year for ten years. But your old roof was in bad shape and further patching might not have worked. So, this could qualify as a legal gray area. To compromise, you concede the deck is an

improvement, but insist that the roof is a repair. If the auditor backs down, you get a deduction of 100% ($5,000) for the roof and 10% ($500) for the deck. While you wanted $10,000, deducting $5,500 beats the auditor's allowing only $1,000 that year. You can still take tax deductions for the balance ($4,500) at $500 per year over nine years.

It may sound odd, but don't talk dollars when negotiating with an auditor. For instance, don't offer 50¢ on the dollar during negotiating. The IRS language of audit negotiation is percentages. See the examples just above.

2. Adjustments in Your Favor—Taking the Offensive

Legally, the auditor must make any and all adjustments whenever found during an audit—even if they are in your favor. This in line with the IRS' contention that the auditor is simply determining the correct amount of tax. Even the most hard-nosed auditor knows that people make tax return mistakes in the IRS' favor or overlook claiming tax benefits. This is another reason to visit a tax pro before meeting with an auditor—to find out if you missed any deductions.

If you didn't claim a tax deduction for some reason—you lost the receipt or did not believe it was available to you—bring it up now. The auditor might accept it, or you might use it as a negotiating chip. Nothing ventured, nothing gained.

Be patient. Don't bring up any item in your favor until the auditor has completed his review and decided on changes for the IRS. Then spring your new deductions on him. If you reveal them any earlier, he might look harder for offsetting adjustments. After he is locked into his report, it can only get better with your newly found deductions. ■

Ending an Office or Field Audit

As mentioned in Chapter 1, the IRS normally has only 36 months to begin and end an audit of your return—beginning on the day you file it. (If the IRS suspects underreporting of income by at least 25%, the IRS has six years to complete the audit. And if the IRS suspects fraud, the IRS has forever to audit you.) The Internal Revenue Manual, however, directs auditors to complete audits within 28 months after you filed your tax return. This allows the IRS an additional eight months to process any appeal you might file.

This means that delays can work in your favor, because the IRS is under deadline. And because the IRS is not the model of efficiency, audits are often delayed for various reasons—backlogs, agent transfers, postponements and lost files. When an old file surfaces, the file may be assigned to a new auditor, who is reluctant to work on a half-done case. The three-year deadline for auditing your return may expire before the file resurfaces. If the file does re-emerge, the more anxious the auditor is to close it. An auditor can be fired for failing to close an audit within the three-year deadline.

A. Slowing Down an Audit

Generally, there is no stopping an audit once it begins. Once the IRS sends an examination notice to your last known address, the audit has begun. Even if you die, your spouse or the executor of your estate is obligated to carry on the audit. You may be able to slow down—or even end—an audit, however, if you ask for a transfer of your file to another IRS District. Audit transfers are discretionary with the IRS, and you need a good reason to get one—such as a more convenient location of your tax documents or nearer to your accountant's office.

Example: Janiel, who lived in one IRS District but had a jewelry business in another, received an audit notice for her residence district. She requested a transfer to the district where her business was located. Janiel told the IRS that her records were at the business location, which was true. The transfer was granted, but the new district's audit plate was already full. They never got around to Janiel's audit. The three-year deadline expired and Janiel's worries came to an end.

B. Extending an Audit

If an auditor hasn't completed her work within 28 months of when you filed your return, she will ask you to sign IRS Form 872, Consent to Extend the Time to Assess Tax, giving the IRS extra time to finish the audit. When you are asked to sign the consent form, you have three options:

- sign
- don't sign, or
- negotiate the terms of the extension.

The auditor will let you know that your options are the first two—to sign or not to sign. If you agree to sign, the auditor will probably ask you to sign an open-ended extension agreement. This will mean that an audit adjustment can be made on any item, at any time in the future.

It's never in your interest to sign an open-ended extension. Instead, refuse to sign or negotiate the terms of the extension. Ask that the form be limited to specific items—those on which the auditor says she needs to do more work—such as rental property or the gain on the sale of securities. Also, agree to a period of extension for no longer than six months. These perfectly reasonable limitations on the auditor narrow your risk and assure finality in the audit.

If your negotiations are unsuccessful or you refuse to sign the extension form, the IRS will take one of two courses of action:

- The auditor will issue simultaneously the Examination (Audit) Report and a Notice of Deficiency explaining your right to contest the audit in Tax Court. This means that you cannot appeal the Examination Report within the IRS but can only contest it without first paying the tax by going to Tax Court. (See Chapter 9.) This is the most likely outcome, but it's not so bad. Taking the IRS to Tax Court isn't very difficult in most cases.

- The IRS may slip up and accidentally let the three-year audit deadline pass—without issuing an audit report—meaning that no audit assessment on this return can ever be made against you. This does not happen very often. The IRS disciplines auditors who blow the deadline. But when it does happen, it's like winning the lottery. Even rarer, the IRS can conclude that you understated your income by more than 25% and determine that the statute of limitations is six years, not three. This determination does not have to be made before the audit begins.

C. Rushing a Field Audit

Although you usually want to slow down any audit, occasionally it makes sense to rush along a field audit. Having the IRS in your life is just plain stressful—and field audits are the worst. Furthermore, the longer the auditor looks, the greater the odds she will find any problem that lies lurking.

One of the best ways to hurry things along is to point out any obvious problems early on—ones the auditor would surely find later.

Example: The auditor hasn't yet seen Philo's bank statement with a mysterious $10,000 deposit. Philo, for reasons of his own that have nothing to do with his taxes, prefers not to talk about it. Philo says, "I've heard that auditors usually find some problems. I hope you try to find them quickly so I can get back to my business." Philo, hoping the auditor will stop looking after she finds a few small adjustments if it's obvious that he won't fight, points out glaring math mistakes in his records.

In addition, each individual auditor seems to have a psychological tax adjustment level—and once they reach that amount, they can close your file. Although you won't know the amount, this may tell you why the audit mysteriously ended when you thought the auditor would continue to dig. This mentality is probably left over from the days when auditors' work was evaluated by the number of dollars per hour they produced in audit adjustments.

Example: Allison claimed a very questionable $2,000 business deduction. The auditor hadn't yet reached that part of the tax return. Nearing the end of the first day of the audit, Allison volunteered that she mistakenly took a $350 deduction that year—she should have taken it the following year when the bill was paid. Because the auditor had already found $3,200 in disallowances, Allison thought she might be satisfied with one more. She was. The auditor closed the audit.

But don't appear too anxious if you know there are big problems that the auditor may find if she takes her time. Auditors are sensitive to overly nervous taxpayers who want to rush things.

D. When the Audit Is Over

At the end of your last or only meeting with the auditor, ask her to specify exactly what adjustments she intends to make. While she may not be willing to commit without further review of your file or discussing it with her supervisor, she should have a pretty good idea. If you can pin her down, you can argue your case on the spot or ask her for time to get more documents together if you disagree with her findings.

1. Receiving the Examination Report

When the auditor is done, she'll either hand or mail you a tentative Examination Report. Don't be concerned if the report doesn't show up shortly after the audit is closed. Four weeks is about average, and three months is not out of the question. Most likely, the report is sitting on the desk of a review person or a manager. The auditor doesn't have the authority to issue a final report without managerial approval.

SAMPLE EXAMINATION REPORT

Department of the Treasury - Internal Revenue Service
Income Tax Examination Changes

Name and Address of Taxpayer	SS or EI Number:		Return Form No. 1040
	Person with whom examination changes were discussed	Name and Title	

1. Adjustments to Income	Tax Year End 12/31/96	Tax Year End	Tax Year End
A. 1099 INT - INTEREST	$ 15.00	$	$
B. SCH C-CAR & TRUCK EXPENSE	5,450.00		
C. SCH C-LEGAL & PROF SVCS	26,300.00		
D. SCH C-MEALS & ENTERTAIN	750.00		
E. SCH C-OTHER EXPENSES	10,010.00		
F. SCH C-RENT-OTHER BUS PROP	2,000.00		
G. SCH C-SUPPLIES	400.00		
H. SE AGI ADJUSTMENT	(3,173.00)		
I.			
J.			
K.			
L.			
M.			
N.			
O.			
P.			
Q.			
R.			
S.			
2. Total Adjustments	41,752.00		
3. Taxable Income Per Return or as Previously Adjusted	653.00		
4. Corrected Taxable Income	42,405.00		
Tax Method	TAX TABLE		
Filing Status	JOINT		
5. Tax	6,666.00		
6. Additional Taxes			
7. Corrected Tax Liability	6,666.00		
8. Less A.			
Credits B.			
C.			
D.			
9. Balance (Line 7 less total of lines 8A through 8D)	6,666.00		
10. Plus A. SELF EMPLOYMENT TAX	7,404.00		
Other B.			
Taxes C.			
D.			
11. Total Corrected Tax Liability (Line 9 + lines 10A to 10D)	14,070.00		
12. Total Tax Shown on Return or as Previously Adjusted	1,157.00		
13. Adjustments to A. Special Fuels Credit			
B. EARNED INCOME CREDIT	(1,606.00)		
14. Deficiency - Increase in Tax or (Overassessment - Decrease in tax) (Line 11 less Line 12 adjusted by Line 13)	14,519.00		
15. Adjustments to Prepayment Credits			
16. Balance Due or Overpayment (Line 14 Adjusted by Line 15) (Excluding Interest and penalties)	$ 14,519.00	$	$

The Internal Revenue Service has agreements with State tax agencies under which information about Federal tax, including increases or decreases, is exchanged with the States. If this change affects the amount of your State income tax, you should file the State form.

You may be subject to backup withholding if you underreport your interest, dividend, or patronage dividend income and do not pay the required tax. The IRS may order backup withholding at 31 percent after four notices have been issued to you over a 120-day period and the tax has been assessed and remains unpaid.

RGS Ver. 4.00.02   Page 1 of 2   Form 4549-CG   (Rev. 1-91)

SAMPLE EXAMINATION REPORT (cont.)

Department of the Treasury - Internal Revenue Service
Income Tax Examination Changes

Name of Taxpayer:	SS or EI Number:	Return Form No. 1040

	Tax Year End 12/31/XX	Tax Year End	Tax Year End
17. Penalties			
A. ACCURACY-IRC 6662	$ 2,903.80	$	$
B.			
C.			
D.			
E.			
F.			
G.			
H.			
I.			
J.			
K.			
L.			
M.			
N.			
18. Total Penalties	2,903.80		
19. Underpayment attributable to negligence: An addition to the tax of 50 percent of the interest due on this underpayment will accrue until paid or assessed.			
20. Underpayment attributable to fraud: An addition to the tax of 50 percent of the interest due on this underpayment will accrue until paid or assessed.			
21. Underpayment attributable to Tax Motivated Transactions: TMT Interest will accrue and be assessed at 120 percent of the underpayment rate in accordance with IRC 6621(c).			

Summary of Taxes, Penalties and Interest:
  A. Balance due or Overpayment of Taxes (line 16, page 1)
  B. Penalties (line 18, page 2) (computed to 02/20/XX)
  C. Interest (IRC 6601) (computed to 02/20/XX)
  D. TMT Interest (computed to 02/20/XX on TMT underpayment)
	14,519.00
	2,903.80
	3,243.72		

E. Amount due or refund (sum of lines A. B. C. and D.)	20,666.52		

Other Information:

Examiner's Signature
Dave Longo
	District
	      Northern California
		Date
		  01/21/XX

  Consent to Assessment and Collection - I do not wish to exercise my appeal rights with the Internal Revenue Service or to contest in United States Tax Court the findings in this report. Therefore, I give my consent to the immediate assessment and collection of any increase in tax and penalties, and accept any decrease in tax and penalties shown above, plus additional interest as provided by law. It is understood that this report is subject to acceptance by the District Director.

PLEASE NOTE: if a joint return was filed, BOTH taxpayers must sign	Signature of Taxpayer	Date	Signature of Taxpayer	Date
By		Title		Date

SAMPLE EXAMINATION REPORT (cont.)

```
Name of Taxpayer:                                        01/21/XX
Identification Number:              TOTAL                4.00.02
```

9612 SCHEDULE SE - COMPUTATION OF SELF-EMPLOYMENT TAX

Primary

135-46-3300

1. Self-employment income	52,400.00
2. Multiply line 1 by 0.9235	48,391.40
3. Farm Optional Method Income	0.00
4. Non Farm Optional Method Income	0.00
5. Earnings subject to self-employment tax (sum of 2, 3, 4)	48,391.40
6. Maximum earnings subject to social security	62,700.00
7. Social Security wages and tips from W-2	0.00
8. Unreported tips from Form 4137	0.00
9. Sum of lines 7 and 8	0.00
10. Line 6 less line 9	62,700.00
11. Multiply the smaller of line 5 or 10 by 0.1240	6,000.53
12. Multiply line 5 by 0.0290	1,403.35
13. Self-Employment Tax (sum of lines 11 and 12)	7,403.88

Secondary

549-25-5112

1. Self-employment income	0.00
2. Multiply line 1 by 0.9235	0.00
3. Farm Optional Method Income	0.00
4. Non Farm Optional Method Income	0.00
5. Earnings subject to self-employment tax (sum of 2, 3, 4)	0.00
6. Maximum earnings subject to social security	62,700.00
7. Social Security wages and tips from W-2	0.00
8. Unreported tips from Form 4137	0.00
9. Sum of lines 7 and 8	0.00
10. Line 6 less line 9	0.00
11. Multiply the smaller of line 5 or 10 by 0.1240	0.00
12. Multiply line 5 by 0.0290	0.00
13. Self-Employment Tax (sum of lines 11 and 12)	0.00

SAMPLE EXAMINATION REPORT (cont.)

```
Name Of Taxpayer:                                              01/21/XX
Identification Number:                    TOTAL                4.00.02
```

9612 SCHEDULE EIC - COMPUTATION OF EARNED INCOME CREDIT

1. Wages, Salaries, Tips, etc.	8,042.00
2. Taxable scholarship or fellowship grant	0.00
3. Line 1 less line 2	8,042.00
4. Nontaxable Earned Income	0.00
5. Net Profit or Loss from Self-Employment	48,698.00
6. Earned Income (Total of lines 3, 4, and 5)	56,740.00
7. Credit allowed using the amount on line 6	0.00
8. Modified Adjusted Gross Income *	0.00
9. Credit allowed using the amount on line 8	0.00
10. Earned Income Credit (smaller of line 7 and 9)	0.00
11. Alternative Minimum Tax	0.00
12. Allowable Earned Income Credit (line 10 less line 11)	0.00

*Modified Adjusted Gross Income is the Adjusted Gross Income increased
by (1) any loss on Schedule D, and (2) one-half any loss claimed
on Schedule C or Schedule F.

SAMPLE EXAMINATION REPORT (cont.)

```
Name of Taxpayer:                                                01/21/XX
Identification Number:              TOTAL                        4.00.02


    9612 FORM 6251 - ALTERNATIVE MINIMUM TAX COMPUTATION

 1. Total Adjustments and Preferences                           6,700.00
 2. Tax Table Income (from Form 1040, line 35)                 50,055.00
 3. Net Operating Loss Deduction                                    0.00
 4. Itemized Deduction Limitation (from Schedule A Worksheet)       0.00
                                                               _____
 5. Combine lines 1 through 4                                  56,755.00

 6. Alternative Tax Net Operating Loss Deduction                    0.00
 7. Alternative Minimum Taxable Income                         56,755.00
 8. Exemption Amount                                           45,000.00
                                                               _____
 9. Subtract line 8 from line 7 (if 0 or less, enter 0)       11,755.00

10. If line 9 is $175,000 or less ($87,500 or less
    if married filing separate) multiply line 9 by 26%         3,056.00
11. Alternative Minimum Tax Foreign Tax Credit                     0.00
                                                               _____

12. Tentative Minimum Tax (Subtract 11 form 10)                3,056.00
13. Regular Tax Before Credits (less Foreign Tax Credit)       6,666.00
14. Alternative Minimum Tax (before credit)                        0.00
15. Empowerment Zone Employment Credit                             0.00
                                                               _____
16. Net Alternative Minimum Tax (line 14 less line 15)             0.00




    EXEMPTION WORKSHEET (Line 8)

    A.  Enter $33,750 ($45,000 if married filing jointly or
        qualifying widow(er), $22,500 if married filling separate)  45,000.00
    B.  Alternative Minimum Taxable Income (line 7)             56,755.00
    C.  Enter $112,500 ($150,000 if married filing jointly or
        qualifying widow(er), $75,000 if married filing separate) 150,000.00
    D.  Subtract line C from line B                                 0.00
    E.  Multiply line D by 25%                                      0.00
    F.  Subtract line E from line A (if zero or less, enter 0) 45,000.00
```

SAMPLE EXAMINATION REPORT (cont.)

```
Name of Taxpayer:                                      01/21/XX
Identification Number:            TOTAL                4.00.02
```

SUMMARY OF THE ACCURACY-RELATED PENALTY

9612 - 20% PENALTY ISSUES - Section 6662(a) and 6662(b)

It has been determined that the underpayment of tax shown on line 5 below is attributable to one or more of the following elements of the accuracy-related penalty: (1) negligence or disregard of rules or regulations, (2) substantial understatement of income tax, or (3) substantial valuation overstatement, therefore, an addition to the tax is imposed as provided by Section 6662(a) of the Internal Revenue Code.

1. Total tax computed with non-penalty adjustments and   14,519.00
   adjustments subject to penalty under Section 6662(b)

2. Total tax computed with non-penalty adjustments only   0.00

3. Line 1 less line 2 - Underpayment to which   14,519.00
   Section 6662(a) applies

4. Allocable Prepayment Credits (other than EIC and   0.00
   Special Fuels Credits included in lines 1 & 2)

5. Line 3 less line 4 - Underpayment subject to penalty   14,519.00

6. Applicable penalty rate   0.200

7. Line 4 multiplied by line 5   2,903.80
8. Previously assessed 20% Accuracy Penalty   0.00
9. Line 7 less line 8 - 20% Accuracy-related penalty   2,903.80

9612 - 40% PENALTY ISSUES - Section 6662(h)

It has been determined that the underpayment of tax shown on line 14 below is attributable to a gross valuation misstatement, therefore, an addition to the tax is imposed as provided by Section 6662(h) of the Internal Revenue Code.

10. Total tax computed with non-penalty adjustments,   0.00
    adjustments subject to penalty under IRC 6662(a)
    and adjustments subject to penalty under IRC 6662(h)

11. Total tax from line 1 above   14,519.00

12. Line 10 less line 11 - Underpayment to which   0.00
    Section 6662(h) applies

13. Allocable Prepayment Credits (other than EIC and   0.00
    Special Fuels Credits included in lines 10 & 11)

14. Line 10 less line 11 - Underpayment subject to penalty   0.00

15. Applicable penalty rate   0.000

16. Line 14 multiplied by line 15   0.00
17. Previously assessed 40% Accuracy Penalty   0.00
18. Line 16 less line 17 - 40% Accuracy-related penalty   0.00

19. Line 9 plus line 18 - Total ACCURACY-RELATED PENALTY   2,903.80

SAMPLE EXAMINATION REPORT (cont.)

```
Name of Taxpayer:                                         01/21/XX
Identification Number:            TOTAL                   4.00.02
_____


        9612 - SUMMARY OF PROPOSED PENALTIES


        DESCRIPTION                          AMOUNT
        _____     _____



        ACCURACY RELATED-IRC 6662            2,903.80
                                             _____

        TOTAL PENALTIES                      2,903.80
```

SAMPLE EXAMINATION REPORT (cont.)

```
Name of Taxpayer:                                          01/21/XX
Identification Number:                TOTAL                4.00.02
```

9612 - TAX PRD INTEREST COMPUTATION TO 02/20/99

```
Total Tax Deficiency                                   14,519.00
Plus Penalties*
-Overvaluation                          0.00
-Substantial Understatement             0.00
-Failure to File                        0.00
-Negligence                             0.00
-Civil Fraud                            0.00
-Accuracy Penalties                 2,903.80
                                    ────────

Total Penalties*                                        2,903.80

Tax Deficiency and Penalties Subject to Interest       17,422.80
```

Type	Effective Dates	Days	Rate	Interest
COMPOUND	04/15/xw-12/31/xw	260	09.00	1,422.79
COMPOUND	01/01/xx-03/31/xx	90	09.00	422.84
COMPOUND	04/01/xy-12/31/xy	275	08.00	1,196.96
COMPOUND	01/01/xz-02/20/xz	51	07.00	201.13

```
                      Total Interest              3,243.72
                      Total Underpayment         14,519.00
                      Total Penalties             2,903.80
                                                 ─────────
                      Total Amount Due           20,666.52
```

    Additional interest will be charged at the current rate compounded daily.
Interest is charged from the original due date of the return to a date 30 days
after an agreement to the additional tax is signed, or to the date of payment,
if earlier. Negligence and fraud penalties, if applicable, will also continue
to be charged. Generally, if notice and demand is made for payment of any
amount, and that amount is paid within 10 days after the date of the notice
and demand, interest on the amount paid will not be charged after the date of
the notice and demand. Since additional tax is due, you may want to pay it now
and limit the interest and penalty charges.
*   Interest on penalties became effective 7/19/84 (1/1/89 for Negligence and
    Civil Fraud) and is computed from the due date of the return unless a valid
    extension was filed. Extension date: 10/15/xw

SAMPLE EXAMINATION REPORT (cont.)

FORM 886-A	EXPLANATION OF ITEMS	SCHEDULE/EXHIBIT ____
NAME OF TAXPAYER		YEAR/PERIOD ENDED 9612

PRELIMINARY REPORT:

This report is a preliminary report showing what adjustments would be proposed if we do not meet with you to review additional information. This report is pending your appointment on ___March 4, 19XX___ .

DEPARTMENT OF THE TREASURY
INTERNAL REVENUE SERVICE

FORM 886-A (REV 4-68)

SAMPLE EXAMINATION REPORT (cont.)

FORM 886-A	EXPLANATION OF ITEMS	SCHEDULE/EXHIBIT _____
NAME OF TAXPAYER		YEAR/PERIOD ENDED 9612

STANDARD PARAGRAPHS:

	PER RETURN	PER EXAM	ADJUSTMENT
1099 INT - INTEREST	0.00	15.00	15.00

We adjusted your interest income to reflect the amounts shown on
Form 1099-INT.

	PER RETURN	PER EXAM	ADJUSTMENT
SCH C-LEGAL & PROF SVCS	26,300.00	0.00	26,300.00

Since you did not establish that the business expense shown on your
tax return was paid or incurred during the taxable year and that the
expense was ordinary and necessary to your business, we have
disallowed the amount shown.

	PER RETURN	PER EXAM	ADJUSTMENT
SCH C-RENT-OTHER BUS PROP	2,000.00	0.00	2,000.00

Since you did not establish that the business expense shown on your
tax return was paid or incurred during the taxable year and that the
expense was ordinary and necessary to your business, we have
disallowed the amount shown.

DEPARTMENT OF THE TREASURY   FORM 886-A (REV 4-68)
INTERNAL REVENUE SERVICE

SAMPLE EXAMINATION REPORT (cont.)

FORM 886-A	EXPLANATION OF ITEMS	SCHEDULE/EXHIBIT _____
NAME OF TAXPAYER		YEAR/PERIOD ENDED 9612

STANDARD PARAGRAPHS:

	PER RETURN	PER EXAM	ADJUSTMENT
SCH C-SUPPLIES	400.00	0.00	400.00

Since you did not establish that the business expense shown on your
tax return was paid or incurred during the taxable year and that the
expense was ordinary and necessary to your business, we have
disallowed the amount shown.

	PER RETURN	PER EXAM	ADJUSTMENT
SCH C-MEALS & ENTERTAIN	750.00	0.00	750.00

Since you did not establish that the business expense shown on your
tax return was paid or incurred during the taxable year and that the
expense was ordinary and necessary to your business, we have
disallowed the amount shown.

	PER RETURN	PER EXAM	ADJUSTMENT
SCH C-OTHER EXPENSES	10,010.00	0.00	10,010.00

Since you did not establish that the business expense shown on your
tax return was paid or incurred during the taxable year and that the
expense was ordinary and necessary to your business, we have
disallowed the amount shown.

DEPARTMENT OF THE TREASURY   FORM 886-A (REV 4-68)
INTERNAL REVENUE SERVICE

SAMPLE EXAMINATION REPORT (cont.)

FORM 886-A	EXPLANATION OF ITEMS	SCHEDULE/EXHIBIT _____
NAME OF TAXPAYER		YEAR/PERIOD ENDED 9612

STANDARD PARAGRAPHS:

	PER RETURN	PER EXAM	ADJUSTMENT
SCH C-CAR & TRUCK EXPENSE	5,450.00	0.00	5,450.00

Since you did not establish that the business expense shown on your tax return was paid or incurred during the taxable year and that the expense was ordinary and necessary to your business, we have disallowed the amount shown.

	PER RETURN	PER EXAM	ADJUSTMENT
SE AGI ADJUSTMENT	529.00	3,702.00	(3,173.00)

The adjustments to your net income from self-employment shown in this report resulted in a change to your self-employment tax. The self-employment tax deduction has been adjusted to one-half of the recomputed amount.

DEPARTMENT OF THE TREASURY
INTERNAL REVENUE SERVICE

FORM 886-A (REV 4-68)

2. Understanding the Examination Report

The Examination Report shows proposed changes to your tax liability—taxes, penalties and interest—for the years under audit. Each change is listed, citing the relevant section of the Tax Code and a generally vague explanation. For example, the explanation may say, "You did not prove the amount shown was a rental expense." In many cases, the explanation doesn't specifically state *how* you failed. If you don't understand what went wrong, call the auditor and ask. She must tell you.

3. Options After Getting the Examination Report

From your viewpoint, the report is a win, loss or draw.

Win. Instead of an Examination Report, you receive a "no change" letter or a refund letter. Congratulations! You can put the book down. There's no need to read any more of the material.

SAMPLE EXAMINATION REPORT – NO CHANGE LETTER

Internal Revenue Service   Department of the Treasury
District Director

Date: November 13, 20XX

                                             Form:
                                             1120
                                             Person to Contact:
                                             Simpson
                                             Contact Telephone Number:
                                             (408) 555-0987
                                             Tax Period(s) Ended:

Dear Taxpayers:

    We are pleased to tell you that our examination of your tax returns for the
above period(s) shows no change is necessary in your reported tax. However, our
examination may not reflect the results of examinations of flow-through entities
(Forms 1120S, 1065, 1041) in which you may have an interest.

    If you have any questions, please write to the person whose name is shown
at the top of this letter or you may call that person at the telephone number
shown. If the number is outside your local calling area, there will be a
long-distance charge to you. If you prefer, you may call the IRS telephone
number listed in your local directory. An employee there may be able to
help you, but the office at the address shown on this letter is most familiar
with your case.

    If you write to us, please provide your telephone number and the most
convenient time for us to call in case we need more information. Please attach
this letter to any correspondence to help us identify your case. Keep the copy
for your records.

    Thank you for your cooperation.

                                 Sincerely Yours,

                                 Bonnie Ohida

                                 District Director

Enclosure:
Copy of this letter

P.O. Box 11013, San Jose, CA   95103   Letter 590(DO) (Rev.3-88)
Case #   CCAGL

SAMPLE EXAMINATION REPORT – NO CHANGE FORM

Department of the Treasury - Internal Revenue Service
Income Tax Examination Changes

Name and Address of Taxpayer	SS or EI Number:		Return Form No: 1120S
	Person with whom examination changes were discussed	FREDERICK DAILY	

1. Adjustments to Income	Tax Year End:	Tax Year End:	Tax Year End:
A.			
B.			
C.			
D.			
E.			
F.			
G.			
H.			
I.			
J.			
K.			
L.			
M.			
N.			
O.			
P.			
2. Total Adjustments			
3. Taxable Income Per Return or as Previously Adjusted	*None*		
4. Corrected Taxable Income Tax Method Filing Status			
5. Tax			
6. Alternative Taxes, If Applicable			
7. Corrected Tax Liability			
8. Less A. Credits B. Total Credits (See attached schedule) C. D.			
9. Balance (Line 7 less total of lines 8A through 8D)			
10. Plus A. Other B. Capital Gains / Built-In Gains Tax Taxes C. D.	2,099.00	0.00	0.00
11. Total Corrected Tax Liability (line 9+line 10A-10D)	2,099.00	0.00	0.00
12. Total Tax Shown on Return or as Previously Adjusted	2,099.00	0.00	0.00
13. Adjustment to: A. B.			
14. Deficiency-Increase in Tax or (Overassessment-Decrease in Tax) (Line 11 less 12 adjusted by 13)	0.00	0.00	0.00
15. Adjustments to Prepayment Credits	0.00	0.00	0.00
16. Balance Due or (Overpayment) (Line 14 adjusted by Line 15) (Excluding interest and penalties)	0.00	0.00	0.00

The Internal Revenue Service has agreements with State tax agencies under which information about Federal tax, including increases or decreases, is exchanged with the States. If this change affects the amount of your State income tax, you should file the State form.

You may be subject to backup withholding if you underreport your interest, dividend, or patronage dividend income and do not pay the required tax. The IRS may order backup withholding at 20 percent after four notices have been issued to you over a 120-day period and the tax has been assessed and remains unpaid.

Form CG-4549

SAMPLE EXAMINATION REPORT – NO CHANGE FORM (cont.)

Department of the Treasury - Internal Revenue Service
Income Tax Examination Changes

Name and Address of Taxpayer	SS or EI Number:		Return Form No: 1120S

17. Penalties	Tax Year End:	Tax Year End:	Tax Year End:
A.			
B.			
C.			
D.			
E.			
F.			
G.			
H.			
I.			
J.			
K.			
L.			
M.			
N.			
18. Total Penalties			
Underpayment attributable to negligence: (1981-1987) A tax addition of 50 percent of the interest due on underpayment will accrue until paid or assessed			
Underpayment attributable to fraud: (1981-1987) A tax addition of 50 percent of the interest due on underpayment will accrue until paid or assessed			
Underpayment attributable Tax Motivated Transactions TMT interest will accrue and be assessed at 120% of underpayment rate in accordance with IRC 6621(c)			
19. Summary of Taxes, Penalties and Interest: A. Balance due or Overpayment Taxes - Line 16, Page 1 B. Penalties (Line 18, Page 2) - computed to 10/27/97 C. Interest (IRC 6601) - computed to 10/27/97 D. TMT Interest-computed 10/27/97 on TMT underpayment			
E. Amount due or refund (sum of lines A, B, C and D)			

Other Information:

Examiner's Signature: H. Simpson *Howard Simpson*	District: Central California	Date: 09/27/XX

Consent to Assessment and Collection - I do not wish to exercise my appeal rights with the Internal Revenue Service or to contest in the United States Tax Court the findings in this report. Therefore, I give my consent to the immediate assessment and collection of any increase in tax and penalties, and accept any decrease in tax and penalties shown above, plus additional interest as provided by law. It is understood that this report is subject to acceptance by the District Director.

PLEASE NOTE: If a joint return was filed, BOTH taxpayers must sign	Signature of Taxpayer	Date	Signature of Taxpayer	Date
		Title		Date

Form CG-4549

Loss. The Examination Report makes changes—you owe more in taxes, plus interest and probably some penalties. The auditor rejected your documentation—such as suspicious handwritten receipts for business purchases—or you didn't provide any. Or, the auditor disagreed with your claim of the tax benefits—such as an exemption for the support of your elderly mother—to which you felt entitled.

Draw. The Examination Report is a mixed bag—the auditor accepted some of your documents but not others. She agreed with your legal position on one item—such as your business entertainment deductions—but not on another—such as the education expense for a surfing course. You owe more money, but not a backbreaking amount.

After you receive the Examination Report, you have three choices in how to proceed.

a. Agree and Get It Over With

If you are willing to accept everything in the report—added taxes, plus any penalties and interest—you can sign and return it along with IRS Form 870, Consent to Proposed Tax Adjustment, and end the audit process. By signing off, you can't appeal within the IRS or go to Tax Court. This scenario, called an "agreed case," is what the IRS hopes for.

When would you want to agree? Obviously, if the IRS missed something big, which could have produced a large adjustment, sign and run. Another reason for signing might include simply getting the IRS out of your life. Maybe the wear and tear on your nerves, along with the time away from your work it would take for an IRS appeal or going to court, is simply not worth it. But before giving in, consider the fact that the larger the tax bill you agree to, the more likely your audit number will come up again. No one knows what the magic figure is, but in my experience, it starts around $5,000 in extra taxes, penalties and interest.

Signing the audit report doesn't mean that you agree to pay the tax bill now—or ever. The auditor will ask for payment and may offer to set up a monthly payment plan, with interest and late payment penalties running. (The interest rate changes every three months, but the combined interest/penalty rate hovered between 12%-16% during the late 1990s.) You can instead tell the auditor that you prefer to wait until the bill comes from the Service Center and then will decide how to pay.

Sometimes, the Service Center bill is less than the audit report figure. The Service Center people may have dropped a penalty, or made or corrected a computation error. If the Service Center made a mistake, let your conscience be your guide about notifying the IRS of its error. If you pay the lesser amount, no one may ever notice. You run the risk, however, of later being billed for the difference.

If the bill is for more than the amount on the report, you can complain. Start by calling the auditor or her manager. They may not be able to help you, but should be able to direct you to the person who can.

If you cannot pay the bill in full, you have several alternatives. You can seek a monthly installment agreement by filing IRS Form 9465. (A copy is in the Appendix. It's also available on the IRS' website at http://www.irs.ustreas.gov/forms_pubs/pubs.html.) Or, you may qualify for an IRS Offer in Compromise, where the bill is reduced—sometimes to only pennies on the dollar. Or, your tax debt may be discharged or paid through the bankruptcy court.

How you plan to handle the tax bill is of no concern to the auditor. Collecting taxes is handled by a completely different division within the IRS.

 If you want more information on your payment options, see *Stand Up to the IRS*, by Frederick W. Daily (Nolo).

⚠ Signing the form may not be the end. All audit reports must be approved by the IRS Audit Review staff. Even if you sign the form, your audit report is not final until approved. Occasionally, an Audit Reviewer kicks back a report to the auditor to further develop issues. If this happens, you'll be contacted. It may seem unfair, but it's not considered being audited twice. The audit was not officially concluded.

b. Talk With the Auditor or Auditor's Manager

Examination Reports are not cast in stone. The report may be just the IRS' first or second or third offer. To find out if there's room to negotiate, call the auditor.

You must point out the specific findings with which you disagree—not because you can't pay the bill. Ask the auditor what additional proof she would need to change the report. Ask for 30 days to get her the missing documents or to reconstruct your records. She is likely to give you time to mail her the materials. You might even ask (repeatedly, if necessary) for another appointment—it forces the auditor to face you again. It also shows that you may not sign the report as is.

If the auditor isn't moved to accept your request to send more documentation, to meet with you again or both, ask to speak to her manager. Tell the manager that the auditor is not being reasonable or cooperative. If the auditor finally grants your request to provide more documentation or to meet with her and accepts the new items on your behalf, you will eventually receive an amended Examination Report. If you don't like the second report, you can repeat the routine.

If your arguments aren't getting anywhere, ask the auditor for a copy of her workpapers. These are case notes the IRS requires an auditor to place in an audit file. Workpapers should provide you with an explanation of the auditor's conclusions on the changes she made. Go over the workpapers with the auditor. Ask her to explain anything that isn't obvious.

The auditor might refuse to show you her workpapers. If that happens, tell the auditor that you know you are entitled to them under the Freedom of Information Act. If she still refuses, complain to her manager. If both the auditor and manager refuse to show you the auditor's workpapers, you can make a written request of them to the IRS Disclosure Officer under the federal Freedom of Information Act. (See Chapter 8.) This may take a lot of time, however.

If, after sending in new materials, meeting a second time and reviewing the workpapers, you cannot get the auditor to alter the report, ask to speak or meet face to face with her manager. Managers have a strong motive to close files handled by their auditors with an "agreed" notation, as this is how managers are evaluated, too.

When you speak with the manager, don't criticize the auditor. The manager might focus on defending his employee, not on trying to reconcile your differences. Explain the adjustments with which you don't agree and suggest a compromise. Even if this doesn't work, the manager's replies may convince you that the IRS' position is correct, or at least point out the weaknesses in your position. If all else fails, calmly say, "I am disappointed. I don't want to appeal or go to court, but I don't know what else to do." Auditor managers want your agreement, so this subtle threat may work.

Instead of meeting with a Group Manager, you may meet with a senior auditor appointed by a Group Manager. This "acting manager" might be familiar with your case, especially if your auditor was a trainee. If she won't bend, you can still insist on talking to the real manager.

c. Appeals Beyond the Examination Division

You don't have to respond to an Examination Report or even IRS phone calls asking you whether or not you will sign an audit report. If you instead ignore the IRS, in a month or two you will probably receive something called a 30-day letter. This is a formal notice that your audit is closed and that you have 30 days to request an administrative appeal within the IRS. (See Chapter 8. The appeal process is also covered in IRS Publication 5, Appeal Rights and Preparation of Protests for Unagreed Cases. A copy of this publication is in the Appendix and available on the IRS' website at http://www.irs.ustreas.gov/forms_pubs/pubs.html.)

The law does not guarantee you the right to an administrative appeal; it is discretionary within the IRS. But the Tax Code does give you the right to contest the result of an audit in court. Before you take the IRS to court, you must be sent a copy of the final audit report along with a Notice of Deficiency. These might not arrive for several months after the audit is over, and will come by certified mail. Once you receive the report and notice, you can contest the audit without making a payment, but only by filing a Petition in Tax Court. (See Chapter 9.)

If you don't file a Petition in Tax Court, the audit bill becomes final after 90 days. Then, you can contest it only by first paying it in full, filing a claim with the IRS for a refund, waiting for a denial and then filing a refund suit in U.S. District Court or the Court of Claims. Very few taxpayers go this route.

■

Appealing Your Audit

Try as you might, you couldn't get the auditor to see things your way. In fact, you thought the Examination Report was downright un-American. You went to the auditor's manager. But again, no luck. So what's next? A formal appeal within the IRS, that's what. Fewer than one in ten audited taxpayers request a formal appeal, although many more should. Appealing isn't especially difficult or time-consuming. Your chance of getting at least some tax reduction is great. You don't have to hire a tax pro to appeal.

ODDS OF WINNING AN APPEAL

Auditors privately call the Appeals Office the "IRS' gift shop." There is even an IRS in-joke that appeals officers work on the 50% rule—they cut auditors' adjustments by half. IRS statistics show that the auditors are exaggerating—but not by much. The typical appeal results in a 40% decrease in taxes, penalties and interest proposed by the auditor.

While you don't have an automatic right to appeal, the IRS normally allows it. In a few instances, you won't be granted the right to appeal, such as if the 36-month deadline for completing the entire audit process has fewer than eight months left to it or you are deemed a tax protestor (someone who believes the income tax system is unconstitutional and refuses to pay taxes on that ground). If the IRS does not grant an appeal, it will send you a 90-day letter, formally called a Notice of Deficiency. This means that the only way to challenge the audit without first paying the additional tax the IRS claims is owed is to go to Tax Court. (See Chapter 9.)

There are three good reasons for appealing, and two relatively insignificant reasons not to:

Pros

• Appealing is simple and costs nothing unless you use a tax pro.

• Appealing, in the majority of cases, results in some tax savings—although rarely a total victory.

• Appealing delays your audit tax bill, buying you time to raise the cash.

Cons

• Interest and maybe penalties on the audit bill continue to run during an appeal. The amount is small, however, when compared with the likely tax savings from appealing.

• An appeals officer can raise issues that the auditor missed, but this almost never happens. Nevertheless, if you are afraid that something might pop up and you'll owe a lot more in taxes, you can skip the appeal and go directly to Tax Court, where new issues can't be raised. (See Chapter 9.) Before you skip the appeal, talk to a tax pro. If you hire an attorney for Tax Court and win your case, you may be able to get your attorney's fees paid by the IRS—but you must have appealed within the IRS first.

A. How to Appeal an Audit

As explained in Chapter 7, after your audit file is closed, the IRS sends an Examination Report with any proposed adjustments—additional taxes, penalties and interest. If you don't sign and return the report within a few weeks, the IRS usually sends a 30-day letter and Publication 5, Appeal Rights and Preparation of Protests for Unagreed Cases, explaining how to appeal. (Publication 5 is in the Appendix and available on the IRS' website at http://www.irs.ustreas.gov/forms_pubs/pubs.html.) The official IRS term for appealing an IRS determination is "filing a protest."

SAMPLE 30-DAY LETTER

Internal Revenue Service   Department of the Treasury

Date: January 21, 20XX   IF YOU WRITE OR CALL US,
                                   refer to this information
                                 Number of this letter: 915(DO)

                                 Tax period(s) ended:

                                 For assistance you may call:
                                 Name:

                                 Telephone Number:

Dear   :

    We are enclosing two copies of our report of income tax examination
changes explaining the action we took on your tax return. Please read this
report and decide whether you agree or disagree.

    IF YOU AGREE with the changes in the report, you should sign, date, and
return one copy to us within 30 days from the date of this letter. If you owe
more tax, please include your payment for the full amount you owe; this will
limit interest and penalty charges.

    IF YOU CAN'T PAY the full amount you owe now, pay as much as you can. If
you want us to consider an installment agreement, please complete the enclosed
Form 9465, Installment Agreement Request. If we approve your request, you
will be charged a $43 user fee to help offset the cost of providing this
service. We will take the fee from your first installment payment. Penalties
and interest will continue to increase until you pay the full amount you owe.

    IF YOU DON'T AGREE, within 30 days from the date of this letter, you
should do one of the following:

    1. Mail us any additional information.
    2. Discuss the report with the examiner.
    3. Discuss your position with the group manager.
    4. Request a conference with an appeals officer, as explained in the
        enclosed Publication 5.

    IF YOU DON'T TAKE ANY OF THE ABOVE ACTIONS within 30 days we will process
your case based on the enclosed report. You will then receive a statutory
notice of deficiency that allows you 90 days to petition the United States Tax
Court. If you allow the 90-day period to expire without petitioning the Tax
Court, we will bill you for any additional tax, interest, and penalties.

                        (Continued on next page)

450 GOLDEN GATE AVENUE

SAN FRANCISCO, CA 94102   Letter 915(DO)(CG) (Rev. 9-96)

SAMPLE 30-DAY LETTER (cont.)

-2-

    If you write us about your case, please include your telephone number and
the most convenient time to call in case we need more information. We've
enclosed an envelope for your convenience. If you prefer, you may telephone
the person shown above.

                      Sincerely,

                      DISTRICT DIRECTOR

Enclosures:
Examination Report (2)
Form 9465
Publication 5
Envelope

450 GOLDEN GATE AVENUE

SAN FRANCISCO, CA 94102   Letter 915(DO)(CG) (Rev. 9-96)

1. How to Start an Appeal

You must file your appeal or protest within 30 days of the date on the 30-day letter—not the date you received it. As discussed in Chapter 7, you can, and usually should, appeal informally to the auditor's manager.

⚠ Informally appealing—that is, contacting the auditor's manager— does not extend the 30-day deadline to file a protest. Be sure to meet the deadline for filing your formal appeal even if you choose to continue discussion with the manager or senior auditor.

Extension. If you can't get your protest letter in within the 30-day deadline, request an extension from the auditor or his manager. Extensions are usually granted, but don't rely on a verbal promise. If the IRS has not sent you notice with the new deadline date, send your own letter stating the terms of the extension and the name of the person who granted it. Typical extensions are for 30–60 days.

The IRS doesn't offer a preprinted form for audit protests—the IRS obviously doesn't want to encourage appeals, given that it has preprinted forms for everything else. You must write a protest letter unless the taxes, interest and penalties the IRS claims you owe from the audit are under $2,500. Then you can orally request an appeal to the auditor. Even so, put it in writing.

Oddly enough, if the IRS sends you a 90-day letter with your Examination Report, thereby denying you the right to formally appeal, and you sue the IRS in Tax Court, your case will be sent to the Appeals Office before the Tax Court any way. You will be offered a meeting with an appeals officer. Unless you are hellbound to meet a Tax Court judge, take the IRS up on the offer. If you still don't settle, your case will be sent back to Tax Court.

a. Writing a Protest Letter

The IRS appeal rules differ slightly on what you need to say in your protest letter depending on the amount being contested.

$2,500 to $9,999. If your audit bill falls between $2,500 and $9,999 (remember, you can orally protest a bill under $2,500), all you need to do is send a letter stating, "I disagree with the Examination Report dated 10/21/xx, and want to appeal." Use this same language for an appeal of under $2,500.

$10,000 or more. If your audit bill is for $10,000 or more, you must send a letter containing a bit more detail:

- your name, or your and your spouse's names, if a joint return was audited

- your Social Security number, or your and your spouse's Social Security numbers, if a joint return was audited

- a statement that you are appealing an Examination Report of certain date

- the specific findings in the Examination Report with which you disagree, including any penalties

- a brief explanation of why the Examination Report is wrong—you can attach copies of documents supporting your explanation, although it isn't necessary

- your signature, or your and your spouse's signatures, if a joint return was audited, under "penalty of perjury" (see sample letter, below), and

- copies of the 30-day letter and the Examination Report.

Even with all those requirements, make the protest letter short and sweet. Stick to the facts. Never criticize the auditor, his manager, the IRS or the tax law. Blowing off steam only detracts from an otherwise valid appeal. You may be disregarded by the IRS as someone considered to be an "irate" taxpayer or just another nut case.

The sample below is a skeleton-type protest letter, meaning it provides only a brief statement of your disagreement. Some tax pros recommend very detailed protest letters with copies of all supporting documents. While commendable, that can be difficult to do correctly in a short period of time. Because you are not a tax expert, go with the bare-bones approach. You will have plenty of time later to provide the appeals officer with the details.

Consult an appeals-experienced tax pro if you are unsure about the appeals process. Ask for advice on drafting the letter and documents to attach. While you're talking to the tax pro, ask for tips on preparing for the appeals hearing. A tax pro who has been there knows what kinds of evidence—documents and statements—the appeals officer looks for.

b. Filing a Protest Letter

Mail your protest letter by certified mail, return receipt requested, to the local IRS District Director. The address is on the Examination Report or 30-day letter. Also send or give a copy to the auditor, just to make sure that everyone knows that you are appealing. Correspondence sometimes gets lost within the IRS.

SAMPLE PROTEST (APPEAL) LETTER

August 15, 20xx

District Director
Internal Revenue Service
P.O. Box 44687 (Stop 11)
Indianapolis, IN 46244

VIA CERTIFIED MAIL—RETURN RECEIPT REQUESTED
PROTEST OF BILLY BOB & PEGGY SUE VALLEY
SSN: 555-55-5555 (Billy Bob Valley)
SSN: 777-77-7777 (Peggy Sue Valley)
66667 Elm Street
Bloomington, IN 47000

Dear Sir/Madam:

We wish to appeal from the Examination Report of 8/1/xx, a copy of which is attached. We request a hearing. The tax years protested are 19xx and 19xy.

The adjustments we disagree with are the disallowance of business expense deductions shown on our Schedule C of $12,999, and penalties and interest in the total amount of $848.

The adjustments were incorrect because the deductions we took were legitimate expenses of Billy Bob's music business, and we were trying to make a profit.

Under penalty of perjury, we declare that the facts presented in this protest and in any accompanying documents are, to the best of our knowledge and belief, true, correct and complete.

Sincerely,

Billy Bob Valley   *Peggy Sue Valley*

cc: Auditor
Enclosures: Copy of 30-Day Letter & Copy of Examination Report

c. Getting the Auditor's File

Under a federal law called the Freedom of Information Act, or FOIA, you are entitled to a copy of almost everything in your IRS auditor's file. You could just contact the auditor and ask him for his notes and workpapers justifying his conclusions. Some auditors will give you copies of their file just for the asking, and some won't.

If you go this route, you will never know if the auditor gave you everything to which you were entitled. For this reason, you are better off making a formal written request for the file under the FOIA. You may not get anything other than what the auditor gave or would have given you—but it's also possible that you might mine a gold nugget, especially items given to you accidentally, that by law the IRS does not have to disclose. For instance, the file may contain something called a Report Transmittal form showing that the auditor initially suspected fraud. Or, you may be able to conclude from the deletions in the file that the IRS investigated other items or had made a criminal referral. If either of these situations is the case, see an experienced tax attorney to discuss any possible implications.

The IRS has not developed a preprinted FOIA request form. Instead, write to the FOIA Disclosure Officer at your local IRS District Office— the same address where you sent your protest letter, but don't send the two letters together. Ask for a copy of your complete audit file by the year under audit. Offer to pay for copying charges. The IRS does not have to make copies for you, although it usually will, and free of charge. Enclose a photocopy of your driver's license or birth certificate. Hand-deliver or send your letter by certified mail, return receipt requested.

Allow several weeks for a response to your FOIA request. If you don't hear from anyone within 30 days, call the Disclosure Officer at the District Office. If your appeals hearing is approaching and you haven't yet received the FOIA material, ask the appeals officer for a postponement. The appeals officer should agree if you are not asking for too much time—a few weeks or so. If she agrees to the postponement over the phone, send her a confirming letter.

SAMPLE FOIA LETTER

August 15, 20xx

District Director
Internal Revenue Service
P.O. Box 44687 (Stop 11)
Indianapolis, IN 46244

VIA CERTIFIED MAIL—RETURN RECEIPT REQUESTED
FOIA REQUEST OF BILLY BOB & PEGGY SUE VALLEY

SSN: 555-55-5555 (Billy Bob Valley)
SSN: 777-77-7777 (Peggy Sue Valley)
66667 Elm Street
Bloomington, IN 47000

Dear Sir/Madam:

Under the Privacy Act of 1974, 5 U.S.C. 552A, and the Freedom of Information Act, 5 U.S.C. 552, we hereby request a copy of all files relevant to the audit of our tax return for years 19xx and 19xy. The examination was handled by Revenue Agent Frump of the Bloomington downtown office and the report was issued on 8/1/xx.

We agree to pay reasonable charges for copying the requested documents, up to $25. If the charges exceed this amount, please contact us for further authorization.

If you determine that any portion of these files is exempt, please identify the portion claimed exempt and the specific exemption that justifies your refusal to release them.

Sincerely,

Billy Bob Valley   *Peggy Sue Valley*

2. Should You Hire a Tax Pro?

Appeals officers respect experienced tax professionals. The officer and your tax pro may know each other well. A good tax pro knows what an appeals officer looks for. Tax professionals should know the law and can get right to the point. Taxpayers on their own tend to get off the subject and frustrate appeals officers by wasting time.

Even so, hiring a tax pro is almost always an economic decision. Attorneys and CPAs charge upwards of $2,500 to handle an appeal, although enrolled agents may charge less. Your other option is to handle the appeal yourself but consult a tax pro. An hour or two of professional time should cost a few hundred dollars, but could mean the difference between winning or losing. Hiring a tax pro to attend the appeals hearing might make sense if you are contesting at least $5,000 to $10,000.

A few non-economic factors may determine whether or not you hire a tax pro to meet the appeals officer, such as the intricacy of the accounting or legal issues, your comfort level in dealing with the government and whether or not you have something to hide.

Before hiring a tax pro, be sure to ask how much IRS appeals experience she has—and the results of her cases. Compare her answers to the advice given here.

B. How the Appeals Office Works

Section 8631 of the Internal Revenue Manual states, "The appeals mission is to resolve tax controversies, without litigation, on a basis which is fair and impartial to the both the government and the taxpayer and in a manner that will enhance voluntary compliance and public confidence in the integrity and efficiency of the [IRS]." The key words are, "to resolve tax controversies, without litigation ..." The Appeals

Office exists to settle cases with taxpayers. You might think that the work of an appeals officer is to raise money for the U.S. Treasury, but he has a different job.

The IRS Appeals Office is completely separate and independent from the District Office that handled your audit. It might even not be in the same city or building. Appeals officers view cases with a fresh perspective. While a few officers rely heavily on the auditor's file, most keep an open mind to your proposals.

The auditor doesn't participate in the appeal. His file is before the appeals officer, but it may lack important details. An appeals officer might contact your auditor to clarify something, but chances are the auditor may have moved on or have long forgotten your case. Many months will have elapsed since the auditor saw that file. If you submit new data to the appeals officer, the officer might ask the auditor to review it, but it's doubtful.

Appeals officers are experienced negotiators. IRS appeals officers are long-time IRS employees. Most have come up from the ranks of auditors to these more prestigious and higher-paying jobs.

Appeals officers are trained to be flexible. They are given more discretion in dealing with taxpayers than auditors have. IRS statistics show that 70% of appeals are settled. Appeals officers' job performance is judged in how many compromises they reach—not how often they uphold IRS auditors.

Appeals officers are aware of legal precedents on routine tax issues. They can rattle off things such as the kinds of documentation legally sufficient to verify business entertainment expenses or a home office deduction. Unless your case is very unusual, the appeals officer will have already researched the applicable legal issues in your case.

Appeals officers can weigh the "hazards of litigation." They often settle cases because the IRS does not want the courts to set any precedents unfavorable to the IRS. Court decisions against the IRS are published and can be relied on by other taxpayers. Bad precedent would cost the government much more in the long run than settling your case at the appeals level would cost.

Appeals officers are realists. They know that about 50% of all taxpayers win at least partial victories in court. Therefore, the appeals officer is alert to any fact that might cause a judge to rule in your favor. In addition, the appeals officer understands that the IRS' personpower is not unlimited. Most Congressional funding to the IRS in the last decade has gone into computerization and hiring collectors—not hiring appeals officers or legal staffs. They don't want small-potatoes cases using up more of the government's resources than is absolutely necessary.

⚠ **An appeals officer can't settle a case based purely on its nuisance value.** She won't cave in just to avoid the trouble of going to court. You must supply a justification for the appeals officer to make a deal. Her work is reviewed by higher-ups, so she must include good arguments in your favor in her report.

C. Preparing Your Presentation

After notifying the IRS of your request to appeal, you will have anywhere from several months to a year before your hearing. It depends on the backlog at your IRS Appeals Office. Use this time to do the following:

- Review everything you presented to the auditor.
- Get a copy of the auditor's file by making your Freedom of Information Act request. (See Section A.1.c, above.)

- Study the file to see if the auditor misrepresented or missed something.

- Read the text of any tax law cited by the auditor in his Examination Report and file to see if it really supports his position. If need be, check it out with a tax pro.

- Re-review the Examination Report. Focus on the issues you need to combat. Don't get bogged down in minor adjustment items—such as $54 of bank interest not reported on your return. Get to the heart of the problem that is costing you real money.

1. Organizing and Presenting Documents

Many audit battles are lost because the taxpayer didn't get her records together. Jumbled papers or messy files may have caused the auditor to throw up his hands and show you the door. Ask yourself if there are better ways to organize and present your supporting materials to the appeals officer. For example, run adding machine tapes for each category of deduction, prepare schedules of items or type up summaries and written explanations, point by point. (See Section C.3, below.)

Get creative. For instance, maybe something else tells your story better than words alone. Charts, graphs and drawings are very effective. A part-time jazz artist whose deductions for his musical business were disallowed when the auditor concluded that his music was a hobby brought a demo tape and player to an appeals hearing. Remember, too, that a picture is worth a thousand words. A photo of your professional-looking home office or a group shot at your business' employee picnic may prove your deduction and win over an appeals officer. Everyone prefers images over written descriptions or oral explanations—appeals officers included.

If neatness, typing, preparing schedules or just plain getting paperwork together is not your forte, find a bookkeeper or friend to do it. The expense is tax deductible.

2. Filling in the Gaps

If any of your records were missing at the audit, try harder to find them. Look back at every location where you might have put your papers. Renew attempts to get copies of checks from banks and duplicate receipts from businesses and people with whom you dealt. If you can't get the documents, reconstruct missing items. (See Chapters 3 and 4 for suggestions.)

3. Focusing on Challenged Items

Make a separate file, page or folder for each item the auditor challenged which you dispute. Write a simple explanation next to each stating why the auditor was wrong. For example, you might write something like, "This deduction of $395 was for a sales training course to help me get more listings for my sideline real estate business, and should be allowed as a business educational expense."

Next, segregate the supporting documents you have—canceled checks, receipts and whatever else—for each item you dispute. Group them with, or attach to each of, your explanations.

A three-ring binder with dividers for each challenged item is one of the best ways to organize your tax materials. Make a duplicate complete copy of the binder for the appeals officer. If you have only one or two disputed issues, and few documents, you can put it all in a file folder. While you give your presentation at the hearing, the officer can follow along. If you lose the appeal, the binder or file folder will do double duty if you go on to court.

4. Finding New Evidence

Think hard. Can you come up with anything new since the audit, such as a statement from someone familiar with a disallowed expense? For example, you hired Connie, a handyperson, to make repairs on your rental property. She didn't have a bank account and insisted on being paid in cash. You couldn't find the receipts for her labor and materials and she has since left town. Now, you could try to prove the work was done through a statement from a tenant, like the one below.

SAMPLE WITNESS STATEMENT

Declaration of Clara Burton

I, Clara Burton, declare that for all of 19XX, I was a tenant in an apartment owned by Alexander Woolf, located at 123 Hannah Road, Appleton, Wisconsin.

Early in the spring of 19XX we had a bad storm. The rain caused plaster to fall from the ceiling in my apartment and ruin the carpet. All the damage was repaired by Connie Williams. She was a nice young woman and I made her coffee every morning. Connie said she wanted to go back to college and I encouraged her to do that. I remember her saying that she wanted to study in Europe.

I moved out of Mr. Woolf's apartment building in November of 19XX to be closer to my nursing job. I now live at 456 Dover in Appleton, Wisconsin. My phone number is 555-1290.

Under penalty of perjury, I declare that the statements of fact contained in this declaration are, to the best of my knowledge and belief, true, correct and complete.

Dated: 6/20/xx   Clara Burton

Perhaps you donated a piece of real estate and claimed the donation as a charitable deduction—and the IRS disputes the value of the real estate (the amount you deducted). Did a real estate appraiser ever make a written report stating the value of real estate? Can an appraiser do so now based on sales of comparable properties that took place around the time of the donation?

D. Meeting the Appeals Officer

Before the hearing, prepare notes of what you are going to say to the appeals officer—an outline of the points you want to make. List the documents and other evidence you want to present. Then try it out by explaining your case to your friends or relatives. Ask if they understand it clearly. Their responses may direct you to weaknesses that you can work on before the hearing.

You'll meet at the appeals office in a private office or meeting room. Seldom is anyone else present from the IRS. An appeals hearing is rather informal, so be yourself. Unlike a court, testimony is not taken under oath and technical rules of evidence don't apply. Tell your story like you would to a friend. The IRS won't tape record the hearing. You have a right to, as long as you inform the appeals officer several days in advance—but taping serves no real purpose. It would likely make the appeals officer speak less candidly than he would otherwise, and reduce your chance of reaching any settlement. If you go on to court, you wouldn't be allowed to play the tape to the judge anyway.

Ask to see the file. If you never received a copy of the auditor's file, ask the appeals officer to show it to you. Take a few minutes to make sure that there isn't anything in it with which you aren't prepared to deal. If there is something new, ask for a postponement. The appeals officer will understand that you were entitled to this information in response to your FOIA request, and should grant you the postponement.

A FORMAL APPEALS HEARING MAY NOT BE NECESSARY TO MAKE A DEAL

Sometimes, cases settle on appeal without a face-to-face meeting with the appeals officer. If the nearest appeals office is hundreds of miles away, it's worth asking to have the appeal handled by mail and telephone. If you prefer the personal touch, ask for a conference at the appeals office.

1. Presenting a Case to an Appeals Officer

Some appeals officers sit back and wait for you to present your case, while others run the show by asking questions. Unless the appeals officer directs otherwise, start with a short statement outlining your case. Point out the specific items in the Examination Report and the auditor's workpapers that are erroneous. Did the auditor ignore documents or leave out facts you presented? Did he misquote you in his workpapers? Here's a sample of how you might address an issue with an appeals officer:

"The auditor was incorrect in finding that I was not entitled to deduct on my tax return costs related to the part of my apartment that I use as a home office for my part-time sales business. I can show, by my testimony and with documents, that my home office deduction is legitimate. The documents include:

- the floor plan of my apartment, showing the space used exclusively for my home office

- a photo of my home office

- my business diary showing that I spent more than 50% of my working hours in the business at my home office, and

- bills and canceled checks for the expenses I incurred in running my home office."

Don't mention the auditor's lack of intelligence or mean-spiritedness. Instead, characterize what you see as errors as "misunderstandings" or "oversights." The appeals officer may take offense at IRS-bashing or be a friend of the auditor.

After the appeals officer hears your side, he may call the auditor, but usually not in your presence. This doesn't mean he will automatically take the auditor's word over yours.

LEGAL ISSUES

Most audits turn on factual issues, like verification of claimed deductions, not on whether you had a legal right to take them. But the auditor may have disallowed an item based on a legal issue. One common tax law issue, for example, is whether your enterprise is a legitimate business or a non-deductible hobby. Appeals officers know the gray areas of tax law more than "black and white legal issue" auditors do. If you researched a legal issue or consulted a tax pro and came up with something favorable, show it to the officer. Ask him to comment on it. If he isn't swayed, ask him why not.

Theoretically, statements made by you to an appeals officer could be considered "admissions against interest," meaning they could later be used by the government against you in a court case. But seldom does an IRS lawyer ask an appeals officer to testify as to what a taxpayer said at an appeals hearing. So, in most appeals hearings, you should acknowledge the weaknesses, as well emphasize the strengths, of your case. Appeals officers appreciate candor, but don't overdo it!

2. Negotiating a Settlement

The odds are great that you will reach a settlement of your case with an appeals officer. The Internal Revenue Manual states, "A settlement may either resolve each issue on the basis of the probable result in litigation or involve mutual concessions of issues based upon the relative strength of the opposing positions where there is substantial uncertainty of the outcome in litigation."

In plain English, the appeals officer wants to deal if there's a possibility of the IRS losing in court. Be sure to write down exactly what you agree to, and compare it to the final settlement papers that the appeals officer prepares.

a. Ask That Penalties Be Removed

One way to start a settlement discussion is to ask the appeals officer to drop any penalties recommended by the auditor. This is the easiest item for an appeals officer to give in on. You'll need an excuse, such as you or your tax preparer made an honest mistake, you weren't trying to cheat the government, you've never been audited before, you didn't understand the tax form or something similar.

b. Accept Some Adjustments

Unless you believe that the auditor was completely wrong on every adjustment, let the appeals officer know that you will accept some changes, without specifying which ones just yet. This breaks the ice and shows the officer you can be reasonable—unlike some of the irrational and irate taxpayers who come through his door. The appeals officer should warm to you. And it is good psychology, any way you slice it.

c. Speak the IRS Lingo

Don't negotiate in terms of how many dollars the audit change would cost you. Use the words "adjustments" or "disallowances" instead, just like the audit report does. It amounts to the same thing. Talk in terms of percentages of disallowances.

Example: An auditor disallowed 80% of Monika's entertainment expenses for her Internet consulting business. The reason was that Monika didn't produce any writings showing the business purpose for each entertainment expense. Monika acknowledged to the appeals officer that her records were incomplete, but emphasized that her records did show that she paid the various expenses and that she was in a legitimate business. Monika offered to accept a 20% disallowance of the entertainment expenses. The appeals officer proposed to allow 50% of the deduction. They talked more and finally agreed on 35%—a far cry from the auditor's disallowance of 80%. Monika never spoke in terms of dollars, only percentages.

Notice that negotiating is an art, not a science. Both sides came out with less than what they wanted, but each side got something.

CASE HISTORY OF AN APPEAL

Mick was a telephone company executive by day and a rock band leader Saturday nights. Four years back he formed the Boohoos. The group never made it to the big time, but Mick enjoyed performing. Bonuses at the phone company allowed Mick to buy new sound gear and a Ford van to haul it to gigs. He became more enthusiastic about his music and hired an agent for the Boohoos. Mick tax-reported his musical income and expenses on his tax returns as a sideline business. The music venture showed overall losses which were claimed to offset Mick's income from his regular job on his tax returns. His total tax bill was lowered.

Sideline Businesses and the Tax Code

Is there a tax problem lurking for Mick? The law says that a sideline business loss can produce a tax write-off for Mick as long as he is honestly trying to make a profit. The Tax Code provides a test for profit motive: If a venture doesn't make money in at least three of five years, it is presumed to be a hobby, and not operated for profit. Hobby losses are personal and cannot be claimed for tax purposes. While this three-of-five-years legal presumption is not final, it puts the burden on Mick to show he was trying to make a profit. As it turned out, Mick had made a small profit in two of the last four years he had been tax-reporting his musical activities.

The hobby loss issue would never arise unless Mick was audited, and, of course, he was. IRS audit classifiers are on the lookout for loss claims that offset income from another job—in effect, a tax shelter. The IRS hunts tax shelters like wolves pursue sheep. When an auditor finds an operation wasn't run to make a profit, he disallows all expenses in excess of income. For example, if Peggy Sue's Scamway distributorship brought in $1,000 and she deducted $3,000 in expenses, the IRS could disallow her $2,000 tax loss—unless the IRS was convinced that Peggy

CASE HISTORY OF AN APPEAL (continued)

Sue was serious about making a profit. The IRS frequently finds the real motive in home sales enterprises is social—entertaining friends and getting home products for personal use. Dabbling in a side business doesn't cut it.

Back to Mick. During the year under audit, Mick's music income was only $1,300, but he claimed $12,300 in business expenses. His largest expenses were the new van and sound system. Under the hobby loss rules, the auditor decided Mick's music expenses were primarily for his personal pleasure. He disallowed the $11,000 tax loss. This meant added taxes, penalties and interest of about $4,500. To make matters worse, he then recommended an audit of two more years.

Mick argued that he had worked hard to make a musical career. Recently he had been getting more jobs for the Boohoos; one hit record would make him millions and the IRS plenty of taxes. The auditor, apparently not a rock fan, was unmoved. An informal appeal—a meeting with Mick and the auditor's manager—went nowhere.

Next, Mick received the Examination Report and appeal notice. He filed his protest letter within the 30-day deadline. Mick felt strongly he had been trying to make money in music, even though he had failed so far. Mick's task was to show the appeals officer a justification for changing the audit result.

Legal Research for Mick's Appeal

The auditor disallowed Mick's deduction of his music equipment as a business loss. His report said that the business expense was not established. Mick called the auditor to ask what tax code section he relied on to reach his decision. The answer was Internal Revenue Code §183.

Mick went to the library and found some simple tax books in the reference section, including The Master Federal Tax Manual. In its index for "IRC 183 and losses," Mick saw the subhead "business" directing him to a definition of a business as "a pursuit or occupation carried on for profit, whether or not profit actually results." There was an excerpt from a Tax Court case stating "an activity may be for profit

CASE HISTORY OF AN APPEAL (continued)

although the investment is not expected to generate profits for several years under the current level of activity." So, the legal principle in Mick's favor is that the profit motive, not the actual result, distinguishes a business from a hobby. The intention to make a profit is sufficient under the tax law, even if the probability of financial success is small or remote. (*Dreicer v. Commissioner of the Internal Revenue*, 78 U.S.T.C. 642 (1982). See also, *Cornfield v. U.S.*, 797 F.2d 1049 (D.C. Cir. 1986).) This meant that Mick's musical activities were not automatically disqualified as a business just because he lost money. Mick photocopied this page.

Mick found more help in *J.K. Lasser's Your Income Tax.* The index lists "Hobby as a Sideline Business," which leads to the following: "If you show a profit in three or more years, the law presumes you are in an activity for profit. The presumption does not necessarily mean that losses will be automatically allowed; the IRS may rebut the presumption." This looked significant because it cited Tax Code §183, the one on which the auditor based his decision. Mick made another photocopy.

In the first two years Mick claimed his music business, he was using his old equipment. He didn't deduct any vehicle expense. The result was that in year one he showed a profit of $120 and in year two he showed a profit of $332. In year three—the audit year—Mick bought the van and the new equipment, causing sizable losses in years three and four. The appeals hearing took place in year five, for which a tax return was not yet due.

So Mick can't be helped by the Tax Code's "three-of-five-year" presumption of profit rule. Mick had only two profitable years out of four. If his appeal hearing were held after he filed a tax return for year five then maybe it would be different. The trick would be to prepare the latest tax return to show a profit—by not taking some expense deductions. This would be perfectly legal, as the law requires you only to report all your income; you are never forced to claim a deduction. Mick could go into the hearing with the benefit of the three-year presumption of profit rule. This would put him in a stronger position for the "profit motive" component, but alone wouldn't assure him an outright win. He still might have to convince the appeals officer that he operated the venture in a businesslike manner.

CASE HISTORY OF AN APPEAL (continued)

Mick's Appeal Hearing

After Mick filed his protest requesting an appeal, the IRS notified him of a conference date. Mick and an appeals officer met. Mick outlined his position. He showed a contract from a talent booking agent who had gotten the Boohoos one job. Mick presented a flyer and event calendar showing the group had performed at public functions twice during the audited year. He didn't mention that one appearance was at an unpaid charity benefit. Mick showed a publicity photo and his calendar showing band rehearsal dates.

Mick understood that appeals are rarely 100% successful. He also didn't want to lose any more time from work and his life by going on to court. His goal was to give the officer justification for compromising, not to walk away clean. In a half hour, Mick finished presenting his case and said, "Let's settle this without going to court. I'll accept a 20% disallowance of my music business losses." Mick was offering to let the IRS reduce his losses from the $11,000 adjustment the auditor made, to $2,200.

The appeals officer replied that he was thinking a 50% disallowance, from $11,000 to $5,500. Mick was in! The IRS accepted the possibility that a court might find that Mick was trying to make a profit. They took a coffee break. On resuming, Mick commented on the photo of the Little Leaguer on the officer's desk. Mick said he had a son, and they talked about parenthood for a few minutes. The appeals officer seemed relieved not to talk taxes for a bit. At 4:30, near IRS quitting time, Mick said that he'd agree to split the difference and accept a 35% disallowance, from $11,000 to $3,850 of his losses and no penalties. Mick also requested the appeals officer not recommend the other two years be opened for audit. The officer agreed. While this was no guarantee of no more audits—appeals officers don't have this authority—their words carry great weight. Several weeks later, Mick received the settlement letter.

> ## CASE HISTORY OF AN APPEAL (continued)
>
> *Post Appeal Wrap-up*
>
> Mick's case is typical of how IRS appeals are handled—and settled.
> If Mick hadn't appealed, he would have owed $11,000 and would have
> been audited for two other years. Mick's appeal didn't require great tax
> expertise. It did involve some effort in research and four or five hours of
> preparation and attendance at the hearing. Most appeals—be they home
> office deductions, entertainment expenses, business auto usage or
> whatever—can be handled successfully like Mick's.

3. Finalizing a Deal

You may not walk away with a deal from the appeals officer at one
sitting. He may want to research an issue before rendering a decision or
accepting a settlement proposal. And if you ask, you will usually be
given time to send more documents or do further legal research. Request
a month to get things in. Appeals officers seem to work at a more
leisurely pace than the rest of the IRS, so he may agree to an even longer
time.

The officer may ask you to sign a waiver extending the normal three-
year limit the IRS has for assessing a tax liability. It is usually okay to
agree to an extension at the appeals level—but certainly not during the
audit. (See Chapter 7, Section B.)

When you and the appeals officer reach a settlement, the appeals
officer does the paperwork. You won't be asked to write anything except
your name. Settlements are formalized on IRS Form 870, Consent to
Proposed Tax Adjustment. Don't expect the settlement papers right
away; the IRS may take several months before finalizing the papers.
Settlements must be approved by a supervisor before leaving the IRS
office.

Make sure you understand the settlement document before signing. Review your notes from the hearing. If the settlement papers don't match, call the officer and hash it out. If you still have questions, run it by a tax pro. She can check computations and explain the details to you. Once you sign, you are barred from going to Tax Court if you change your mind.

⚠️ **Appeals settlement figures may not include the government-mandated interest.** Ask the appeals officer to figure this in to get the bottom line cost. Otherwise, the final bill may come as a shock.

4. If You Don't Settle on Appeal

If you and the appeals officer can't reach a settlement at the end of your meeting, maybe he needs further convincing. Keep trying. Ask what else you can do to change his mind. Maybe he needs further documentation or supporting legal precedent. If so, request time to get it to him before his decision is final. If in doubt how to follow through, see a tax pro.

If you never settle, you'll get a letter denying your appeal. It will come with a form called a 90-day letter, or Notice of Deficiency, advising you of your right to go to Tax Court. If you don't act, after 90 days the audit report becomes final. The tax is assessed and a tax bill from the IRS Service Center will arrive within a few months. (If you want to go to Tax Court, see Chapter 9.)

SAMPLE NOTICE OF DEFICIENCY LETTER

INTERNAL REVENUE SERVICE   DEPARTMENT OF THE TREASURY

Western Region   San Francisco Appeals Office
                                                  160 Spear Street, Suite 800
                                                  San Francisco, CA 94105

Date: July 18 20XX

                                                  AP:SF:90D:GC:JC

                                                  S.S.N./E.I.N.:

                                                  Person to Contact:

                                                  Telephone Number:

                                                  CERTIFIED MAIL

Tax Year(s) Ended	Increase In Tax	IRC § 6662(a)
December 31, 19XY	$10,410.00	$2,072.00

NOTICE OF DEFICIENCY

Dear Taxpayer:

    We determined that you owe an additional amount, as shown above. This letter is your NOTICE OF DEFICIENCY, as required by law. The enclosed statement shows how we figured the deficiency.

    If you want to contest this deficiency in court before making any payment, you have 90 days from the above mailing date of this letter (150 days if addressed to you outside the United States) to file a petition with the United States Tax Court for a redetermination of the deficiency. To get a petition form and the rules for filing a petition, write to: United States Tax Court, 400 Second Street, NW, Washington, D.C. 20217.

    Send the completed petition form, a copy of this letter and a copy of all statements and schedules you received with this letter to the Tax Court at the same address.

    The time you have to file a petition with the Court (90 or 150 days) is fixed by law. The Court cannot consider your case if you file the petition late.

    If this letter is addressed to both husband and wife, and both want to petition the Tax Court, both must sign and file the petition or each must file a separate, signed petition. If only one of you petitions the Tax Court, the full amount of the deficiency will be assessed against the non-petitioning spouse.

Small Tax Cases

    The Tax Court has a simplified procedure for small tax cases, when the amount in dispute is $50,000 or less for any one tax year. You can get information about this procedure, as well as a petition form, by writing to the Clerk of the United States Tax Court at the court address shown in the second paragraph above. You should write promptly if you intend to file a petition with the court.

    If you decide not to file a petition with the Tax Court, please sign and return the enclosed waiver form. This will permit us to assess the deficiency quickly and will limit the accumulation of interest. The enclosed envelope is for your convenience.

SAMPLE NOTICE OF DEFICIENCY LETTER (cont.)

- 2 -

If you are a "C" corporation, under Internal Revenue Code Section 6621(c), large corporate underpayments may be subject to a higher rate of interest than the normal rate of interest for underpayments.

If you decide not to sign and return the waiver, and you don't file a petition with the Tax Court within the time limit, the law requires us to assess and bill you for the deficiency after 90 days from the above mailing date (150 days if this letter is addressed to you outside the United States).

If you have questions about this letter, you may call or write to the person whose name is shown above. If the telephone number is outside your local calling area, you will be charged for a long distance call. If you write, please attach a copy of this letter to help us identify your account. Also, include your daytime telephone number so we can call you if necessary.

Sincerely,

Chancy O'Rourke
Commissioner
by

Associate Chief

Enclosures:
    Copy of this letter
    Waiver
    Statement
    Envelope

SAMPLE NOTICE OF DEFICIENCY LETTER (cont.)

FORM 5278 (REV. MAY 1982	Department of Treasury - Internal Revenue Service Statement of INCOME TAX CHANGES	RETURN FORM 1040	SCHEDULE 1
Name of Taxpayer:		NOTICE OF DEFICIENCY	

Tax Years Ended	19XY		
1. Adjustments to Income			
a.			
b. SCH - E PASSIVE LOSSES	$37,744		
c. ITEMIZED DEDUCTIONS (EXHIBIT A)	$946		
d.			
e.			
f.			
g.			
i.			
2. Total Adjustments	$38,690		
3. Taxable Income - PER RETURN	$37,372		
4. Taxable Income - as revised	$76,062		
5. Tax from: TAX TABLES (JOINT)	$16,361		
6. Alternative Tax (if applicable from:)			
7. Corrected Tax Liability	$16,361		
8. Less Credits			
a			
b			
c			
9. Balance (line 7 less lines 8a 8b 8c)	$16,361		
10. Plus			
a ALTERNATIVE MINIMUM TAX (SCH 2)	$0		
b			
c			
11. Total Corrected Income Tax Liability	$16,361		
12. Total Tax Per Return or As adjusted	$5,951		
13. Adjustment to A. Earned Income Credit B. Special Fuels Credit	$0		
13. INCREASE (DECREASE)	$10,410		
14. Additions to the Tax:			
SECTION 6662(a) (SCHEDULE 3)	$2,072		

i11698　　　　　　　　　　　　　　　　　Form 5278 (rev) 5-82)

SAMPLE NOTICE OF DEFICIENCY LETTER (cont.)

SCH94,WK4   EXHIBIT A

TAXPAYERS:

19XY SCHEDULE A - ITEMIZED DEDUCTIONS

	PER RETURN	PER EXAM	ADJUSTMENT
1. MEDICAL, DENTAL AND INSURANCE PREMIUMS	$3,249	$3,249	
2. 7.5% OF AGI	$5,127	$7,958	
3. NET MEDICAL AND DENTAL EXPENSE	$0	$0	
4. TAXES	$8,901	$8,901	
5. HOME INTEREST EXPENSE	$9,418	$9,418	
6. INVESTMENT INTEREST	$0	$0	
7. OTHER INTEREST EXPENSE	$0	$0	
8. TOTAL INTEREST EXPENSE	$9,418	$9,418	
9. CONTRIBUTIONS	$4,771	$4,580	
10. CASUALTY AND THEFT LOSSES	$0	$0	
11. MOVING EXPENSE	$0	$0	
12. MISCELLANEOUS DEDUCTIONS SUBJECT TO AGI LIMIT	$4,362	$4,362	
13. 2% OF ADJUSTED GROSS INCOME	$1,367	$2,122	
14. EXCESS MISCELLANEOUS DEDUCTIONS	$2,995	$2,240	
15. OTHER MISCELLANEOUS DEDUCTIONS	$0	$0	
16. TOTAL ITEMIZED DEDUCTIONS (SUM OF LINES 3, 4, 8, 9,10, 11, 14, AND 15)	$26,085	$25,139	$946
ADJUSTED GROSS INCOME	$68,357	$106,101	

ITEMIZED DEDUCTIONS WORKSHEET

A. TOTAL OF LINES 3, 4, 8, 9, 10, 11, 14 AND 15	$25,139
B. TOTAL OF LINES 3, 6, 10, (PLUS ANY GAMBLING LOSSES INCLUDED ON LINE 15)	$0
C. LINE A LESS LINE B	$25,139
D. MULTIPLY THE AMOUNT ON LINE C BY 80%	$20,111
E. ADJUSTED GROSS INCOME FROM FORM 1040	$106,101
F. $111,800 (OR $55,900 IF MARRIED FILING SEPARATE)	$111,800
G. LINE E LESS LINE F	$0
H. MULTIPLY THE AMOUNT ON LINE G BY 3%	$0
ENTER THE SMALLER OF LINE D OR LINE H	$0

SAMPLE NOTICE OF DEFICIENCY LETTER (cont.)

ALTMIN94.WK4   SCHEDULE 2

19XY ALTERNATIVE MINIMUM TAX COMPUTATION

TAXPAYERS:

1. TOTAL ADJUSTMENTS AND PREFERENCES	$24,861
2. TAX TABLE INCOME (FROM FORM 1040, LINE 35)	$80,962
3. NET OPERATING LOSS DEDUCTION	$0
4. ITEMIZED DEDUCTION LIMITATION (FROM SCH A)	$0
5. COMBINE LINES 1 THROUGH 4	$105,823
6. ALTERNATIVE TAX NET OPERATING LOSS DEDUCTION	$0
7. ALTERNATIVE MINIMUM TAXABLE INCOME	$105,823
8. EXEMPTION AMOUNT	$45,000
9. SUBTRACT LINE 8 FROM LINE 7	$60,823
10. IF LINE 9 IS $150,000 OR LESS MULTIPLY LINE 9 BY 26%	$15,814
11. ALTERNATIVE MINIMUM TAX FOREIGN TAX CREDIT	$0
12. TENTATIVE MINIMUM TAX (SUBTRACT 11 FROM 10)	$15,814
13. REGULAR TAX BEFORE CREDITS (LESS FTC)	$16,361
14. ALTERNATIVE MINIMUM TAX (BEFORE CREDIT)	$0
15. OTHER CREDITS	$0
16. NET ALTERNATIVE MINIMUM TAX (LINE 14 LESS LINE 15)	$0

SAMPLE NOTICE OF DEFICIENCY LETTER (cont.)

NEGL.WK4   SCHEDULE 3

TAXPAYERS:

TAX YEAR: 19XY

NEGLIGENCE PENALTY - SECTION 6662(c)

1. TOTAL CORRECTED TAX LIABILITY	$16,361
2. TOTAL TAX SHOWN ON THE RETURN	$5,951
3. TOTAL UNDERPAYMENT (LINE 1 LESS LINE 2)	$10,410
4. ADJUSTMENT TO PREPAYMENT CREDITS	$0
5. UNDERPAYMENT NOT DUE TO NEGLIGENCE	$50
6. LINE 3 LESS LINE 4 & 5 (UNDERPAYMENT DUE TO NEGLIGENCE)	$10,360
7. APPLICABLE PENALTY RATE	20.00%
8. LINE 6 MULTIPLIED BY LINE 7 - NEGLIGENCE PENALTY	$2,072
9. PREVIOUSLY ASSESSED NEGLIGENCE PENALTY	$0
10. NEGLIGENCE PENALTY (LINE 8 LESS LINE 9)	$2,072

SAMPLE EXPLANATION OF ADJUSTMENTS

Statement

EXPLANATION OF ADJUSTMENTS

1. a. It is determined that you do not meet the rules for taxpayers in real property businesses outlined in IRC section 469(c)(7). You have not shown that you spent more than 750 hours in real property businesses and that the number of hours spent in the real property businesses is more than half of your personal services. Therefore, the passive activity loss limitations apply. Your allowable rental loss is $14,633.00 rather than the $52,377.00 shown on your 19XY income tax return. Your taxable income is increased by $37,744.00 in taxable year 19XY.

It is determined that your claimed section 179 depreciation deduction is not allowable. The section 179 election only applies to property used in a trade or business and does not apply to rental property.

b. It is determined that your charitable contribution deduction is $4,580.00 rather than the $4,771.00 shown on your 19XY income tax return. Therefore, your taxable income is increased by $191.00 in taxable year 19XY.

Due to changes in your 19XY adjusted gross income, your itemized deductions is reduced by $191.00. Therefore, your taxable income is increased by $755.00 in taxable year 19XY.

See Exhibit A for computation of these changes.

10. a. Due to the above changes, your alternative minimum tax is zero rather than the $345.00 shown on your 19XY income tax return. Therefore, your tax is reduced by $345.00 in taxable year 19XY.

14. Since all the underpayment of tax for taxable year ended December 31, 19XY is attributable to one or more of (1) negligence or disregard of rules or regulations, (2) any substantial understatement of income tax, or (3) any substantial valuation overstatement, an addition to the tax is charged as provided by section 6662(a) of the Internal Revenue Code. The penalty is twenty (20) percent of the portion of the underpayment of tax attributable to each component of this penalty. In addition, interest is computed on this penalty from the due date of the return (including any extensions.)

E. Limits on IRS Settlements on Appeal

In a few situations, the Internal Revenue Manual restricts appeals settlements. If the appeals officer mentions any of the following, you are limited in negotiating with appeals officers or may have to go to Tax Court:

- Your audit was part of a large group of similar taxpayers with identical issues, and the IRS wants to treat everyone uniformly. In this situation, the IRS may make a "standard" non-negotiable settlement proposal to everyone. If you don't accept the settlement, the IRS is prepared to let the judge decide.

- A past court decision or Revenue Ruling directly on point and supporting the IRS' position exists, according to the appeals officer. Because you can argue that rarely are two cases ever exactly alike, this shouldn't prevent you from settling with an appeals officer. If an appeals officer raises this issue, ask for some time to do some research or talk to a tax professional.

- Your case has tax crime potential.

- You are a part of a group of investors who claim tax benefits from investment losses—tax shelters—the IRS concludes were not legitimate business deals, but were tax dodges.

- You formed what the IRS calls "abusive trusts" in order to avoid tax liability.

- You refuse to comply with the tax laws based on moral, political, constitutional, religious or similar grounds.

Going To Court

You lost your audit and didn't do any better with your appeal. You are ready to swallow hard and accept your fate. But before pulling out your checkbook and turning over your life savings to the IRS, consider going to Tax Court.

Each year, over 30,000 taxpayers who lose their audits go to Tax Court. It isn't difficult and can be done inexpensively. You may not need a lawyer. Your chance of winning—at least partially reducing an audit bill—is excellent. Filing a case in court shows the IRS you mean business. Once the IRS receives notice of your Tax Court petition, the government often compromises. Over 80% of Tax Court cases filed settle without ever seeing a judge.

Even if the IRS doesn't settle, you might win at least a tax reduction from the judge. More than 50% of all petitions filed in Tax Court bring some tax relief. In cases with $50,000 or less at stake, 47% of all taxpayers win something. In cases with over $50,000 at stake, 60% of taxpayers come out ahead. Tax Court isn't a total panacea, however; the chance of a complete victory over the IRS is only 5%.

In addition, filing in Tax Court delays your audit bill for a year or longer. Even if you lose, you will have bought time to get your finances in order without worrying that the tax collector will ride off in your new Ford pickup truck. Of course, interest does accrue during this period, which is the downside. But given that more than one out of two people get an audit bill reduced in Tax Court, this trade-off is usually worth it.

Tax Court is not part of the IRS. Tax Court judges are federal judges appointed by the president for 15-year terms. They are lawyers with experience in tax matters, usually gained working for the IRS or in private practice. Don't let the fact that many Tax Court judges are ex-IRS employees dissuade you. The judges are not automatically pro-IRS. In general, they disapprove of auditors who don't give taxpayers a fair shake. You'll get as impartial a trial here as you would in any other court. The impartiality of the judge is very important because you do not have the right to a jury trial in Tax Court.

A. When Not to Go to Tax Court

A person who uses the Tax Court to protest the tax system as unconstitutional or who refuses to file tax returns can be penalized for filing a frivolous lawsuit. These people may be fined $5,000 or more, but hardly anyone ever is. You can almost always find a legitimate reason for disagreeing with an audit report. So don't hesitate in going to Tax Court if you have legitimate grounds to dispute the audit report.

As mentioned, one minor drawback of Tax Court is that interest continues to run on your tax bill if you lose. Alternatively, you could pay the bill in advance to stop the interest accrual. Label the check "deposit/cash bond" on the memo line in the lower left-hand corner. Send a cover letter stating that you are making a deposit/cash bond. If you win your case, you'll get a refund—but the government does not pay you interest for the time it had your money.

DID YOU WAIT TOO LONG?

The envelope you send to the Tax Court with your Petition and other papers must bear a U.S. mail postmark within 90 calendar days of the date on the Notice of Deficiency. If it arrives in Washington after day 90, that's okay, as long as it's postmarked within the 90-day period. Note that 90 days does not mean three calendar months.

Contact the Tax Court clerk for a set of forms and rules as early as possible after receiving your 90-day letter. (See Section B.1, below.) Don't wait until day 83 before contacting the clerk. If you don't have enough time, see a tax pro to get the current forms or use the ones in the Appendix—these forms are not available on the Internet. The Tax Court will most likely accept an out-of-date Petition form. It will even accept a late filing, but the IRS will file a motion to dismiss which the Tax Court judge must grant.

B. Tax Court Small Cases

The small case division of the Tax Court hears audit contests when additional taxes and penalties proposed for any one tax year are $50,000 or less. If you're audited for three years and the IRS claims you owe $50,000 for each year—a total of $150,000—your case still qualifies as a small case. It is given an "S" case designation by the Tax Court.

In S cases, Tax Court operates much like your local small claims court. You tell your story, show your evidence and don't have to know legal procedures. Even if you lose, you have the satisfaction of knowing you had your day in court.

If your case qualifies as a small case, it automatically will be treated as such unless you check a box on the Tax Court Petition rejecting the S designation. Seldom, if ever, would you want to reject S status and deal with the more complex legal and court rules for regular cases. (See Section C, below.) About the only reason you'd reject an S court designation is if you wanted to preserve your right to appeal to a higher court. Neither you nor the IRS has the right to appeal an S case. But appealing may be of little benefit to you. Unlike an administrative appeal within the IRS, fewer than 10% of all Tax Court appeals are successful.

1. Preparing the Forms

The Appendix contains three documents you need to begin your Tax Court case: Tax Court Petition, Designation of Place of Trial form and Election of Small Tax Case Procedure and Preparation of Petitions booklet. If you have enough time, write the Clerk, U.S. Tax Court, 400 Second St., NW, Washington, DC 20217, or call 202-606-8754 and ask for a current set of forms and rules booklet. Amazingly, the Tax Court office is remarkably responsive. There is no charge for these items, which will be sent promptly.

Begin by reading the Election of Small Tax Case Procedure and Preparation of Petitions booklet. Then make several photocopies of the blank Tax Court Petition and Designation of Place of Trial form. This way you will have extra copies to use as drafts and in case you make errors on the forms you type up.

a. Tax Court Petition

Below are a completed sample Tax Court Petition and line-by-line instructions.

Don't worry about minor errors—the Tax Court will overlook them or give you a chance to make corrections. If it's at all possible, type your Tax Court Petition and Designation of Place of Trial form. Handwriting invites misinterpretations.

Top. Type your name exactly as it appears on the audited tax returns. If the IRS audited one or more joint tax returns, add your spouse's name, too, exactly as it appears on the audited tax returns.

In the first blank, fill in all the years for which the IRS made adjustments following the audit which you contest. For example, if your 1997 and 1998 tax returns were audited but you are contesting only the 1998 adjustments, you would enter 1998 in this blank. In the second blank, enter the date from the upper right-hand portion of the Notice of Deficiency (90-day letter). In the third blank, enter the city and state from which the IRS sent you the Notice of Deficiency. It's on the front of the Notice of Deficiency.

Where requested, enter your Social Security number. If the IRS audited joint tax returns, add your spouse's Social Security number as well.

Now let's move to the columns. In the first one, type in the years contested—the same years listed in the first blank. Normally you'll list all years in which adjustments were made.

In the second column, list the exact amount of the tax disputed for each corresponding year. This may not be the whole adjustment made by the IRS for that year. For instance, if the adjustment includes tax on $120 of interest from Xavier Bank for 1998 that you simply forgot to report, you shouldn't contest it.

In the third column, list any penalty you are disputing for each year. Penalties are separately listed in the Notice of Deficiency under "additions to tax." Contest all penalties, even if you are not contesting the tax adjustment because you admit you made a mistake. You don't protest interest, because interest is never listed in a Notice of Deficiency.

The fourth column applies only in the unlikely event you are seeking a refund for an overpayment of taxes for the audited year. This might happen, for instance, if during your audit you found deductions that you forgot to include on the tax return, you would have been entitled to a refund and the auditor rejected the new deductions. You'll have to recalculate your income tax liability for the year and state it here. A tax preparer can help you come up with this figure.

Next, the form asks you to specify the findings in the Examination Report with which you disagree. Don't be concerned with legal technicalities. The Tax Court doesn't expect you to write or act like a tax lawyer. Just make sure your points are clear, for example, "I disagree with the $1,200 deduction disallowed by the IRS. I incurred this expense as the rent I pay on the portion of my apartment I use for my home office." The form also asks you to state why you disagree with the adjustments, but this isn't really necessary in an S case Petition. Don't go into the details of your case. There will be plenty of chances to do this later. The more you write now, the more you are likely to misstate something. Remember, too, not to write down the items you concede, such as the bank interest income you accidentally omitted from your tax return.

Bottom. Sign and date the Petition. If the IRS audited one or more joint tax returns, your spouse must sign, too. Type your address and daytime phone number.

SAMPLE TAX COURT PETITION FORM

UNITED STATES COURT

(FIRST)   (MIDDLE)   (LAST)

Andrew & Malia Lawrence

PLEASE TYPE OR PRINT)   Petitioner(s)

V.

COMMISSIONER OF INTERNAL REVENUE
     Respondent   Docket No.

PETITION

1. Petitioner(s) disagree(s) with the tax deficiency(ies) for the year(s) **19XY, 19XZ** as set forth in the NOTICE OF DEFICIENCY dated , **September 17, 20XX** _____ A COPY OF WHICH IS ATTACHED. The notice was issued by the Office of the Internal Revenue Service at **Austin, Texas**
       (CITY AND STATE)

2. Petitioner(s) taxpayer identification (e.g. social security) number(s) is (are)
555-12-3456; 555-56-7890

3. Petitioner(s) disputes(s) the following:

Year	Amount of Deficiency Disputed	Addition to Tax (Penalty) if any, Disputed	Amount Over-payment Claimed
19XY	$2,766	$632	
19XZ	$517	$109	

4. Set forth those adjustments, i.e. changes, in NOTICE OF DEFICIENCY with which you disagree and why you disagree.

For 19XY, we disagree with the disallowance of $1,710 in expenses against Andrew's royalty income. As a writer, Andrew incurs significant travel expenses to research and promote his books. For 19XZ, we disagree with the disallowance of our $325 donation to the Church of Questionability as a charitable contribution. The Church of Questionability is a legitimate religion with a 501 (c) (3) non-profit corporations status.

Petitioner(s) request(s) that this case be conducted under the "small tax case" procedures to provide the taxpayer(s) with an informal, prompt and inexpensive hearing. A decision in a "small tax case" is final and cannot be appealed to a Court of Appeals by the Internal Revenue Service or the Petitioner(s). If you do not want this case conducted as a "small tax case" place an "X" in the following box.

Andrew Lawrence 10/4/XX 33678 Johnson Dr.
SIGNATURE OF PETITIONER DATE (PRINT) PRESENT ADDRESS-STREET
        Austin, TX 78700 (512) 555-9030
        CITY STATE ZIP CODE AREA CODE TELEPHONE NO.

Malia Lawrence 10/4/XX Same as above
SIGNATURE OF PETITIONER (SPOUSE) DATE (PRINT) PRESENT ADDRESS-STREET
        ( )
        CITY STATE ZIP CODE AREA CODE TELEPHONE NO.

SIGNATURE, NAME ADDRESS, TELEPHONE NO., AND TAX COURT BAR NUMBER OF COUNSEL, IF RETAINED BY PETITIONER(S)

T.C. FORM 2 (REV 4/92)

b. Designation of Place of Trial

Completing the Designation of Place of Trial is simple. First, type your name and your spouse's if the IRS audited a joint return. Then select the city nearest to you in which Tax Court trials take place. The list of these cities is found on pages 4 and 5 of the Small Tax Case Procedure and Preparation of Petitions booklet. Finally, sign your name; your spouse must sign, too, if the IRS audited a joint return.

2. Filing the Tax Court Forms

Below are the six simple steps to follow to file your case in Tax Court. This information is accurate as of August, 1999, with no changes anticipated. To be safe, however, contact the clerk of the Tax Court (see Section B.1, above) for verification.

1. Make three photocopies of the following:
   - completed Tax Court Petition
   - completed Designation of Place of Trial
   - Notice of Deficiency (90-day letter) you received from the IRS with the Examination Report attached.

2. Put one copy each of the Tax Court Petition, Designation of Place of Trial and Notice of Deficiency in your files.

3. Staple the original Notice of Deficiency to the original Tax Court Petition; do the same with the two sets of copies.

4. Make out a personal or business check or get a money order for $60 to "Clerk, U.S. Tax Court."

5. Place the original and two copies of the Tax Court Petition and the Notice of Deficiency, the original and two copies of the Designation of Place of Trial and your check or money order in a large envelope. Don't enclose anything else.

6. Take the packet to the post office and mail it certified, return receipt requested to Clerk, U.S. Tax Court, 400 Second St., NW, Washington, DC 20217. It isn't necessary to send it by express or overnight delivery. Remember—the packet must be postmarked within 90 days of the date on the Notice of Deficiency; the Tax Court need not receive it within the 90 days. Get a receipt from the postal clerk.

Within seven days of receiving your papers, the Tax Court will send you confirmation of receipt and will assign you a case number. Whenever you write or call the Tax Court or the IRS, refer to your case number.

SAMPLE NOTIFICATION OF RECEIPT OF PETITION LETTER

```
                    UNITED STATES TAX COURT
                    400 SECOND STREET, N.W.
                    WASHINGTON, D.C.  20217


        Frederick W. Daily
        Law Offices of F. W. Daily
        302 Warren Drive
        San Francisco, CA 94131


                NOTIFICATION OF RECEIPT OF PETITION


        Docket No.  : XX-13-2893-98

        Name of Case:

        On February  17, 20XX  the Court received and filed a
        PETITION in the above case.

        Further:
        (X) Filing Fee Paid
        (X) Designation of Place of Trial filed for San Francisco, CA

        Petition served on respondent on February  18,20XX


            All papers and correspondence MUST bear the
                 DOCKET NUMBER given above.



                            Charles S. Castro
                            --------------------
                            Clerk of the Court


        Date: February  18, 20XX
```

⚠ **The IRS may respond by filing a document titled Answer.** In this unlikely event, you may need to file a legal paper called a Reply. Alternatively, the IRS might file a Motion to Dismiss. In either situation, you will probably need the advice of a tax attorney.

3. Receiving Notice of the Trial Date

After you file your Petition and receive confirmation, you probably won't hear back from the Tax Court for another four to ten months. Then, you will receive a Notice Setting Case for Trial. It gives you the place, date and time of your court date. It orders you to cooperate with the IRS in certain matters before the trial. And you are warned that if you don't show up for the trial, your case will be dismissed.

SAMPLE NOTICE SETTING CASE FOR TRIAL

U N I T E D   S T A T E S   T A X   C O U R T
Washington, D.C. 20217

August 28, 20XX

Petitioner,

v.   Docket No.: XX-13-2893-98

COMMISSIONER OF INTERNAL REVENUE,
            Respondent.   Trial At: Room 2-1408, Federal Building
                                       and U. S. Courthouse
                                       450 Golden Gate Avenue
                                       San Francisco, CA 94102

NOTICE SETTING CASE FOR TRIAL

The parties are hereby notified that the above-entitled case is set
for trial at the Trial Session beginning on February 01, 20XY

The calendar for that Session will be called at 10:00 A.M. on that
date and both parties are expected to be present at that time and be
prepared to try the case. YOUR FAILURE TO APPEAR MAY RESULT IN DISMISSAL
OF THE CASE AND ENTRY OF DECISION AGAINST YOU.

Your attention is called to the Court's requirement that, if the
case cannot be settled on a mutually satisfactory basis, the parties,
before trial, must agree in writing to all facts and all documents about
which there should be no disagreement. Therefore, the parties should
contact each other promptly and cooperate fully so that the necessary
steps can be taken to comply with this requirement. YOUR FAILURE TO
COOPERATE MAY ALSO RESULT IN DISMISSAL OF THE CASE AND ENTRY OF DECISION
AGAINST YOU.

If there are a number of cases to be tried, the Court will fix the
time of each trial at the end of the calendar call. The Court makes
every effort to suit the convenience of the petitioners in fixing trial
times, but because of conflicting requests received from petitioners,
the final determination of trial times must rest in the Court's
discretion.

                                   Charles S. Castro
                                   Clerk of the Court

Frederick W. Daily
Law Offices of F. W. Daily
302 Warren Drive
San Francisco, CA 94131

SAMPLE NOTICE OF SETTING CASE FOR TRIAL (cont.)

UNITED STATES TAX COURT

WASHINGTON, DC 20217

NOTICE

To: Petitioners (Taxpayers) and Respondent (I.R.S) in the attached Notice of Trial:

1. Status of Tax Court. This Court hears disputes between taxpayers and the Internal Revenue Service. It is not a part of, or connected with, the Internal Revenue Service.

2. Settlement Conferences. Before the calendar call date, the parties should meet and try to settle the case. "Settle" means that the petitioner and the Internal Revenue Service will agree on an amount of the tax due, or that there is no tax due, without a court trial. Settlement documents should be presented to the Court prior to the call of the calendar.

3. Readiness for Trial. If the parties have not submitted to the Court signed settlement documents, the case will be called at the calendar call at the date and time set forth in the notice of trial. After the calendar call, the parties must be ready for trial at any time during the session. The session of the Court may last as short as one day or as long as two weeks.

   a. Cases will not be continued other than under exceptional circumstances.

   b. Failure to appear may result in a dismissal of the case and a decision against the non-appearing party.

4. Stipulation Conference. The parties are to enter into a written agreement about all material facts and documents that are not in dispute. Deliberate failure or refusal by a party to stipulate may result in a finding against that party.

5. The Trial. The parties are responsible for presenting all evidence to the Court at the time of trial. The evidence consists of the stipulation of facts, sworn testimony at trial, and any documentary evidence accepted by the Court as exhibits at the trial. Accordingly, the parties should bring to court all books and records, and any other documents upon which they intend to rely.

The time of trial is the only opportunity for the parties to present their evidence to the Court. Information or documents previously presented to the Internal Revenue Service are not before this Court. Therefore, at trial, the parties must present all documents and the testimony of all witnesses that they want the Court to consider in deciding the case, even though this evidence may have previously been presented to the Internal Revenue Service.

Clerk of the Court

Dated: June 16, 20XY

In most cases, the trial won't be held for at least six months or more from when you filed your Tax Court Petition date. It's highly unlikely that the trial would be more than a year from when you filed your papers. In major cities, Tax Court hearings are held year-round, except summers. In smaller places, Tax Court meets only once a year for a week or two. This six-to twelve-month delay doesn't mean that nothing is happening before your trial date.

You will receive two other notices from the Tax Court:

Standing Pre-Trial Order. This is a notice from the judge assigned to your case. It comes three or four months prior to your trial date and orders you and the IRS to discuss settlement (Section B.4, below), and states that if you don't compromise, you must prepare written stipulations (again, Section B.4). You are advised that obtaining a postponement of the trial date is not easy. Finally, you are told that you and the IRS must exchange lists of witnesses who may testify at least 15 days before the trial date.

SAMPLE STANDING PRE-TRIAL ORDER

UNITED STATES TAX COURT
WASHINGTON, D. C.

STANDING PRE-TRIAL ORDER

To the parties in the Notice of Trial to which this Order is attached:

Policies

You are expected to begin discussions as soon as practicable for purposes of settlement and/or preparation of a stipulation of facts. Valuation cases and reasonable compensation cases are generally susceptible of settlement, and the Court expects the parties to negotiate in good faith with this objective in mind. All minor issues should be settled so that the Court can focus on the issue(s) needing a Court decision.

If difficulties are encountered in communicating with another party, or in complying with this Order, you should promptly advise the Court in writing, with copy to each other party, or in a conference call among the parties and the trial judge.

Continuances will be granted only in exceptional circumstances. See Rule 133 (formerly Rule 134), Tax Court Rules of Practice and Procedure. Even joint motions for continuance will not routinely be granted.

If any unexcused failure to comply with this Order adversely affects the timing or conduct of the trial, the Court may impose appropriate sanctions, including dismissal, to prevent prejudice to the other party or imposition on the Court. Such failure may also be considered in relation to disciplinary proceedings involving counsel. See Rule 202(a).

Requirements

To effectuate the foregoing policies and an orderly and efficient disposition of all cases on the trial calendar, it is hereby

ORDERED that all facts shall be stipulated to the maximum extent possible. All documentary and written evidence shall be marked and stipulated in accordance with Rule 91(b), unless the evidence is to be used to impeach the credibility of a witness. Objections may be preserved in the stipulation. If a complete stipulation of facts is not ready for submission at trial, and if the Court determines that this is the result of either party's failure to fully cooperate in the preparation thereof, the Court may order sanctions against the uncooperative party. Any documents or materials which a party expects to utilize in the

SAMPLE STANDING PRE-TRIAL ORDER (cont.)

- 2 -

event of trial (except for impeachment), but which are not stipulated, shall be identified in writing and exchanged by the parties at least 15 days before the first day of the trial session. The Court may refuse to receive in evidence any document or material not so stipulated or exchanged, unless otherwise agreed by the parties or allowed by the Court for good cause shown. It is further

ORDERED that unless a basis of settlement has been reached, each party shall prepare a Trial Memorandum substantially in the form attached hereto and shall submit it directly to the undersigned and to the opposing party not less than fifteen (15) days before the first day of the trial session. It is further

ORDERED that witnesses shall be identified in the Trial Memorandum with a brief summary of the anticipated testimony of such witnesses. Witnesses who are not identified will not be permitted to testify at the trial without leave of the Court upon sufficient showing of cause. Unless otherwise permitted by the Court upon timely request, expert witnesses shall prepare a written report which shall be submitted directly to the undersigned and served upon each other party at least 30 days before the first day of the trial session. An expert witness' testimony may be excluded for failure to comply with this Order and the provisions of Rule 143(f). It is further

ORDERED that, where a basis of settlement has been reached, stipulated decisions shall be submitted to the Court prior to the first day of the trial session. Additional time for filing of settlement documents will be granted only where it is clear that settlement has been approved by both parties, and the parties shall be prepared to state for the record the basis of settlement and the reasons for delay in filing documents. The Court will specify the date by which settlement documents will be due and expect proposed decisions to be submitted by such date. It is further

ORDERED that all parties shall be prepared for trial at any time during the term of the trial session unless a specific date has been previously set by the Court. It is further

ORDERED that every pleading, motion, letter or other document submitted to the Court by any party subsequent to the date of the notice of trial shall be served upon every other party or counsel for a party and shall contain a certificate of service as specified in Rule 21(b).

Myra Starr
Myra Starr
Judge

Dated:　Washington, D. C.
　　　　August 28, 20XY

Trial Memorandum. Several months before your trial date, you'll be sent a blank form and told to complete and mail it to the Tax Court at least 15 days before the trial. On the form, you must state the issues to be decided by the court, the names of your witnesses, a brief summary of what they will say and an estimate of how long the trial will last. Don't be concerned about mistakes when filling out this form. The judge realizes you aren't an attorney.

Take a look at the filled-in sample. If you are worried about completing it—maybe forms scare you—ask a tax pro for help. But, the judge doesn't expect more than the minimum.

Starting at the top, notice that you are always the "Petitioner" and the Commissioner of Internal Revenue is always the "Respondent." Under Name of Case, write your (and your spouse's, if applicable) name. Under Docket Number, write the number that's on the notice from the Tax Court.

Write "none" in the space for the Petitioner's attorney. Leave blank the space for the name of the Respondent's attorney.

Amounts in dispute. Take this information from paragraph 3 of your Petition.

Stipulation of facts. Section B.4, below, explains stipulations. If the IRS has completed the stipulations by the time you send back this form, check "completed." Otherwise, check "in process."

Issues. Take this information from paragraph 4 of your Petition.

Witnesses you expect to call. Give their names and addresses, along with one or two sentences explaining what they know about your case.

Current estimate of trial time. Generally, you will need at least an hour for your testimony and presentation of evidence and the IRS attorney's questions. And, for every witness you will call, add on another half hour. It's all right to guess, but always ask for more time than you think you'll need to be safe.

Summary of facts. Be brief, but if you feel you must, you can attach a separate statement. Simply state what you did that the IRS is disputing. This is not the time or place to refute anything or present your argument.

Brief synopsis of legal authorities. Unless you are confident of your tax research skills or have talked to a tax pro, leave this space blank. This space is used mostly to alert the judge to some exotic tax issue the judge has never likely encountered before. Chances are the judge has seen the issues in your case many times before.

Evidentiary problems. It's not necessary to fill this in. But, if you think you might have a problem getting a witness to court on the date of the trial notice, bring it up.

Do you wish to discuss this case with the settlement judge? This question is not on every form. If it is on your form, say "yes."

Sign and date the form, and mail it back to the Tax Court.

SAMPLE TRIAL MEMORANDUM

Trial Calendar: SAN FRANCISCO, CALIFORNIA
Date: MARCH 17, 20XX

TRIAL MEMORANDUM FOR ((Petitioner)/Respondent)
Please type or print legibly
(This form may be expanded as necessary)

NAME OF CASE   DOCKET NO. (S).

Billy Bob & Sue Valley, Petitioners   *6666-99*
                        vs.
Commissioner of Internal Revenue, Respondent

ATTORNEYS:
    Petitioner: *None*   Respondent: *(Leave Blank)*
    Tel. No.: *(414) 555-5555*   Tel. No.: _____

AMOUNTS IN DISPUTE:

Year(s)	Deficiencies	Additions	Damages
19XZ	*$12,407*	*$2,481*	*(Leave Blank)*

STIPULATION OF FACTS: Completed _____   In Process ___✗___
                        (If you have signed it, mark "Completed," otherwise "In Process")
ISSUES:

1. Was Peggy Sue Valley's Scamway venture a business or a hobby in 19XZ?

2. Was Billy Bob Valley allowed to deduct entertainment expenses for taking 20 of his best restaurant and bar business customers to the Super Bowl?

WITNESS(ES) YOU EXPECT TO CALL (Name and brief summary of expected
    testimony) *(List everyone other than yourself and spouse)*

(1) Bonita Biziodi, neighbor who helped Peggy Sue run her Scamway parties at home.

(2) Horace Soljerz, customer of Billy Bob's restaurant who ran up a bar tab of $11,187 in 19XZ.

CURRENT ESTIMATE OF TRIAL TIME: *2 - 4 hours* (make estimate, judge won't hold you to it)

(Continued on back)

SAMPLE TRIAL MEMORANDUM (cont.)

<u>SUMMARY OF FACTS</u>
(Attach separate pages, if necessary, to inform Court of
facts in chronological narrative form)

1. *Peggy Sue has been a Scamway dealer since 19XY. In some years the business has been profitable, but in 19XZ it was not. In 19XZ Peggy Sue was sick with pneumonia for three months, so could not sell Scamway products.*

2. *Billy Bob's bar and restaurant has been operated by the Valleys since 19XT. Most of the profits are made from regular patrons of the bar, many of whom are there seven days a week. Billy Bob took the top twenty big spenders to the Super Bowl to keep them as customers. The twenty customers spent about $110,000 total in the business in 19XZ.*

<u>BRIEF SYNOPSIS OF LEGAL AUTHORITIES</u>
(Attach separate pages, if necessary, to discuss fully your
legal position)

1. *Since Peggy Sue had a profit motive in operating Scamway, it was not a hobby under IRC 183 and so she can tax-deduct a business loss for 19XZ.*

2. *Entertainment expenses which serve a business purpose are deductible under IRC 274 and so Billy Bob can deduct the costs of the Super Bowl trip in 19XZ.*

<u>EVIDENTIARY PROBLEMS</u>

Horace Solierz is a long distance truck driver. He can be in court on December 9, but will be on the road December 7, the first day of trial week.

<u>DO YOU WISH TO DISCUSS THIS CASE WITH THE SETTLEMENT JUDGE</u>?

Yes (This question may or may not be in your form, if it is, answer "Yes")

DATE: _____9/9/xx_____   *Billy Bob Valley & Sue Valley*
                                              (Petitioner)/Respondent

Return to: Judge Stephen J. Swift
            United States Tax Court
            Room 316
            400 Second Street, N.W.
            Washington, D.C. 20217
            (202) 606-8731

4. Meeting With the IRS Before the Trial

Often, Tax Court S cases are sent to the IRS Appeals Office before being sent to the IRS' lawyers who would prepare for the trial. The goal is for an appeals officer to consider settlement. The IRS lawyers, called a district counsel, won't work on your case file until they know it is not likely to be settled by an appeals officer. If your case is sent to the Appeals Office, you'll be notified. Be sure to read Chapter 8 before meeting with an appeals officer.

If you don't settle with the appeals officer or your case isn't sent there, you will be contacted by the IRS attorney handling your case at least 30 days before the trial. She will request a meeting at her office or by telephone. She wants to discuss the documents and other evidence—both yours and the IRS'—to be presented in court. She'll explain how she is labeling her documents, called exhibits. She must tell you the names and addresses of any witnesses that may testify. You must do the same. She may even tell you what her witnesses will say.

In addition, she'll ask you to agree in writing to any undisputed facts. These are called stipulations, and cover routine things like identification of your tax return, that signatures on various documents are yours and the accuracy of bank or other records. Tax Court judges require parties to stipulate to as many facts as possible before trial. If you agree to certain facts, the lawyer will offer to prepare a joint "Stipulations of Facts" for you to sign. Any facts not stipulated to must be proven in court.

Ordinarily, you should sign an IRS-prepared Stipulation of Facts. Judges get upset if you waste the court's time by requiring the IRS to produce witnesses unnecessarily, such as calling a bank records custodian to testify that a certain account is yours. Occasionally, an IRS attorney may try to slip something by you. If anything appears on the stipulation which you don't understand, ask the IRS lawyer to explain or delete it. Or see a tax pro for advice before signing.

SAMPLE APPEALS OFFICE LETTER

INTERNAL REVENUE SERVICE

Western Region

Department of the Treasury

San Francisco Appeals Office
160 Spear Street, Suite 800
San Francisco CA 94105
Telephone: 415-744-9271

Date: April 20, 20XY

Re: **1040 / 19XZ** _____ v Commissioner, **Docket No. 2893-98**

Dear Petitioner:

You have petitioned the United States Tax Court to hear disagreements that arose from the examination of your **19XZ** federal income tax return. The Court requires both parties to make every reasonable effort to settle cases without trial, and it is a mutual advantage to both, taxpayer and government.

Consequently, the Tax Court referred your case to the San Francisco Appeals Office for settlement. This case has been assigned to our office for a limited time so that we can meet, discuss issues in the case and resolve any disagreements. Therefore, an Appeals hearing is scheduled for:

DATE: May 11, 20XX
Time: 9:30 A.M.
Place: 160 Spear Street, Suite 800
       San Francisco CA

Please **CONFIRM, the Appeals hearing date and time in WRITING** within the next seven (7) calendar days from the date of this letter. The hearing is your oppurtunity to present any documentary evidence or legal authority for the disputed issues. At the meeting you should plan to bring all records relating to the disputed issues. In addition, the evidence must be organized and categorized to amounts as claimed on the filed tax return.

If we are unabe to reach agreement, the case will be forwarded to our legal staff for trial. For questions, the Appeals Officer can be contacted **before** the hearing at the above indicated telephone number.

Sincerely,

David Collingsworth

David Collingsworth
Appeals Officer

In general, you don't have to worry about this meeting. The IRS attorney isn't likely to raise new issues, make threats or try to trap you into saying something harmful to your case.

> **HIRING A TAX PRO VERSUS DOING IT YOURSELF**
>
> The discussion in Chapter 8, Section A.2, generally applies here. Hiring a tax pro is almost entirely an economic decision. Good tax help for Tax Court is not cheap. An alternative to turning the case over to a professional is using a tax pro as a coach. He can work in the background or accompany you to meetings with the IRS lawyers before your court date. A tax pro's presence shows you are in earnest about your day in court.
>
> IRS attorneys usually welcome a tax pro if it might help reach a settlement and keep from having to prepare your case for trial. The pro doesn't have to be admitted to practice before the Tax Court—usually attorneys only—as long as he doesn't sign any court papers on your behalf.

5. Proposing a Settlement

The IRS attorney may not say so, but she would like to settle the case, rather than go to trial. It is less work for her. So, consider the meeting with the lawyer as an opportunity to deal. Review the negotiation tips in Chapter 6, Section D and Chapter 8, Section D.2. Present your case as if she were an auditor or appeals officer. Stress any new reasons for her to compromise—maybe you located new documents or witnesses.

Remember that most cases settle before the trial. The IRS lawyer might turn you down now, but later change her stance. You and the IRS lawyer can settle the case at any time. As time progresses, the lawyer may review the case and decide you have a better chance to win than she first thought. Perhaps a witness is not available or a document is lost.

If you make a deal, the IRS will prepare something called a Stipulated Tax Court Decision. You, the IRS attorney and the judge must sign it. It is a technical document, so if you don't understand it, before signing, ask that the lawyer explain it to you or have it reviewed by your tax pro. Once you sign the Stipulated Tax Court Decision, it will be nearly impossible to back out of the deal.

6. Preparing Your Case for Trial

If you don't settle, you must start preparing for the trial—even if you eventually do settle the case. Begin preparing several months before the trial date.

You are in a position to start over. Although you have the facts down cold and have met with an auditor, the auditor's manager, the appeals officer and the IRS lawyer, Tax Court is a whole new ballgame. It is a brand new hearing before a judge who knows nothing about your case.

a. Make a Trial Notebook

The best way to arrange your materials is the way lawyers do, with a trial notebook. This is a three-ring binder or a series of file folders. Each section contains information about the stages of the trial and the points you want to prove. List your documents or testimony evidence backing up the point.

 Keep in mind that you must prove your case—by convincing the judge that the IRS is wrong. The IRS doesn't have to prove it is right.

Your trial notebook should contain the following:

Opening statement. The first item in your notebook should be the opening statement you'll give at the beginning of the trial. Summarize the case—create a roadmap of where you will go to prove that the IRS is wrong. Make it brief—no more than five minutes. Speak to the judge as if you were talking to a friend.

Example One: *"Your Honor, the IRS auditor found that I was not serious about making money in my side business as a Scamway home products distributor. She said that the sales presentations in my home were really social gatherings and so she disallowed my $6,492 in losses. I will show the court the evidence of my profit motive and that I operated in a businesslike manner, even though my business showed a loss that year."*

Example Two: *"Your Honor, the Examination Report is incorrect in finding that I was not entitled to claim my children, Katie and Rick, as exemptions on my tax return. I will testify that the children lived with me for the greater part of the year. I will show the court copies of school records proving the children were in school close to my home. I will present canceled checks showing that I paid for their clothing, medical care and other needs. My next door neighbor, Corrine Rogers, will testify that the children were living with me."*

Your testimony. Anytime you relate facts to the judge, you are testifying under oath. Write down your main points so you won't forget any.

Example: *To prove you tried to make a profit with Scamway, you might write:*
"Started Scamway distributorship in 1992."
"First two years, made small profits."
"In-home presentations strictly followed the guidelines of Scamway."
"Third year. Lost money overall but made sales in February, May, June and October."

Make only an outline of your testimony, not a word-for-word recital. That sounds too artificial unless you are a trained actor.

Your evidence. Every tangible thing that helps tell your story to the judge—tax returns, canceled checks, receipts, bills, adding machine tapes, letters, photographs, charts, musical tapes, declarations of witnesses (a sample witness statement is in Chapter 8, Section C.4)—is your evidence. Arrange these documents in a similar binder, separate from your trial notebook. Put them in the order in which you want the judge to see them. Keep the originals in your evidence binder and make two complete copies, one for the judge and one for the IRS attorney.

Example: *Where you are trying to show your Scamway distributorship profit motive, include in your trial notebook the following documents:*

- *Schedule C, Business Income and Expense Form, of two non-audited tax returns showing a profit*
- *the Scamway home presentation guidelines*
- *a videotape of one of your presentations, and*
- *guest lists of the people attending the presentations.*

As mentioned earlier, the formal rules of evidence don't apply in S tax cases. Judges want to get to the bottom of the dispute and will generally consider anything you want to show them.

Preparation always pays, even if you never get before the judge. Your trial notebook and evidence binder should be done before you meet the IRS attorney, so show them to her. If you are well organized and might make a good impression in court, the lawyer might agree to settle. If she's not impressed with your work, she might tell you where you've missed the boat, giving you a chance to fix it before the trial.

Legal authority. Most Tax Court cases are factual disputes, not disputes over the meaning of the Tax Code. This means you rarely have to do legal research. For instance, whether or not you operated your Scamway venture in a businesslike manner is a factual issue. But some questions, such as which parent is legally entitled to claim a child as an exemption, is a legal one and may require research. If you do any research and find something helpful, put copies of the cases or other legal authority in your trial notebook and your evidence binder. (See Chapter 10 for basic tax research advice.)

Closing argument. The last thing in your trial notebook is your closing argument or statement—the summing up at the end of the trial. Like the opening statement, be brief and to the point.

Example: *"Your Honor, you have heard the evidence and can understand why I disagree with the auditor's report. I believe I should owe only $412, not the $4,721 the government says.*

"I explained my efforts to make profits in the music business. I showed the court receipts and canceled checks for music expenses. Although some of my records were missing, I am in substantial compliance with the tax law. I showed flyers promoting my appearances. The Declaration of my booking agent, Irving R. Schwartz, states he made valiant efforts to get my band more performances.

"After hearing my evidence, it should be clear that I had a profit motive. I operated in a businesslike manner. Even though I enjoyed my work, it was not a hobby, as the IRS contends. Therefore, my business losses should have been allowed by the auditor, and I should only owe tax for the additional interest I forgot to report of $412.

"Thank you for hearing my case."

After you are done preparing your case for trial, practice your presentation in front of relatives or friends, or at least a mirror. Concentrate on making your points clearly and logically explaining your documents. Rehearsing gives you confidence in court.

b. Prepare Your Witnesses

In an S case, you might be the only one testifying. Written witness statements are okay if you don't bring people to court. But live witnesses are always more impressive.

In deciding between live witnesses or written statements, consider the following.

Persuasiveness. A person whose testimony is extremely supportive—such as the stranger who purchased items at your Scamway presentation and has no motive to lie—should testify in person. She'll be more persuasive in person than on paper in testifying as to your businesslike manner of operation.

Convenience. Don't seriously inconvenience someone or he may retaliate in court. For instance, if the person at your Scamway presentation is a pilot scheduled to be 40,000 feet above ground on the trial date, settle for a written statement.

Cost. Some people are too expensive to bring to court. Suppose your trial focuses on work done on your rental property which was deducted as a repair. The IRS disallowed the repair deduction, saying that it was an improvement. You want to bring to court the contractor who did your job, and have him testify as to the condition of the property. The law requires you pay a witness a fee for his time and for mileage from his house to court, which could add up if he must travel a long way, then sit in the hall awaiting his turn to testify. Just bring his statement.

Harm. If you're concerned that your witness might say something harmful to your case, then provide a statement. If a witness is a real character, and you aren't sure what might come out of her mouth, think twice. The IRS attorney gets to ask questions, too.

GETTING WITNESSES FOR COURT

There are two ways to get a witness to attend a trial: ask them or subpeona them. You can probably depend on friendly witnesses to be at your trial without giving them formal notice. But if you want to be sure that a witness will show up, you must have her served with a subpoena. This form is available from the Tax Court Clerk in Washington. Call or write for the form well before the trial. (Contact information is in Section B.1.) Enter the case number, witness' name and address and time and place of the trial. You must complete a separate subpeona for each witness.

The subpoena must be served on—hand-delivered to—the witness. Anyone over 18 can serve the subpoena—except you or your spouse. But the rules of what constitutes proper service are strict rules, and so you might visit the federal courthouse and have the U.S. Marshal's office do the serving. Be prepared to give the witness a check for the witness fee and mileage. Ask the clerk the current witness fee and mileage rate when you request the subpoena.

If you decide to have witnesses testify, list them in your trial notebook. Make sure you give the IRS attorney their names and addresses on the Trial Memorandum before the trial. The attorneys for the IRS have the right to talk to taxpayers' witnesses before trial, but seldom do.

7. Arguing Your Case in Court

Come to court a little early; judges hate tardiness. It will also give you time to find parking and the right room, and to orient yourself.

Court sessions are held weekdays during normal business hours—no evenings or weekends. Proceedings are usually held in a federal building. The judge sits in an elevated area, called the bench, or at the end of a conference table. It's hard to generalize about Tax Court judges.

Most are patient souls, giving you all the time needed to present your case. Judges are assigned randomly, so there is no way you can pick a particular one, or request a change. It's doubtful you'd ever know a Tax Court judge anyway. The rest of the cast of characters present are the judge's clerk, a stenographer called a court reporter and the IRS lawyer.

Don't expect to have your trial that day. Instead, the judge is likely to assign a specific date and time to come back for the trial—usually later that week or in the next one. You might be told to call in or to expect a phone message with the exact date and time of your hearing. If the date is impossible for you or your witnesses, ask for another. Most judges are flexible a few days, one way or another. If your witnesses have limited time, don't have them come with you the first time you go to the court. Have them on telephone standby, however, in case the judge has you proceed that day or you need to check their availability for a later date.

If you live far from the Tax Court trial city or have trouble with your work schedule, call the court clerk or IRS lawyer in the week before your court day. Ask for permission not to appear until the day your case will actually be heard. Whether your request is granted depends on the judge. Most try to be accommodating in S cases.

If you get cold feet at the last minute, hire a tax pro. He doesn't have to be a lawyer—some enrolled agents and CPAs are admitted to practice before the Tax Court. But if your tax pro can't formally represent you, he may be able to sit with you during the trial. Ask the judge for permission. The tax pro cannot speak directly to the judge unless the judge allows it.

When you return for your actual trial, again come early to observe and get comfortable with the surroundings. Wait for the clerk to call your name. When that happens, answer that you are present and ready for trial. If you have a problem, ask that your case be continued. You must have a very, very good reason—a serious illness, death in the family or catastrophe like an accident involving a crucial witness on his way to court. Any lesser excuse won't do. The judge came from Washington, DC, to hear your case come hell or high water.

You will be invited to sit at one of two tables facing the judge. The IRS lawyer will be at one, so finding your spot won't be difficult. Bring your trial notebook and evidence binder and arrange them on the table. If anyone is assisting you or there for support, tell the judge who they are and ask permission to have them with you at the table. Your witnesses should be sitting in the public area.

 If you and your spouse were audited, only one must attend the trial. But it makes a better impression when both of you are present.

Although Tax Court trials are open to the public, few spectators attend and trials aren't usually newsworthy. In fact, they are deadly dull affairs to everyone but you, and far removed from TV trial dramas. But for you, the trial is your opportunity to tell your side of the story.

The typical S case trial lasts less than two hours. The judge will grant you more time to present your case if you need it. He's not likely to recess the trial, however, if you have some kind of problem, such as forgetting documents or not getting a witness to court.

COURTROOM TIPS

Address the judge as "your honor" or "judge."
- Stand when you speak, unless the judge asks you to remain seated.

- Refer to your notes, but avoid reading the verbatim; tell your story conversationally, in your own words.

- Get to the point; the judge doesn't want to hear your life story or anti-IRS rhetoric.

- Be polite. Never interrupt the judge or the IRS lawyer.

- Appear to be well organized. Don't fumble with your papers.

The judge knows little about your case before the trial begins. His file contains only your Petition (with the Notice of Deficiency and Examination Report attached), Trial Memorandum and Stipulation of Facts. The judge doesn't have any IRS files. Neither will he have anything that you submitted to the auditor or appeals officer. You must start from scratch in educating the judge.

To begin the trial, you and your witnesses are placed under oath to tell the truth. Next, you're asked to present your case. Ask if you can give an opening statement. The judge will tell you to proceed. Don't read it word for word—that's stiff and unnatural. You'll be okay if you rehearsed it at home or in front of friends. The judge doesn't expect you to be a lawyer or tax law expert.

After making your opening statement, pass out your evidence binders.

The judge wants to hear your story and see your evidence. Don't leave out any relevant details. Start with the preparation of your tax return that was audited. If you are giving too much detail, the judge will let you know. At the appropriate times during your presentation, direct the judge and IRS lawyer to evidence or legal authority in the binder. The judge or IRS attorney may want to look at your originals.

As you tell your story, call your witnesses to testify. For example, say, "I'd like to call Ms. Scarlet to the stand." The judge will grant permission for the witness to come forward.

Your witness doesn't simply tell what she knows. You must ask questions. This is a courtroom technique that will seem awkward to you, so write out the questions ahead of time.

Example: *Recall the Scamway distributor whose losses were disallowed by the IRS. Here are sample questions for Scarlet, a neighbor and friend:*
Please tell the court your name and address.
Are you familiar with me and my Scamway business?
Did you come to my home for presentations?

Describe how those presentations were conducted.
Who else was present?
How many times have you bought Scamway products from me?
Did other people buy products at the presentations you attended?
Have you seen Scamway products stored in my house?
Do you know if I have a home office?"

After you finish questioning your witness, the IRS attorney and the judge may ask a few.

Once you are done presenting your case, it's the IRS' turn. The lawyer's presentation will be much like yours. If the IRS lawyer calls any witnesses, you can ask them questions. Do not interrupt the IRS lawyer. Respectfully and quietly listen to her presentation.

Once the IRS finishes, ask permission to sum up the case—to give your closing statement.

8. Awaiting the Judge's Decision

While the judge may announce his decision at the end of your trial, don't count on it. Judges don't announce their decisions in court to avoid debates with sore losers. Instead, expect to receive the decision in the mail within a few months.

In S cases, judges often don't give detailed explanations of why you won or lost. The decision won't show the final amount owed to the IRS, either, interest gets added on later in your bill from the Service Center.

The judge's decision is final. You cannot appeal an S case decision.

SAMPLE CASE DECISION

<u>UNITED STATES TAX COURT</u>

PETITIONER,	)))))
v.	) DOCKET NO. 20320-97
COMMISSIONER OF INTERNAL REVENUE,	))
RESPONDENT.	)

<u>DECISION</u>

Pursuant to the agreement of the parties in the above-entitled case, it is

ORDERED AND DECIDED: That there are deficiencies due from the petitioner for the taxable years 19XX and 19XY in the amounts of $4,336.00 and $2,641.00, respectively; and

That there are no additions to tax due from the petitioner under the provisions of I.R.C. section 6662(a) for the taxable years 19XX and 19XY.

(Signed) **Susan Cohen**
Judge

Entered: **Mar 31 20XX**

*   *   *   *   *

It is stipulated that the Court may enter the foregoing decision in the above-entitled case.

C. Tax Court Regular Cases

If you want to contest in Tax Court an audit outcome of over $50,000 for any one year, your case will be considered a regular case. While most people hire a lawyer to represent them when arguing a regular case, 40% of all taxpayers proceed pro se—without a lawyer. Most cases settle before ever reaching a judge, which may be why so many people are able to represent themselves. You can appeal a regular case decision to a higher court.

If your case reaches the trial stage, the judge may not be that patient with a taxpayer representing himself. Strict court procedures and rules of evidence apply. After the trial, you must submit a formal legal brief. This is a highly technical document and anything but brief. You must comment on evidence produced at trial, legal theories and tax law precedents. The only way to avoid the complicated brief writing is by asking the judge for a bench decision at the end of the trial. If the IRS attorney doesn't object, the judge can rule without legal briefs if he is satisfied that the facts and law are clear-cut—either for or against you. If the IRS attorney objects or the judge denies your request for a bench decision, you will probably lose if you don't submit a brief.

If your audit bill is over the limit for an S case, you might still use the S case procedure. You must give up disputing anything over $50,000 per year. For example, Ronnie's audit report claims he owes $62,000 for 1998 and $29,500 for 1999. Ronnie can proceed with an S case if he contests only $50,000 for 1998, agreeing to owe the $12,000 overage. He can contest all of the $29,500 for 1999.

If you decide to hire a lawyer to represent you, understand that it probably won't be cheap. You are not entitled to a court-appointed attorney in Tax Court, although a nearby law school may offer free student help or a legal clinic. You might also check with your local bar association for a free or low-cost lawyer referral service for advice.

If you win the case, you might be able to get the IRS to pay your lawyer's fees. (Internal Revenue Code §7430.) Your lawyer must show that the IRS' position is not substantially justified. This means convincing a judge the IRS knew or should have known that it was dead wrong—on either the facts or the law.

While there is no maximum you can get, you won't be entitled to more than $125 per hour for the attorney's time. There is one exception: You might qualify for a higher rate if the case was unusually difficult and your attorney normally charges more. The second part is easy—tax attorneys charge from $150 to $400 per hour.

Example: Tom lost his audit after supplying documents which were ignored by the IRS. He showed the same records to a Tax Court judge and won. The judge awarded him $17,000 in legal expenses incurred in fighting the unreasonable tax assessment. (Tinsley v. Commissioner of Internal Revenue, *TC Memo 1992-195 (1992).*)

D. Other Federal Courts

Instead of going to Tax Court, you can contest an audit from the IRS in two or possibly three other federal courts: a U.S. District Court, the U.S. Court of Federal Claims or a U.S. Bankruptcy Court. (Bankruptcy courts are covered in Section E.)

District Courts follow strict rules of procedure, even more intense than Tax Court Regular cases—you'll need a tax lawyer from start to finish. The Court of Federal Claims is more like the Tax Court with somewhat relaxed rules of procedure. Its judges are friendlier to people representing themselves than are District Court judges.

The unpopular feature of these two forums is that before suing, you must pay the tax bill, file IRS Form 843, Claim for Refund (a copy is in the Appendix or available on the IRS' website at http://www.irs.ustreas.

gov/forms_pubs/pubs.html) and then wait six months until the IRS officially denies your request. Your lawsuit then becomes one for a refund of overpaid taxes.

Unlike Tax Court, where some CPAs and enrolled agents can appear on your behalf, only a lawyer can represent you in a District Court or the Court of Claims. If you win, however, the IRS may be ordered to pay your attorney's fees. (See Section C, above.)

If you are disputing $50,000 or more and can pay first, talk to a tax attorney about filing in a District Court or the Court of Claims. There are several potential advantages to filing in one of these courts. First, they rule in favor of taxpayers more often than the Tax Court does. Second, because of the quirkiness of our judicial system, you might be able to shop around for the federal court that has historically been most kind to your tax situation. Third, you get a jury trial in a District Court (but not the Court of Claims)—a jury of your peers who are sufficiently upset with the IRS or the tax law might give you a break. Finally, unlike Tax Court, the government lawyers defending the IRS in District Court or the Court of Claims do not work directly for the IRS. They work for the Justice Department and often are more reasonable in settling cases than are the IRS' lawyers.

E. Bankruptcy Court

If you are a serious candidate for bankruptcy, talk to a bankruptcy lawyer with tax experience or a tax lawyer with bankruptcy experience. In a bankruptcy case, you can ask the judge to determine a tax dispute. Bankruptcy courts have made some very favorable tax rulings. Another advantage of bankruptcy court—you don't have to pay the IRS first.

F. Appealing to Higher Courts

As mentioned earlier, you cannot appeal a Tax Court S case. All other cases—Tax Court regular cases and those filed in a District Court, Court of Federal Claims or bankruptcy court—can be appealed to a U.S. Circuit Court of Appeals. You will need a lawyer and can expect to pay legal fees starting at $50,000. Your statistical chance of winning is less than 10%. If you lose again, the U.S. Supreme Court might agree to hear your case, but your chance of winning ranks up there with winning your state lottery.

■

CHAPTER 10

Help Beyond This Book

This book gives you strategies for preparing for an audit, appealing within the IRS and appealing your audit in Tax Court. If you need more help, try any of these:

- *Tax Professionals (tax pros).* An Enrolled Agent, Certified Public Accountant or tax attorney can provide tax information, guidance or representation before the IRS.

- *IRS.* The IRS has free tax publications, telephone prerecorded and live information, Internet access and taxpayer service representatives at many offices.

- *Library.* You can research tax questions in larger public libraries and law libraries in your community.

- *Internet.* You can do much research on tax issues at the IRS' and others' websites.

A. Finding and Using a Tax Pro

You can successfully take on the IRS alone most of the time. But if you feel over your head or want professional reassurance, consider consulting or hiring a tax pro.

Under a federal law called the Taxpayers' Bill of Rights, you can have a representative handle any IRS matter for you. You never have to face the IRS alone if you hire a tax pro. You also have the right to call time out to consult a tax pro during the process whenever you are taking on the IRS by yourself.

Consultation and advice. A tax pro can analyze your situation and identify the strengths and weaknesses. Once you know this, you can better prepare for your audit or appeal. Of course, a tax pro might pitch her services. Weigh the pro's advice against what you have learned by reading this book and your own judgment.

Negotiation. Tax pros often possess negotiating skills. And, an experienced tax pro should know what kinds of deals can and can't be made with the IRS.

Representation. Tax pros know IRS procedures and how to maneuver around the IRS bureaucracy. They can neutralize the intimidation factor the IRS knows it holds over you. And, if you have something to hide, a tax pro usually can keep the lid on it better than you can.

1. The Right Type of Tax Pro

Enrolled Agent (EA). An EA is usually a full-time tax advisor and tax preparer who is licensed to practice before the IRS. Most EAs cannot represent you in Tax Court, however. They earn the designation En-rolled Agent by either passing a difficult IRS exam or having at least five years of experience working for the IRS. They also must participate in continuing education programs to retain their EA designations.

There are approximately 24,000 EAs in the U.S., 6,000 of whom are members of the National Association of Enrolled Agents. EAs are the least expensive of all tax pros. For a cost-effective approach to handling an audit or appeal within the IRS, consider an EA.

Tax attorney. Tax attorneys are lawyers who do various types of tax-related work. Some specialize in complex tax and estate planning, others focus on IRS dispute resolution and some do tax return preparation. To assure competence, look for a tax attorney with either a special tax law degree (LLM-Tax) or a certification as a tax law specialist from a State Bar Association. If a great deal of money is at stake, the IRS is accusing you of committing fraud or you're headed to court, call a tax attorney.

Certified Public Accountant (CPA). Like attorneys, CPAs are licensed and regulated in all states. They do sophisticated accounting and inter-nal audit work, and prepare tax returns. To become a CPA, an accoun-tant must have a college degree and experience with a CPA firm, and must pass a rigorous examination. Some CPAs have a great deal of IRS experience, but many don't ever deal with the IRS. CPAs charge about the same or even a little less than attorneys. As a rule, CPAs are not as aggressive as tax lawyers when facing IRS personnel.

Using an Enrolled Agent can be a cost-effective choice if you want representation in a straightforward audit or appeal. But if you face complex legal or accounting issues, hire a tax attorney or CPA. In some cases you may need both.

An immediate family member or business partner or employee can represent you at an audit. You must give written permission on IRS Form 2848, a copy of which is in the Appendix. While there's no harm in bringing any of these people along for support, you are better off hiring a tax pro or representing yourself at the audit.

2. How to Choose a Tax Pro

There are several ways to find a good tax pro. Asking the IRS is not one of them.

Personal referrals. This is frequently the best source. Ask friends, relatives and acquaintances whose judgment you trust for the names of tax pros who helped them. If their tax pros can't help, ask for a referral.

Your tax preparer or accountant. Your tax return preparer or accountant might have a good recommendation of a tax pro who can help you deal with an IRS problem outside of their expertise.

Audit assistance or preparer guarantees. Some tax preparers offer audit assistance free with their return preparation service. One chain says they will go with you to the IRS to explain how a return was prepared. This service may fall short of actual representation. And there is no guarantee the person going with you prepared your return or knows anything about the tax law. Not all tax preparers are created equal—not by a long shot.

Advertising. Various directories, including phone books and newspapers, carry lists of tax pros. Look under Accountants, Tax Return Preparers, Tax Consultants and Attorneys—Tax. Some tax pros offer a first consultation by phone or in their office at no charge. Bear in mind, however, that anyone heavily advertising or giving away her time may be new to the game.

Professional associations and referral panels. Most local bar associations will give out the names of tax attorneys who practice in your area. But, bar associations don't meaningfully screen the attorneys listed; those who are listed may not be experienced or competent. To find an EA in your area, call the National Association of Enrolled Agents referral line at 800-424-4339. To find a CPA, try calling a local or state CPA society.

3. What to Look for in a Tax Pro

Once you have the name of a tax pro, call and ask to speak with him directly. If he is too busy to talk to you—and your call isn't transferred to another tax specialist—assume the office is too busy to handle your case. Call the next person on your list.

When you speak to a tax pro, try to develop a rapport. Mention how you got his name, especially if it was a personal referral. Then get to the point—tell him your tax problem. If he doesn't handle your type of case, ask for the names of professionals who do.

Here are some other suggestions for making a good match:

- Don't rush to hire the first tax pro you speak to. Your decision is important, and rarely is there only one person for the job. Talk to a few. Choose the one you communicate with best—do you understand her advice and answers to your questions?

- Question the tax pro carefully about her IRS experience. No matter how well she knows the tax code, prior IRS dealings is key. Previous IRS employment is not always a plus; it may have forever impressed the IRS point of view on her. Also, be skeptical if she hasn't been in practice at least five years.

- Does the tax pro seem to be aggressive or timid in discussing your case? If she seems awed by the IRS, find someone else.

- Does the tax pro give you a feeling of confidence? Ask her the likely outcome of your case. While no one can predict the future, her answer should create trust. Look for an honest response, not necessarily a rosy picture.

a. Tax Pro Help Before an Audit

If you consult a tax pro before your audit, bring your audit notice, tax return and documents on which the return was prepared to the first meeting. If you face an *office* audit, go over the audit letter checklist with the tax pro—explain why you reported your income as you did or took the deductions that the IRS is now questioning. Ask the tax pro what documentation will help you prove your position.

If you face a *field* audit, your audit won't be limited to any pre-prepared list of items to be examined. This makes a field audit more difficult to prepare for than an office audit. Show the tax pro your return and ask which items he would expect the IRS to question. Next, ask him if he sees any legal problem areas and how to deal with them. You might ask the tax pro to photocopy some supporting tax law authority or to prepare a memorandum of law pertaining to your case to show the auditor.

Finally, ask the tax pro for suggestions on how best to explain and present your documents to the auditor. You may want his assistance in making summaries or spreadsheets showing your business or investment transactions. The more clearly you present information, the less time you will spend with the auditor. Auditors appreciate and, more importantly, reward well-prepared taxpayers.

If your tax pro was the preparer of the tax return, ask her to explain all figures and schedules to you. If she has workpapers or notes used to prepare your return, ask for copies and interpretations, if needed. You won't necessarily show them to the auditor—they may be just for your reference.

b. Tax Pro Help After an Audit

If you handled your own audit and it did not turn out well, you might ask a tax pro why. He can analyze the Examination Report, tax return and documents you produced at the audit. Tell him what you said and what the auditor said about items that are disputed. The tax pro can then evaluate the strengths and weaknesses of your legal position.

If the tax pro believes you are at least in a legal gray area, he may examine the quality of the documents and consider the credibility of your explanations. In an hour or so, he should be able to decide whether you should contest the IRS' report. He may advise you to try again with the auditor or her manager, or to make a formal appeal or go to Tax Court.

4. Tax Pros' Fees

Get an understanding about the tax pro's fees at your first meeting. Does she charge by the hour or a flat fee? Most professionals charge $35 to $350 per hour, depending on where you live, the type of case and the tax pro. To some extent, you can control costs: Tax pros can be either hired as consultants, meaning you handle your own case and ask for advice as needed, or hired to represent you start to finish. In other words, hiring a tax pro need not be an all-or-nothing affair.

Although uncertainty about open-ended fee arrangements leaves most folks uncomfortable, many good tax pros won't quote a flat fee. But most tax pros should be able to ballpark a range of hours necessary for your case. For example, I usually figure 5–15 hours of my time for full representation in an office audit. For appeals, field audits and Tax Court cases, I put in 10–40 hours.

Most tax pros require a fee and cost retainer paid in advance, often equal to the minimum time estimated as needed on the case. For example, on a typical collection case, I require a $1,500 retainer.

TIPS ON CONTROLLING A TAX PRO'S FEES

- If you like the tax pro but not her fee, ask if she can do it for less. If she isn't very busy, she may be flexible on fee and payment arrangements. Small tax firms or solo practitioners are more likely than professionals in large offices to negotiate their fee.

- Ask for a written fee agreement and monthly billings with itemized statements of time and services rendered. This will keep the tax pro honest and keep the large bill fee shock down. In many states, attorneys are required to give you a written fee agreement before starting work.

- If you disagree with a bill, call the tax pro. If the firm is interested in retaining your business, it should listen to your concerns, adjust the bill or work toward satisfying you. If the tax pro won't budge, call your state or local CPA society or your state's bar association. Many groups have panels that help professionals and clients mediate fee disputes.

B. Researching Tax Questions

Although most tax matters require no research, some do. Your auditor may go beyond looking at your records. For instance, the question may be whether or not the deductions are legally allowable. Your home office expenses may be disallowed not because you didn't prove them, but because the auditor says that you don't qualify for a home office deduction. To find out if the IRS is correct, you must know what are the legal requirements to qualify for a home office.

There are many good sources to augment the information in this book.

1. Free IRS Information

The IRS offers free publications, as well as telephone and face-to-face help. To meet with someone from the IRS in person, call your nearest local IRS office. There, you can talk to a Taxpayer Service Representative. Just don't expect any sophisticated advice from the IRS.

a. IRS Publications

The IRS distributes free taxpayer pamphlets, nicknamed pubs, numbered from 1 to 1000. Pubs contain tax information on all kinds of issues—from the IRS' point of view, of course. For example, Publication 334, Tax Guide for Small Businesses, covers a variety of rules from how to claim depreciation of a business vehicle to reporting losses on the sale of assets.

These pubs are free at most IRS offices, by calling 800-829-3676 or downloading them off the IRS' website at http://www.irs.ustreas.gov/prod/forms_pubs/index.html. Start with Publication 910, Guide to Free Tax Services, to request the tax information you need. Order as many pubs as you need. Expect to wait several weeks to get them by mail.

b. IRS Telephone Information

The IRS offers a Taxpayer Assistance toll-free line at 800-829-1040 or 800-829-8815. This service is staffed with live people, and is for questions on tax preparation and tax notice questions. Have your Social Security or Employer ID number handy if you need information about your account. The IRS also has a toll-free prerecorded tax information line, Tele-Tax, at 800-829-4477.

The best thing I can say about these telephone services is that they are free. They will give you only the official IRS position, which is conservative and not necessarily beneficial—and many times the answers are misleading or outright wrong. Start, but don't stop here, with your tax law research.

c. Tax Information on the Internet

Many legal and tax resources are available online through the Internet. There are a number of ways to use the Internet to search for material, but by far the most important and common tool for doing research on the Internet is the World Wide Web, or the Web.

A wide variety of sources intended for both lawyers and the general public have been posted on the Internet by publishers, law schools and firms. If you are on the Web, for example, a good way to find these sources is to visit any of the following websites, each of which provides links to legal information by specific subject:

- *http://www.nolo.com* includes a vast amount of legal information for consumers. This includes sets of FAQs (frequently asked questions) on a wide variety of legal topics and articles on legal issues. Nolo's Legal Encyclopedia includes a section devoted exclusively to tax issues.

- *http://www.findlaw.com* is an easy-to-use website that points to legal resources on the Web.

- *http://www.law.cornell.edu/lii.table.html* is another law pointer, maintained by Cornell Law School.

- *http://www.law.indiana.edu/law/v-lib/lawindex.html* is a third useful pointer, maintained by Indiana University's School of Law at Bloomington.

Specific tax information is available at a several websites. Start your research at either of the following:

- *http://www.irs.ustreas.gov*. This is the home page for the IRS. You can read articles on current topics, download IRS forms and publications, peruse summaries of many tax topics and read tax statistics or tax regulations. You can also email simple tax questions to the IRS; you'll get an email response in a few days. The response will be fairly generic, but will help you get started researching a question. You need an application called Adobe Acrobat to download the IRS forms. If you don't already have it, the site has a link to where you can download Adobe Acrobat.

- *http://www.el.com/elinks/taxes/.* Essential Links' tax section points you toward every conceivable tax site on the Internet. The links are categorized as follows:
    —Major Tax Sites
    —Tax Information
    —Tax Forms
    —State Taxes
    —International Taxes
    —Tax Code
    —Tax Law
    —Tax Tips
    —Tax Software
    —Tax Preparation
    —Associations
    —Publications
    —Commercial Tax Sites
    —Tax Professionals
    —News
    —Discussion
    —Links
    —Calculators
    —Potpourri.

2. Private Tax Guides

Numerous privately published tax guides can answer your tax questions.

a. Popular Guidebooks

You've probably seen the annual tax guides, including *The Arthur Young Tax Guide* (Ballantine Books), *J.K. Lasser's Your Income Tax* (Prentice Hall), *The Arthur Andersen Tax Guide* (Perigle Books) and *Consumer Reports Tax Guide* (Consumer Reports Books).

These guides cover the most current tax rules for income reporting and deduction taking. They are easier to read than IRS publications and have better examples of how the tax law works. I favor *The Arthur Young Tax Guide* because it's the most complete, although it is not the easiest to understand. These guides are inexpensive—$10 to $20—and found in most libraries as well.

In preparing for an audit, appeal within the IRS or Tax Court, find a tax book covering the year your audited return was prepared. This isn't always possible—stores carry the most recent books. Libraries, however, may have prior editions. If you can't find a book for an earlier year, a later one should be okay, as the tax law on most audit issues rarely changes from year to year.

b. Tax Pro Deskbooks and Guides

Accountants and attorneys use more sophisticated tax deskbooks. The three top professional guides are *Master Tax Guide* (Commerce-Clearing House), *Master Federal Tax Manual* (Research Institute of America) and the *Federal Tax Guide* (Prentice-Hall). They are all about 600 pages of fine print. Don't let this scare you, as you may need to read only a few pages. These deskbooks summarize the law on the most common tax law problems. They are available in libraries, especially law libraries, and sell in bookstores for about $25.

IRS personnel seem to prefer *Master Tax Guide*. If you have a choice of which of the three to consult, you may want to use that one.

3. Other Research Materials—Using the Library or Internet

The original source materials for the tax law are the Internal Revenue Code (Tax Code) and Congressional Committee Reports. IRS Regulations and federal court decisions interpret the law and show how it is applied to a set of facts. The IRC and Reports are found in federal building libraries, large public libraries and law libraries and on the Internet. Most are technical in the extreme and are only recommended as a cure for insomnia. The guidebooks listed in Section B.2, above, are an attempt to make sense out of this mass of legalese, and are your better bets.

Nevertheless, if you want to look at court decisions or legal treatises, find a law library or a computer with Internet access. To find a library, call your local courthouse or college or a lawyer and ask where the nearest law library open to the public is located. Many private law libraries restrict access to lawyers, judges and law students.

If you go to a library, look in the card catalogue or computer database for:

- Internal Revenue Code

- IRS Regulations

- U.S. Tax Court and other federal court opinions, and

- books by research companies and legal scholars explaining the tax law, such as this book and tax guides mentioned earlier.

Use the Internet site http://www.el.com/elinks/taxes to get this material on the Internet.

Start your research with the number of an Internal Revenue Code section, an IRS Regulation or a name of a case you have run across.

In the library, once armed with the call numbers and the citation or topic, head for the material or throw yourself on the mercy of the library staff. Tell the librarian that you need tax law information. Ask that you be pointed in the right direction. She might even show you how to use the books. But few law librarians have great familiarity with tax law, so don't expect too much.

FURTHER READING AND REFERENCE LIST FOR DEALING WITH IRS PROBLEMS

- *IRS Practice Advisor Report* (Tax Management Inc.), 800-372-1033. This is the most authoritative monthly service on IRS issues. Highly recommended for serious tax pros.

- *IRS Practice & Procedure,* by Michael I. Saltzman (Warren, Gorham & Lamont). This text book is the bible on IRS procedure.

- *Representing the Audited Taxpayer Before the IRS and Representation Before the Appeals Division of the IRS* (West Publishing Co.). Both are loose-leaf and supplemented annually. They are written clearly by experienced people in the field.

- *How to Defend Yourself Against the IRS,* Sandor Frankel and Robert S. Fink (Simon & Schuster). The book was originally published in 1985 and may be difficult to find or out of print.

- *Peyron Tax Accountants Communique* (monthly newsletter, 502-637-7483). This can keep you up to date on new IRS policies and tax cases.

- *Tax Management Tax Practice Series* (Bureau of National Affairs, 800-223-7270). This is a top-of-the-line research resource tool on CD-ROM. It is most likely to be found at a law library or a tax pro's office. The cost depends on the version you purchase.

- *Tax Hotline* (Bottom Line Publications, 800-328-8477). This monthly newsletter is full of tax tips from experts all over the U.S.

Appendix

Form **843**
(Rev. January 1997)

Department of the Treasury
Internal Revenue Service

Claim for Refund and Request for Abatement

▶ See separate instructions.

OMB No. 1545-0024

Use Form 843 only if your claim involves **(a)** one of the taxes shown on line 3a or **(b)** a refund or abatement of interest, penalties, or additions to tax on line 4a.

Do not use Form 843 if your claim is for—
- An overpayment of income taxes;
- A refund of fuel taxes;
- An overpayment of excise taxes reported on Form 720, 730, or 2290 (see **General Instructions**).

Please type or print		
Name of claimant		Your social security number
Address (number, street, and room or suite no.)		Spouse's social security number
City or town, state, and ZIP code		Employer identification number
Name and address shown on return if different from above		Daytime telephone number ( )

1 Period—prepare a separate Form 843 for each tax period
From   , 19   , to   , 19

2 Amount to be refunded or abated
$

3a Type of tax, penalty, or addition to tax:
☐ Employment   ☐ Estate   ☐ Gift   ☐ Excise (unless reported on Form 720, 730, or 2290—see instructions.)
☐ Penalty—IRC section ▶ _____

b Type of return filed (see instructions):
☐ 706   ☐ 709   ☐ 940   ☐ 941   ☐ 943   ☐ 945   ☐ 990-PF   ☐ 4720   ☐ Other (specify) _____

4a Request for abatement or refund of:
☐ Interest caused by IRS errors or delays (if applicable—see instructions).
☐ A penalty or addition to tax as a result of erroneous advice from the IRS.

b Dates of payment ▶

5 **Explanation and additional claims.** Explain why you believe this claim should be allowed, and show computation of tax refund or abatement of interest, penalty, or addition to tax.

Signature. If you are filing Form 843 to request a refund or abatement relating to a joint return, both you and your spouse must sign the claim. Claims filed by corporations must be signed by a corporate officer authorized to sign, and the signature must be accompanied by the officer's title.

Under penalties of perjury, I declare that I have examined this claim, including accompanying schedules and statements, and, to the best of my knowledge and belief, it is true, correct, and complete.

....
Signature (Title, if applicable. Claims by corporations must be signed by an officer.)   Date

....
Signature   Date

For Paperwork Reduction Act Notice, see separate instructions.   Cat. No. 10180R   Form **843** (Rev. 1-97)

Form **2848**
(Rev. December 1997)
Department of the Treasury
Internal Revenue Service

**Power of Attorney
and Declaration of Representative**

▶ See the separate instructions.

OMB No. 1545-0150

For IRS Use Only
Received by:
Name _____
Telephone _____
Function _____
Date ___ / ___ / ___

Part I **Power of Attorney** (Please type or print.)

1 **Taxpayer information** (Taxpayer(s) must sign and date this form on page 2, line 9.)

Taxpayer name(s) and address	Social security number(s)	Employer identification number
	Daytime telephone number	Plan number (if applicable)

hereby appoint(s) the following representative(s) as attorney(s)-in-fact:

2 **Representative(s)** (Representative(s) must sign and date this form on page 2, Part II.)

Name and address	CAF No. .... Telephone No. .... Fax No. .... Check if new: Address ☐ Telephone No. ☐
Name and address	CAF No. .... Telephone No. .... Fax No. .... Check if new: Address ☐ Telephone No. ☐
Name and address	CAF No. .... Telephone No. .... Fax No. .... Check if new: Address ☐ Telephone No. ☐

to represent the taxpayer(s) before the Internal Revenue Service for the following tax matters:

3 **Tax matters**

Type of Tax (Income, Employment, Excise, etc.)	Tax Form Number (1040, 941, 720, etc.)	Year(s) or Period(s)

4 **Specific use not recorded on Centralized Authorization File (CAF).** If the power of attorney is for a specific use not recorded on CAF, check this box. (See instruction for **Line 4—Specific uses not recorded on CAF.**) . . . . ▶ ☐

5 **Acts authorized.** The representatives are authorized to receive and inspect confidential tax information and to perform any and all acts that I (we) can perform with respect to the tax matters described on line 3, for example, the authority to sign any agreements, consents, or other documents. The authority does not include the power to receive refund checks (see line 6 below), the power to substitute another representative unless specifically added below, or the power to sign certain returns (see instruction for **Line 5—Acts authorized**).

List any specific additions or deletions to the acts otherwise authorized in this power of attorney: ---------------------------

----

Note: In general, an unenrolled preparer of tax returns cannot sign any document for a taxpayer. See Revenue Procedure 81-38, printed as Pub. 470, for more information.

Note: The tax matters partner of a partnership is not permitted to authorize representatives to perform certain acts. See the instructions for more information.

6 **Receipt of refund checks.** If you want to authorize a representative named on line 2 to receive, **BUT NOT TO ENDORSE OR CASH**, refund checks, initial here _____ and list the name of that representative below.

Name of representative to receive refund check(s) ▶

For Paperwork Reduction and Privacy Act Notice, see the separate instructions.   Cat. No. 11980J   Form **2848** (Rev. 12-97)

Form 2848 (Rev. 12-97)   Page **2**

7   **Notices and communications.** Original notices and other written communications will be sent to you and a copy to the first representative listed on line 2 unless you check one or more of the boxes below.

   a   If you want the first representative listed on line 2 to receive the original, and yourself a copy, of such notices or communications, check this box . . . . ▶ ☐

   b   If you also want the second representative listed to receive a copy of such notices and communications, check this box . . . . ▶ ☐

   c   If you do not want any notices or communications sent to your representative(s), check this box . . . . ▶ ☐

8   **Retention/revocation of prior power(s) of attorney.** The filing of this power of attorney automatically revokes all earlier power(s) of attorney on file with the Internal Revenue Service for the same tax matters and years or periods covered by this document. If you **do not** want to revoke a prior power of attorney, check here. . . . . ▶ ☐
YOU MUST ATTACH A COPY OF ANY POWER OF ATTORNEY YOU WANT TO REMAIN IN EFFECT.

9   **Signature of taxpayer(s).** If a tax matter concerns a joint return, **both** husband and wife must sign if joint representation is requested, otherwise, see the instructions. If signed by a corporate officer, partner, guardian, tax matters partner, executor, receiver, administrator, or trustee on behalf of the taxpayer, I certify that I have the authority to execute this form on behalf of the taxpayer.

   ▶ **IF NOT SIGNED AND DATED, THIS POWER OF ATTORNEY WILL BE RETURNED.**

_____	_____	_____
Signature	Date	Title (if applicable)
_____		
Print Name		
_____	_____	_____
Signature	Date	Title (if applicable)
_____		
Print Name		

Part II   **Declaration of Representative**

Under penalties of perjury, I declare that:
- I am not currently under suspension or disbarment from practice before the Internal Revenue Service;
- I am aware of regulations contained in Treasury Department Circular No. 230 (31 CFR, Part 10), as amended, concerning the practice of attorneys, certified public accountants, enrolled agents, enrolled actuaries, and others;
- I am authorized to represent the taxpayer(s) identified in Part I for the tax matter(s) specified there; and
- I am one of the following:

   a   Attorney—a member in good standing of the bar of the highest court of the jurisdiction shown below.
   b   Certified Public Accountant—duly qualified to practice as a certified public accountant in the jurisdiction shown below.
   c   Enrolled Agent—enrolled as an agent under the requirements of Treasury Department Circular No. 230.
   d   Officer—a bona fide officer of the taxpayer's organization.
   e   Full-Time Employee—a full-time employee of the taxpayer.
   f   Family Member—a member of the taxpayer's immediate family (i.e., spouse, parent, child, brother, or sister).
   g   Enrolled Actuary—enrolled as an actuary by the Joint Board for the Enrollment of Actuaries under 29 U.S.C. 1242 (the authority to practice before the Service is limited by section 10.3(d)(1) of Treasury Department Circular No. 230).
   h   Unenrolled Return Preparer—an unenrolled return preparer under section 10.7(c)(viii) of Treasury Department Circular No. 230.

▶ **IF THIS DECLARATION OF REPRESENTATIVE IS NOT SIGNED AND DATED, THE POWER OF ATTORNEY WILL BE RETURNED.**

Designation—Insert above letter **(a–h)**	Jurisdiction (state) or Enrollment Card No.	Signature	Date

Instructions for Form 2848

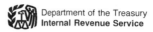

Department of the Treasury
Internal Revenue Service

(Rev. December 1997)

Power of Attorney and Declaration of Representative

Section references are to the Internal Revenue Code unless otherwise noted.

General Instructions

Purpose of Form

Use Form 2848 to grant authority to an individual to represent you before the IRS and to receive tax information. You may file this form ONLY if you want to name a person(s) to represent you and he or she is a "person recognized to practice before the Service." See Part II, Declaration of Representative, items **a-h**. Any person not listed in Part II is not authorized to practice before the IRS under the provisions of Treasury Department Circular No. 230 and cannot act as your representative. However, you can use **Form 8821,** Tax Information Authorization, to authorize any person or organization to receive and inspect confidential tax return information under the provisions of section 6103. For additional information about this or any other matter concerning practice before the IRS, get **Pub. 216,** Conference and Practice Requirements.

Fiduciaries

A fiduciary (trustee, executor, administrator, receiver, or guardian) stands in the position of a taxpayer and acts as the taxpayer. Therefore, a fiduciary does not act as a representative and should not file a power of attorney. **Form 56,** Notice Concerning Fiduciary Relationship, should be filed to notify the IRS of the existence of a fiduciary relationship. If a fiduciary wishes to authorize an individual to represent or perform certain acts on behalf of the entity, a power of attorney must be filed and signed by the fiduciary acting in the position of the taxpayer.

Authority Granted

This power of attorney authorizes the individual(s) named to perform any and all acts you can perform, such as signing consents extending the time to assess tax, recording the interview, or executing waivers agreeing to a tax adjustment. However, authorizing someone as your power of attorney does not relieve you of your tax obligations. Delegating authority or substituting another representative must be specifically stated on line 5. However, the authority granted to an unenrolled preparer may not exceed that allowed under Revenue Procedure 81-38, printed as **Pub. 470,** Limited Practice Without Enrollment.

The power to sign tax returns can only be granted in limited situations. See **Line 5—Acts authorized** on page 2 for more information.

Filing the Power of Attorney

File the original, photocopy, or facsimile transmission (fax) of the power of attorney with each IRS office with which you deal. If the power of attorney is filed for a matter currently pending before an office of the IRS, such as an examination, file the power of attorney with that office.

Otherwise, file it with the service center where the related return was, or will be, filed. Refer to the instructions for the related tax return for the service center addresses.

Substitute Form 2848

If you want to prepare and use a substitute Form 2848, get **Pub. 1167,** Substitute Printed, Computer-Prepared, and Computer-Generated Tax Forms and Schedules. If your substitute Form 2848 is approved, the form approval number must be printed in the lower left margin of each substitute Form 2848 you file with the IRS.

Specific Instructions

Part I—Power of Attorney

Taxpayer Information

Individuals. Enter your name, SSN (and/or EIN, if applicable), and street address in the space provided. If a joint return is involved, and you and your spouse are designating the same representative(s), also enter your spouse's name and SSN, and your spouse's address if different from yours.

Corporations, partnerships, or associations. Enter the name, EIN, and business address. If this form is being prepared for corporations filing a consolidated tax return (Form 1120), do not attach a list of subsidiaries to this form. Only the parent corporation information is required on line 1. Also, line 3 should only list Form 1120 in the Tax Form Number column. A subsidiary must file its own Form 2848 for returns that are required to be filed separately from the consolidated return, such as **Form 720,** Quarterly Federal Excise Tax Return, and **Form 941,** Employer's Quarterly Federal Tax Return.

Employee plan. Enter the plan name, EIN of the plan sponsor, three-digit plan number, and business address of the sponsor.

Trust. Enter the name, title, and address of the trustee, and the name and EIN of the trust.

Estate. Enter the name, title, and address of the decedent's executor/personal representative, and the name and identification number of the estate. The identification number for an estate includes both the EIN, if the estate has one, and the decedent's SSN.

Line 2—Representative(s)

Enter the name of your representative(s). Only individuals may be named as representatives. Use the identical name on all submissions. If you want to name more than three representatives, indicate so on this line and attach a list of additional representatives to the form.

Enter the nine-digit Centralized Authorization File (CAF) number for each representative. If a CAF number has not been assigned, enter "None," and the IRS will issue one directly to your representative. The CAF number is a unique nine-digit identification number (not the SSN, EIN, or enrollment card number) that the IRS assigns to representatives. The CAF number is not an indication of authority to practice. The representative should use the assigned CAF number on all future powers of attorney. CAF numbers will not be assigned for employee plans and exempt organizations application requests (EP/EO).

Check the appropriate box to indicate if either the address or telephone number is new since a CAF number was assigned. Enter your representative's fax telephone number, if available.

If the representative is a former employee of the Federal Government, he or she must be aware of the postemployment restrictions contained in 18 U.S.C., section 207 and in Treasury Department Circular No. 230, section 10.26. Criminal penalties are provided for violation of the statutory restrictions, and the Director of Practice is authorized to take disciplinary action against the practitioner.

Line 3—Tax Matters

You must enter the type of tax, the tax form number, and the year(s) or period(s) in order for the power of attorney to be valid. For example, you may list "income tax, Form 1040" for calendar year "1997" and "Excise tax, Form 720" for the "1st, 2nd, 3rd, and 4th quarters of 1997." A general reference to "All years," "All periods," or "All taxes" is **not** acceptable. Any power of attorney with a general reference will be returned.

You may list any tax years or periods that have already ended as of the date you sign the power of attorney. However, you may include on a power of attorney only future tax periods that end no later than 3 years after the date the power of attorney is received by the IRS. You must enter the type of tax, the tax form number, and the future year(s) or period(s).

If the matter relates to estate tax, enter the date of the taxpayer's death instead of the year or period. If the type of tax, tax form number, or years or periods does not apply to the matter (i.e., representation for a penalty or filing a ruling request or determination), specifically describe the matter to which the power of attorney pertains and enter "Not Applicable" in the appropriate column(s).

Line 4—Specific Uses Not Recorded on CAF

Generally, the IRS records all powers of attorney on the CAF system. However, a power of attorney will not be recorded on the CAF if it does not relate to a specific tax period or it is for a specific issue. Examples of specific issues include but are not limited to the following:

- Civil penalty issues,
- Trust fund recovery penalty,
- Request for a private letter ruling,
- Application for an EIN,
- Claims filed on **Form 843,** Claim for Refund and Request for Abatement,
- Corporation dissolutions,
- A request to change accounting methods, and
- A request to change accounting periods.

Check the specific-use box on line 4 if the power of attorney is for a use that will not be listed on the CAF. If the box on line 4 is checked, the representative should bring a copy of the power of attorney to each meeting with

the IRS. A specific-use power of attorney will not automatically revoke any prior powers of attorney.

Line 5—Acts Authorized

If you want to modify the acts that your named representative(s) can perform, describe any specific additions or deletions in the space provided. The authority to substitute another representative or delegate authority must be specifically stated on line 5.

If you want to authorize your representative to sign an income tax return, this authorization must be specifically listed and the requirements of Regulations section 1.6012-1(a)(5) must be satisfied. In general, this regulation only permits a representative to sign your return if you are unable to make the return by reason of:
(a) Disease or injury,
(b) Continuous absence from the United States (including Puerto Rico), for a period of at least 60 days prior to the date required by law for filing the return, or
(c) Specific permission is requested of and granted by the district director for other good cause.

If you want to authorize a person other than a representative (an agent) to sign an income tax return, you must:

　　1. Complete the information on lines 1–3,
　　2. Check the box on line 4, and
　　3. Write the statement below on line 5 and insert reason **(a), (b),** or **(c)** (see above) in the statement where shown:

"This power of attorney is being filed pursuant to Regulations 1.6012(a)(5), by reason of [insert (a), (b), or (c)], which requires a power of attorney to be attached to a return if a return is signed by an agent. No other acts on behalf of the taxpayer are authorized."

The agent **does not** complete Part II, Declaration of Representative.

Unenrolled return preparer. An unenrolled return preparer is:

- An individual other than an attorney, CPA, enrolled agent, or enrolled actuary who prepares and signs a taxpayer's return.
- An individual who prepares but is not required (by the instructions to the return or regulations) to sign the return.

If any representative you name is an unenrolled return preparer, the acts that person can perform on your behalf are limited by Revenue Procedure 81–38. Generally, an unenrolled return preparer who signs a return as its preparer is:

　　1. Permitted to appear as your representative **only** before revenue agents and examining officers of the Examination Division and not before other offices such as the Collection Division or the Appeals Division of the IRS.

　　2. Limited to discuss tax issues for the taxable year or period covered by that return.

　　3. Not permitted to extend the statutory period, execute waivers, delegate authority, or substitute another representative.

　　Get Pub. 470 (Revenue Procedure 81-38), for more details.

Tax matters partner. The tax matters partner (TMP) (as defined in section 6231(a)(7)) is authorized to perform various acts on behalf of the partnership. The following are examples of acts performed by the TMP that **cannot** be delegated to the representative:

- Binding nonnotice partners to a settlement agreement under section 6224 and, under certain circumstances, binding all partners to a settlement agreement under Tax Court Rule 248;
- Filing a petition for readjustment of partnership items in the Tax Court, District Court, or Claims Court, under section 6226, based on the issuance of a notice of final partnership administrative adjustment by the IRS;
- Filing a request for administrative adjustment on behalf of the partnership under section 6227;
- Filing a petition for adjustment of partnership items with respect to an administrative request in the Tax Court, District Court, or Claims Court, under section 6228; and
- Extending the statute of limitations on assessment of any tax attributable to partnership items (and affected items) under section 6229.

Line 6—Receipt of Refund Checks

If you want to authorize your representative to receive, but not endorse, refund checks on your behalf, you must initial and enter the name of that person in the space provided. Section 10.31 of Treasury Department Circular No. 230 prohibits an attorney, CPA, or enrolled agent, any of whom is an income tax return preparer, from endorsing or otherwise negotiating a tax refund check.

Line 7—Notices and Communications

Original notices and other written communications will be sent to you and a copy to the first representative listed, unless you check one or more of the boxes. If you check:

   1. Only box (a). The original will be sent to the first representative and a copy to you.

   2. Only box (b). The original will be sent to you and copies to the first two listed representatives.

   3. Both boxes (a) and (b). The original will be sent to the first representative and copies to you and the second representative listed.

   4. Only box (c). The original will be sent to you. No copies will be sent to any representatives.

Line 8—Retention/Revocation of Prior Power(s) of Attorney

If there is any existing power(s) of attorney you **do not** want to revoke, check the box on this line and attach a copy of the power(s) of attorney.

If you want to revoke an existing power of attorney and do not want to name a new representative, send a copy of the previously executed power of attorney to each IRS office where the power of attorney was filed. The copy of the power of attorney must have a current signature of the taxpayer under the signature already on line 9. Write "REVOKE" across the top of the form. If you do not have a copy of the power of attorney you want to revoke, send a statement to each IRS office where you filed the power of attorney. The statement of revocation must indicate that the authority of the power of attorney is revoked and must be signed by the taxpayer. Also, the name and address of each recognized representative whose authority is revoked must be listed.

A representative can withdraw from representation by filing a statement with each office of the IRS where the power of attorney was filed. The statement must be signed by the representative and identify the name and address of the taxpayer(s) and tax matter(s) from which the representative is withdrawing. Include your CAF No. on the statement if one has been assigned to you.

The filing of a Form 2848 **will not** revoke any Form 8821 that is in effect.

Line 9—Signature of Taxpayer(s)

Individuals. You must sign and date the power of attorney. If a joint return has been filed and both husband and wife will be represented by the same individual(s), both must sign the power of attorney unless one spouse authorizes the other, in writing, to sign for both. In that case, attach a copy of the authorization. However, if a joint return has been filed and husband and wife will be represented by different individuals, each taxpayer must execute his or her own power of attorney on a separate Form 2848.

Corporations or associations. An officer having authority to bind the taxpayer must sign.

Partnerships. All partners must sign unless one partner is authorized to act in the name of the partnership. A partner is authorized to act in the name of the partnership if, under state law, the partner has authority to bind the partnership. A copy of such authorization must be attached. For purposes of executing Form 2848, the tax matters partner is authorized to act in the name of the partnership. For dissolved partnerships, see Regulations section 601.503(c)(6).

Other. If the taxpayer is a dissolved corporation, deceased, insolvent, or a person for whom or by whom a fiduciary (a trustee, guarantor, receiver, executor, or administrator) has been appointed, see Regulations section 601.503(d).

Part II—Declaration of Representative

The representative(s) you name must sign and date this declaration and enter the designation (i.e., items **a–h**) under which he or she is authorized to practice before the IRS. In addition, the representative(s) must list the following in the "Jurisdiction" column:

a Attorney—Enter the two-letter abbreviation for the state (e.g., "NY" for New York) in which admitted to practice.

b Certified Public Accountant—Enter the two-letter abbreviation for the state (e.g., "CA" for California) in which licensed to practice.

c Enrolled Agent—Enter the enrollment card number issued by the Director of Practice.

d Officer—Enter the title of the officer (i.e., President, Vice President, or Secretary).

e Full-Time Employee—Enter title or position (e.g., Comptroller or Accountant).

f Family Member—Enter the relationship to taxpayer (i.e., spouse, parent, child, brother, or sister).

g Enrolled Actuary—Enter the enrollment card number issued by the Joint Board for the Enrollment of Actuaries.

h Unenrolled Return Preparer—Enter the two-letter abbreviation for the state (e.g., "KY" for Kentucky) in which the return was prepared.

Note: *If the representation is outside the United States, conditions* **a–h** *do not apply.*

Privacy Act and Paperwork Reduction Act Notice. We ask for the information on this form to carry out the Internal Revenue laws of the United States. Form 2848 is provided by the IRS for your convenience and its use is voluntary. If you choose to designate a representative to act on your behalf, under section 6109 you must disclose your social security number (SSN) or your employer identification number (EIN). The principal purpose of this disclosure is to secure proper identification of the taxpayer. We also need this information to gain access to your tax information in our files and properly respond to your request. If you do not disclose this information, the IRS may suspend processing the power of attorney and may not be able to fill your request until you provide the number.

You are not required to provide the information requested on a form that is subject to the Paperwork Reduction Act unless the form displays a valid OMB control number. Books or records relating to a form or its instructions must be retained as long as their contents may become material in the administration of any Internal Revenue law. Generally, tax returns and return information are confidential, as required by section 6103.

The time needed to complete and file this form will vary depending on individual circumstances. The estimated average time is: **Recordkeeping,** 20 min.; **Learning about the law or the form,** 29 min.; **Preparing the form,** 29 min.; **Coping, assembling, and sending the form to the IRS,** 35 min.

If you have comments concerning the accuracy of these time estimates or suggestions for making this form simpler, we would be happy to hear from you. You can write to the Tax Forms Committee, Western Area Distribution Center, Rancho Cordova, CA 95743-0001. **DO NOT** send this form to this address. Instead, see **Filing the Power of Attorney** on page 1.

Form 4700. Examination Workpapers.

Examination Workpapers

Taxpayer's name, address, SSN (Use pre-addressed label or show changes)	Date		Year(s)	
	Examiner			Grade
	Taxpayer(s)	Home Phone		Work Phone
	Reviewer			

A

Initial Interview

1. Examination technique: ☐ Correspondence
   ☐ Undeliverable mail   ☐ No show
   ☐ Interview with:

2. Receipt of Publication 1 ☐
3. Appeal rights and Privacy Act explained ☐
4. Continue on Form 4700-A, B or C

B

Representative - Power of Attorney   ☐ Yes   ☐ No
Name   Phone

Closed No Change

Issue: ☐ Letter 590   ☐ Letter 1156   ☐ Other

Examiner

C

Examination Reminders

1. Proforma Worksheets utilized where applicable
2. Alternative minimum tax
3. Inspection of prior and subsequent year return, IRM 4215
4. Probe for unreported deductions and credits
5. Scope of Examination, IRM 4253.2
6. Automatic adjustments resulting from AGI change(s)

Case Processing Reminders

1. Claim Case - Forms 2297 and 3363
2. Information Reports (IRM 4219) - Form 5346
3. FICA, Self-Employment or Tip Income Adjustments
   Forms 885-E, 885-F, and 885-T
4. Inequities, Abuses, Loopholes - Form 3558
5. Inadequate Records Notice (IRM 4271)
6. Special Handling Notice 3198

D

(Items to be considered, explored, verified)	Year	Per Return	Corrected	Adjustment	Workpapers Index

E

	Year	Per Return	Corrected	Adjustment	Workpapers Index

Form 4700 (Rev. 2-80)   Department of the Treasury — Internal Revenue Service

Form 4700-A. Form 4700 Supplement.

Form 4700 Supplement

Taxpayer		Year(s)
Examiner		Date

		Yes	No	Comments
1. Preparer Information	A. Was return prepared for Compensation? (If Yes, complete remaining items)			
	B. Identification Penalties required?			
	C. Did preparer negotiate refund?			
	D. Did taxpayer receive a copy of return?			

2. Prior IRS Contacts or Prior Audits	☐ None ☐ Yes — Year(s)	Do Repetitive Audit Procedures apply? ☐ Yes ☐ No
	Issues/Reasons:	Was Amended Return(s) filed? ☐ Yes ☐ No

3. All Due Returns Filed?		Yes	No	N/A	Comments
	Individual				
	Household help				
	Employment				
	Excise				

4. Income Probe

If reported or received none, enter (√) in block. If received but not reported, enter (X) in block and comment below.

Interest (S&L) Banks, 2nd Mortgage)	Alimony	Gifts, Inheritance
	Partnerships	Scholarship, Fellowship, Grant
Dividends	Sick Pay	Loans
Sale of assets	Child support	Social Security
Other jobs	Prizes, awards, bonuses	Welfare
Investments	Gambling/Lotteries	Unemployment compensation
Tips	Insurance	VA benefits
Commission	Estate/Trusts	Military allowance
Hobbies	State/Local Tax Refund	Foreign Bank Accounts
Rent/Royalty	Employer Reimbursement	Pensions, Annuities, Profit -Sharing
Comments should indicate nature and extent of income probe		IRA/Keogh Distributions

5. Bartering	Exchange of personal services or merchandise?	Yes	No
	Belong to any bartering clubs or organizations?	Yes	No
	If Yes, explain fully		

6. Foreign Accounts and Foreign Trusts	Is the Foreign Accounts and Foreign Trusts question appearing on the tax return answered correctly? If No, explain fully.	Yes	No	☐ N/A

7. Exemptions	Name	Age	Relationship	Other Information

Form **4700-A** (Rev. 9-84)   *(over please)*   Department of the Treasury — Internal Revenue Service

Form 4700-A. Form 4700 Supplement. (cont'd)

	Complete Remaining Items After Examination
8. Solicit Payment	Payment solicited: Payment received — Include Interest Computation
	Payment solicited: Taxpayer desires to be billed

9. Prior/ Subsequent Year Return

Prior/subsequent year audit recommended?

☐ Yes — Date of AIMS Request _____ Date Information Report Submitted _____

☐ No — State reason:

10. Penalties Recommended For Taxpayer

Type	Asserted	Reason
Negligence	☐ Yes	Indicate issue(s) on which 50% interest is applicable.
	☐ No	
Delinquency	☐ Yes	
	☐ No	
Fraud	☐ Yes	Indicate issue(s) on which 50% interest is applicable.
	☐ No	
Other (State penalty)	☐ Yes	
	☐ No	

11. Preparer Conduct Penalties

Any indications of preparer negligence or fraud?	Yes	No

If Yes, explain:

12. Unagreed Case

Group Manager Involvement in Unagreed Case:

☐ Taxpayer Offered Conference with Group Manager. Date _____

Form **4700-A** (Rev. 9-84)   GPO : 1986 0 – 161–268   Department of the Treasury — Internal Revenue Service

Form 4700-B. Form 4700 Business Supplement.

Form 4700 Business Supplement

	Taxpayer	Year
	Examiner	Date

1. Brief Discription of Day-to-Day Business Operation				
2. Business History	How long in business			
	Number of employees	Full-Time		Part-Time
3. Accounting Method	☐ Cash	☐ Accrual		☐ Hybrid
	Who keeps the books?			

4. Cash on Hand		Beginning of Year	End of Year
	Home	$	$
	Business	$	$
	Elsewhere	$	$

5. Where do You Maintain Your Bank Account(s)?	Business	Account Number	Personal	Account Numb

6. Banking Practices	Were all business and personal expenses kept separately?
	Were all business receipts deposited? To which account?
	How are business expenses paid?

7. Safety Deposit Box	Location	Contents

8. Purchases	Any withdrawals of purchases for personal use?

9. Related Transactions	Any transactions between you and relative or related parties? If so, explain.

10. Gross Receipts	How were gross receipts calculated?

Workpaper Index _____

Form **4700-B** (Rev. 8-83)   Department of the Treasury — Internal Revenue Service

Form 4700-B. Form 4700 Business Supplement. (cont'd)

	Are inventories material? ☐ Yes ☐ No			
	a. Did beginning and ending balances agree with prior/subsequent returns?		Yes	No
11. Inventories	b. Were there any changes in method of valuing inventories?		Yes	No
	c. When taken:			
	How:			
	d. Include year-end purchases?		Yes	No
	e. Any write-offs or write downs?		Yes	No

12.	Loans, notes, mortgages payable:	AMOUNT	Per	Bus.	PAGE, EXHIBIT, SCHEDULE

13.	Capital items sold:	AMOUNT	PURCHASER	PAGE, EXHIBIT, SCHEDULE

14.	Capital items purchased:		SELLER	

Form **4700-B** (Rev. 8-83)   U S GOVERNMENT PRINTING OFFICE 1983 - 381-141/5424   Department of the Treasury — Internal Revenue Service

Form **8822**
(Rev. Oct. 1997)
Department of the Treasury
Internal Revenue Service

Change of Address

▶ Please type or print.

▶ See instructions on back.   ▶ Do not attach this form to your return.

OMB No. 1545-1163

Part I   Complete This Part To Change Your Home Mailing Address

Check ALL boxes this change affects:

1 ☐ Individual income tax returns (Forms 1040, 1040A, 1040EZ, 1040NR, etc.)
   ▶ If your last return was a joint return and you are now establishing a residence separate
     from the spouse with whom you filed that return, check here . . . . ▶ ☐

2 ☐ Gift, estate, or generation-skipping transfer tax returns (Forms 706, 709, etc.)
   ▶ For Forms 706 and 706-NA, enter the decedent's name and social security number below.

▶ Decedent's name   ▶ Social security number

3a Your name (first name, initial, and last name)	3b Your social security number
4a Spouse's name (first name, initial, and last name)	4b Spouse's social security number

5 Prior name(s). See instructions.

6a Old address (no., street, city or town, state, and ZIP code). If a P.O. box or foreign address, see instructions.	Apt. no.
6b Spouse's old address, if different from line 6a (no., street, city or town, state, and ZIP code). If a P.O. box or foreign address, see instructions.	Apt. no.
7 New address (no., street, city or town, state, and ZIP code). If a P.O. box or foreign address, see instructions.	Apt. no.

Part II   Complete This Part To Change Your Business Mailing Address or Business Location

Check ALL boxes this change affects:

8 ☐ Employment, excise, and other business returns (Forms 720, 940, 940-EZ, 941, 990, 1041, 1065, 1120, etc.)
9 ☐ Employee plan returns (Forms 5500, 5500-C/R, and 5500-EZ). See instructions.
10 ☐ Business location

11a Business name	11b Employer identification number
12 Old mailing address (no., street, city or town, state, and ZIP code). If a P.O. box or foreign address, see instructions.	Room or suite no.
13 New mailing address (no., street, city or town, state, and ZIP code). If a P.O. box or foreign address, see instructions.	Room or suite no.
14 New business location (no., street, city or town, state, and ZIP code). If a foreign address, see instructions.	Room or suite no.

Part III   Signature

Daytime telephone number of person to contact (optional) ▶ (   )

**Please
Sign
Here**

▶ _____   ▶ _____
  Your signature   Date   If Part II completed, signature of owner, officer, or representative   Date

▶ _____   ▶ _____
  If joint return, spouse's signature   Date   Title

For Privacy Act and Paperwork Reduction Act Notice, see back of form.   Cat. No. 12081V   Form **8822** (Rev. 10-97)

Form **9465**
(Rev. January 1996)
Department of the Treasury
Internal Revenue Service

Installment Agreement Request

▶ **See instructions below and on back.**

OMB No. 1545-1350

Note: *Do not file this form if you are currently making payments on an installment agreement. You must pay your other Federal tax liabilities in full or you will be in default on your agreement.*

If you can't pay the full amount you owe, you can ask to make monthly installment payments. If we approve you request, you will be charged a $43 fee. **Do not include the fee with this form.** We will deduct the fee from your first payment after we approve your request, unless you choose **Direct Debit** (see the line 13 instructions). We will usually let you know within 30 days after we receive your request whether it is approved or denied. But if this request is for tax due on a return you filed after March 31, it may take us longer than 30 days to reply.

To ask for an installment agreement, complete this form. Attach it to the front of your return when you file. If you have already filed your return or you are filing this form in response to a notice, see **How Do I File Form 9465?** on page 2. If you have any questions about this request, call 1-800-829-1040.

Caution: *A Notice of Federal Tax Lien may be filed to protect the government's interest until you pay in full.*

1	Your first name and initial	Last name	**Your social security number**
	If a joint return, spouse's first name and initial	Last name	**Spouse's social security number**
	Your current address (number and street). If you have a P.O. box and no home delivery, show box number.		Apt. number
	City, town or post office, state, and ZIP code. If a foreign address, show city, state or province, postal code, and full name of country.	

2 If this address is new since you filed your last tax return, check here . . . . ▶ ☐

( ) _____ _____
Your home phone number / Best time for us to call

( ) _____ _____ _____
Your work phone number / Ext. / Best time for us to call

Name of your bank or other financial institution:

Your employer's name:

Address

Address

City, state, and ZIP code

City, state, and ZIP code

7 Enter the tax return for which you are making this request (for example, Form 1040). But if you are filing this form in response to a notice, don't complete lines 7 through 9. Instead, attach the bottom section of the notice to this form and go to line 10 . . . . ▶ _____

8 Enter the tax year for which you are making this request (for example, 1995) . . . . ▶ _____

9 Enter the total amount you owe as shown on your tax return . . . . ▶ $ _____

10 Enter the amount of any payment you are making with your tax return (or notice). See instructions . ▶ $ _____

11 Enter the amount you can paym each month. **Make your payments as large as possible to limit interest and penalty charges.** The charges will continue until you pay in full . . . . ▶ $ _____

12 Enter the date you want to make your payment each month. Do not enter a date later than the 28th ▶ _____

13 If you would like to make your monthly payments using **Direct Debit** (automatic withdrawals from your bank account), check here. . . . . ▶ ☐

Your signature	Date	Spouse's signature. If a joint return, BOTH must sign.	Date

Cat. No. 14842Y   Form **9465** (Rev. 1-96)

Form 9465 (Rev. 1-96)　　　　　　　　　　　　　　　　　　　　　　　　　　　Page **2**

The time needed to complete and file this form will vary depending on individual circumstances. The estimated average time is: **Learning about the law or the form,** 2 min.; **Preparing the form,** 24 min.; and **Copying, assembling, and sending the form to the IRS,** 20 min.

If you have comments concerning the accuracy of this time estimate or suggestions for making this form simpler, we would be happy to hear from you. You can write to the Tax Forms Committee, Western Area Distribution Center, Rancho Cordova, CA 95743-0001. **DO NOT** send the form to this address. Instead, see **How Do I File Form 9465?** on this page.

General Instructions

If you cannot pay the full amount you owe shown on your tax return (or on a notice we sent you), you can ask to make monthly installment payments. But before requesting an installment agreement, you should consider other less costly alternatives, such as a bank loan.

You will be charged interest and may be charged a late payment penalty on any tax not paid by its due date, even if your request to pay in installments is granted. To limit interest and penalty charges, file your return on time and pay as much of the tax as possible with your return (or notice).

You will be charged a $43 fee if your request is approved. **Do not include the fee with this form.** We will send you a letter telling you your request has been approved, how to pay the fee, and how to make your first installment payment. After we receive each payment, we will send you a letter showing the remaining amount you owe, and the due date and amount of your next payment.

By approving your request, we agree to let you pay the tax you owe in monthly installments instead of immediately paying the amount in full. In return, you agree to make your monthly payments on time. **You also agree to meet all your future tax liabilities.** This means that you must have adequate withholding or estimated tax payments so that your tax liability for future years is paid in full when you file your return. If you do not make your payments on time or have an outstanding past-due amount in a future year, you will be in default on your agreement and we may take enforcement actions to collect the entire amount you owe.

Bankruptcy—Offer-in-Compromise. — If you are in bankruptcy or we have accepted your offer-in-compromise, **do not** file this form. Instead, call your local IRS District Office Special Procedures function. You can get the number by calling 1-800-829-1040.

Specific Instructions

Line 1

If you are making this request for a joint tax return, show the names and SSNs in the same order as on your tax return.

Line 10

Even if you can't pay the full amount you owe now, you should pay as much of it as possible to limit penalty and interest charges. If you are filing this form with your tax return, make the payment with your return. If you are filing this form by itself, for example, in response to a notice, include a check or money order payable to the Internal Revenue Service with this form. **Do not** send cash. On your payment, write your name, address, social security number, daytime phone number, and the tax year and tax return for which you are making this request (for example, "1995 Form 1040").

Line 11

You should try to make your payments large enough so that your balance due will be paid off by the due date of your next tax return.

Line 12

You can choose the date your monthly payment is due. For example, if your rent or mortgage payment is due on the first of the month, you may want to make your installment payments on the 15th. When we approve your request, we will tell you the month and date that your first payment is due. If we have not replied by the date you choose for your first payment, you may send the first payment to the Internal Revenue Service Center at the address shown on this page for the place where you live. Make your check or money order payable to the Internal Revenue Service. See the instructions for line 10 for what to write on your payment.

Line 13

Check the box on line 13 if you want your monthly payments automatically deducted **(Direct Debit)** from your bank account. If your installment agreement request is approved, we will send you the required Direct Debit enrollment form and you must include the $43 fee when you return it.

How Do I File Form 9465?

● If you haven't filed your return, attach Form 9465 to the front of your return.

● If you have already filed your return, you are filing your return electronically, or you are filing this form in response to a notice, mail it to the **Internal Revenue Service Center** at the address shown below for the place where you live. No street address is needed.

If you live in:	Use this address:
Florida, Georgia, South Carolina	Atlanta, GA 39901
New Jersey, New York (New York City and counties of Nassau, Rockland, Suffolk, and Westchester)	Holtsville, NY 00501
New York (all other counties), Connecticut, Maine, Massachusetts, New Hampshire, Rhode Island, Vermont	Andover, MA 05501
Illinois, Iowa, Minnesota, Missouri, Wisconsin	Kansas City, MO 64999
Delaware, District of Columbia, Maryland, Pennsylvania, Virginia	Philadelphia, PA 19255
Indiana, Kentucky, Michigan, Ohio, West Virginia	Cincinnati, OH 45999
Kansas, New Mexico, Oklahoma, Texas	Austin, TX 73301
Alaska, Arizona, California (counties of Alpine, Amador, Butte, Calaveras, Colusa, Contra Costa, Del Norte, El Dorado, Glenn, Humboldt, Lake, Lassen, Marin, Mendocino, Modoc, Napa, Nevada, Placer, Plumas, Sacramento, San Joaquin, Shasta, Sierra, Siskiyou, Solano, Sonoma, Sutter, Tehama, Trinity, Yolo, and Yuba), Colorado, Idaho, Montana, Nebraska, Nevada, North Dakota, Oregon, South Dakota, Utah, Washington, Wyoming	Ogden, UT 84201
California (all other counties), Hawaii	Fresno, CA 93888
Alabama, Arkansas, Louisiana, Mississippi, North Carolina, Tennessee	Memphis, TN 37501
American Samoa Guam: Nonpermanent residents only* Puerto Rico (or if excluding income under section 933) Virgin Islands: Nonpermanent residents only* Foreign country (or if a dual-status alien): U.S. citizens and those filing Form 2555, 2555-EZ, or 4563 All APO and FPO addresses	Philadelphia, PA 19255

*Permanent residents of Guam and the Virgin Islands cannot use Form 9465.

♻ Printed on recycled paper

IRS

Department of the Treasury
Internal Revenue Service

Publication 1
(Rev. December 1998)

Catalog Number 64731W

www.irs.ustreas.gov

Your Rights as a Taxpayer

The first part of this publication explains some of your most important rights as a taxpayer. The second part explains the examination, appeal, collection, and refund processes.

Declaration of Taxpayer Rights

I. Protection of Your Rights

IRS employees will explain and protect your rights as a taxpayer throughout your contact with us.

II. Privacy and Confidentiality

The IRS will not disclose to anyone the information you give us, except as authorized by law. You have the right to know why we are asking you for information, how we will use it, and what happens if you do not provide requested information.

III. Professional and Courteous Service

If you believe that an IRS employee has not treated you in a professional, fair, and courteous manner, you should tell that employee's supervisor. If the supervisor's response is not satisfactory, you should write to your IRS District Director or Service Center Director.

IV. Representation

You may either represent yourself or, with proper written authorization, have someone else represent you in your place. Your representative must be a person allowed to practice before the IRS, such as an attorney, certified public accountant, or enrolled agent. If you are in an interview and ask to consult such a person, then we must stop and reschedule the interview in most cases.

You can have someone accompany you at an interview. You may make sound recordings of any meetings with our examination, appeal, or collection personnel, provided you tell us in writing 10 days before the meeting.

V. Payment of Only the Correct Amount of Tax

You are responsible for paying only the correct amount of tax due under the law — no more, no less. If you cannot pay all of your tax when it is due, you may be able to make monthly installment payments.

VI. Help With Unresolved Tax Problems

The National Taxpayer Advocate's Problem Resolution Program can help you if you have tried unsuccessfully to resolve a problem with the IRS. Your local Taxpayer Advocate can offer you special help if you have a significant hardship as a result of a tax problem. For more information, call toll-free 1–877–777–4778 (1–800–829–4059 for TTY/TDD users) or write to the Taxpayer Advocate at the IRS office that last contacted you.

VII. Appeals and Judicial Review

If you disagree with us about the amount of your tax liability or certain collection actions, you have the right to ask the Appeals Office to review your case. You may also ask a court to review your case.

VIII. Relief From Certain Penalties and Interest

The IRS will waive penalties when allowed by law if you can show you acted reasonably and in good faith or relied on the incorrect advice of an IRS employee. We will waive interest that is the result of certain errors or delays caused by an IRS employee.

THE IRS MISSION

PROVIDE AMERICA'S TAXPAYERS TOP QUALITY SERVICE BY HELPING THEM UNDERSTAND AND MEET THEIR TAX RESPONSIBILITIES AND BY APPLYING THE TAX LAW WITH INTEGRITY AND FAIRNESS TO ALL.

Examinations, Appeals, Collections, and Refunds

Examinations (Audits)

We accept most taxpayer's returns as filed. If we inquire about your return or select it for examination, it does not suggest that you are dishonest. The inquiry or examination may or may not result in more tax. We may close your case without change; or, you may receive a refund.

The process of selecting a return for examination usually begins in one of two ways. First, we use computer programs to identify returns that may have incorrect amounts. These programs may be based on information returns, such as Forms 1099 and W-2, on studies of past examinations, or on certain issues identified by compliance projects. Second, we use information from outside sources that indicates that a return may have incorrect amounts. These sources may include newspapers, public records, and individuals. If we determine that the information is accurate and reliable, we may use it to select a return for examination.

Publication 556, *Examination of Returns, Appeal Rights, and Claims for Refund*, explains the rules and procedures that we follow in examinations. The following sections give an overview of how we conduct examinations.

By Mail

We handle many examinations and inquiries by mail. We will send you a letter with either a request for more information or a reason why we believe a change to your return may be needed. You can respond by mail or you can request a personal interview with an examiner. If you mail us the requested information or provide an explanation, we may or may not agree with you, and we will explain the reasons for any changes. Please do not hesitate to write to us about anything you do not understand.

By Interview

If we notify you that we will conduct your examination through a personal interview, or you request such an interview, you have the right to ask that the examination take place at a reasonable time and place that is convenient for both you and the IRS. If our examiner proposes any changes to your return, he or she will explain the reasons for the changes. If you do not

agree with these changes, you can meet with the examiner's supervisor.

Repeat Examinations

If we examined your return for the same items in either of the 2 previous years and proposed no change to your tax liability, please contact us as soon as possible so we can see if we should discontinue the examination.

Appeals

If you do not agree with the examiner's proposed changes, you can appeal them to the Appeals Office of IRS. Most differences can be settled without expensive and time-consuming court trials. Your appeal rights are explained in detail in both Publication 5, *Appeal Rights and Preparation of Protests for Unagreed Cases*, and Publication 556, *Examination of Returns, Appeal Rights, and Claims for Refund*.

If you do not wish to use the Appeals Office or disagree with its findings, you may be able to take your case to the U.S. Tax Court, U.S. Court of Federal Claims, or the U.S. District Court where you live. If you take your case to court, the IRS will have the burden of proving certain facts if you kept adequate records to show your tax liability, cooperated with the IRS, and meet certain other conditions. If the court agrees with you on most issues in your case, and finds that our position was largely unjustified, you may be able to recover some of your administrative and litigation costs. You will not be eligible to recover these costs unless you tried to resolve your case administratively, including going through the appeals system, and you gave us the information necessary to resolve the case.

Collections

Publication 594, *The IRS Collection Process*, explains your rights and responsibilities regarding payment of federal taxes. It describes:

- What to do when you owe taxes. It describes what to do if you get a tax bill and what to do if you think your bill is wrong. It also covers making installment payments, delaying collection action, and submitting an offer in compromise.

- IRS collection actions. It covers liens, releasing a lien, levies, releasing a levy, seizures and sales, and release of property.

Publication 1660, *Collection Appeal Rights for Liens, Levies, Seizures, and Installment Agreement Terminations*, explains your collection appeal rights.

Innocent Spouse Relief

Generally, both you and your spouse are responsible, jointly and individually, for paying the full amount of any tax, interest, or penalties due on your joint return. However, you may not have to pay the tax, interest, and penalties related to your spouse (or former spouse).

New tax law changes make it easier to qualify for innocent spouse relief and add two other ways for you to get relief. For more information, see Publication 971, *Innocent Spouse Relief*, and Form 8857, *Request for Innocent Spouse Relief (And Separation of Liability and Equitable Relief)*.

Refunds

You may file a claim for refund if you think you paid too much tax. You must generally file the claim within 3 years from the date you filed your original return or 2 years from the date you paid the tax, whichever is later. The law generally provides for interest on your refund if it is not paid within 45 days of the date you filed your return or claim for refund. Publication 556, *Examination of Returns, Appeal Rights, and Claims for Refund*, has more information on refunds.

Tax Information

The IRS provides a great deal of free information. The following are sources for forms, publications, and additional information.

- **Tax Questions: 1–800–829–1040** (1–800–829–4059 for TTY/TDD users)

- **Forms and Publications: 1–800–829–3676** (1–800–829–4059 for TTY/TDD users)

- **Internet: www.irs.ustreas.gov**

- **TaxFax Service:** From your fax machine, dial **703–368–9694.**

- **Small Business Ombudsman:** If you are a small business entity, you can participate in the regulatory process and comment on enforcement actions of IRS by calling **1–888–REG–FAIR.**

- **Treasury Inspector General for Tax Administration:** If you want to confidentially report misconduct, waste, fraud, or abuse by an IRS employee, you can call **1–800–366–4484** (1–800–877–8339 for TTY/TDD users). You can remain anonymous.

Your Appeal Rights and How To Prepare a Protest If You Don't Agree

Department of the Treasury
Internal Revenue Service

www.irs.ustreas.gov

Publication 5 **(Rev. 01-1999)**
Catalog Number **46074I**

Introduction

This Publication tells you how to appeal your tax case if you don't agree with the Internal Revenue Service (IRS) findings.

If You Don't Agree

If you don't agree with any or all of the IRS findings given you, you may request a meeting or a telephone conference with the supervisor of the person who issued the findings. If you still don't agree, you may appeal your case to the Appeals Office of IRS.

If you decide to do nothing and your case involves an examination of your income, estate, gift, and certain excise taxes or penalties, you will receive a formal Notice of Deficiency. The Notice of Deficiency allows you to go to the Tax Court and tells you the procedure to follow. If you do not go to the Tax Court, we will send you a bill for the amount due.

If you decide to do nothing and your case involves a trust fund recovery penalty, or certain employment tax liabilities, the IRS will send you a bill for the penalty. If you do not appeal a denial of an offer in compromise or a denial of a penalty abatement, the IRS will continue collection action.

If you don't agree, we urge you to appeal your case to the Appeals Office of IRS. The Office of Appeals can settle most differences without expensive and time-consuming court trials. [Note: Appeals can not consider your reasons for not agreeing if they don't come within the scope of the tax laws (for example, if you disagree solely on moral, religious, political, constitutional, conscientious, or similar grounds.)]

The following general rules tell you how to appeal your case.

Appeals Within the IRS

Appeals is the administrative appeals office for the IRS. You may appeal most IRS decisions with your local Appeals Office. The Appeals Office is separate from - and independent of - the IRS Office taking the action you disagree with. The Appeals Office is the only level of administrative appeal within the IRS.

Conferences with Appeals Office personnel are held in an informal manner by correspondence, by telephone or at a personal conference. There is no need for you to have representation for an Appeals conference, but if you choose to have a representative, see the requirements under *Representation.*

If you want an Appeals conference, follow the instructions in our letter to you. Your request will be sent to the Appeals Office to arrange a conference at a convenient time and place. You or your representative should prepare to discuss all issues you don't agree with at the conference. Most differences are settled at this level.

In most instances, you may be eligible to take your case to court if you don't reach an agreement at your Appeals conference, or if you don't want to appeal your case to the IRS Office of Appeals. See the later section *Appeals To The Courts.*

Protests

When you request an appeals conference, you may also need to file a formal written protest or a small case request with the office named in our letter to you. Also, see the special appeal request procedures in Publication 1660, Collection Appeal Rights, if you disagree with lien, levy, seizure, or denial or termination of an installment agreement.

You need to file a written protest:

- In all employee plan and exempt organization cases without regard to the dollar amount at issue.

- In all partnership and S corporation cases without regard to the dollar amount at issue.

- In all other cases, unless you qualify for the small case request procedure, or other special appeal procedures such as requesting Appeals consideration of liens, levies, seizures, or installment agreements. See Publication 1660.

How to prepare a protest:

When a protest is required, **send it within the time limit specified in the letter you received.** Include in your protest:

1) Your name and address, and a daytime telephone number,

2) A statement that you want to appeal the IRS findings to the Appeals Office,

3) A copy of the letter showing the proposed changes and findings you don't agree with (or the date and symbols from the letter),

4) The tax periods or years involved,

5) A list of the changes that you don't agree with, and why you don't agree.

6) The facts supporting your position on any issue that you don't agree with,

7) The law or authority, if any, on which you are relying.

8) You must sign the written protest, stating that it is true, under the penalties of perjury as follows:

"**Under the penalties of perjury, I declare that I examined the facts stated in this protest, including any accompanying documents, and, to the best of my knowledge and belief, they are true, correct, and complete."**

If your representative prepares and signs the protest for you, he or she must substitute a declaration stating:

1) That he or she submitted the protest and accompanying documents and

2) Whether he or she knows personally that the facts stated in the protest and accompanying documents are true and correct.

We urge you to provide as much information as you can, as this will help us speed up your appeal. This will save you both time and money.

Small Case Request:

If the total amount for any tax period is not more than $25,000, you may make a small case request instead of filing a formal written protest. In computing the total amount, include a proposed increase or decrease in tax (including penalties), or claimed refund. For an offer in compromise, in calculating the total amount, include total unpaid tax, penalty and interest due. For a small case request, follow the instructions in our letter to you by: sending a letter requesting Appeals consideration, indicating the changes you don't agree with, and the reasons why you don't agree.

Representation

You may represent yourself at your appeals conference, or you may have an attorney, certified public accountant, or an individual enrolled to practice before the IRS represent you. Your representative must be qualified to practice before the IRS. If you want your representative to appear without you, you must provide a properly completed power of attorney to the IRS before the representative can receive or inspect confidential information. Form 2848, Power of Attorney and Declaration of Representative, or any other properly written power of attorney or authorization may be used for this

Your Rights as a Taxpayer

The first part of this section explains some of your most important rights as a taxpayer. The second part explains the examination, appeal, collection, and refund processes.

Declaration of Taxpayer Rights

I. Protection of your rights. IRS employees will explain and protect your rights as a taxpayer throughout your contact with us.

II. Privacy and confidentiality. The IRS will not disclose to anyone the information you give us, except as authorized by law. You have the right to know why we are asking you for information, how we will use it, and what happens if you do not provide requested information.

III. Professional and courteous service. If you believe that an IRS employee has not treated you in a professional manner, you should tell that employee's supervisor. If the supervisor's response is not satisfactory, you should write to your IRS District Director or Service Center Director.

IV. Representation. You may either represent yourself, or with proper written authorization, have someone else represent you in your place. You can have someone accompany you at an interview. You may make sound recordings of any meetings with our examination or collection personnel, provided you tell us in writing 10 days before the meeting.

V. Payment of only the correct amount of tax. You are responsible for paying only the correct amount of tax due under the law—no more, no less.

VI. Help from the Problem Resolution Program. The Taxpayer Advocate's Problem Resolution Program can help you with unresolved tax problems and can offer you special help if

you have a significant hardship as a result of a tax problem. For more information, call 1–877–777–4778 (1–800–829–4059 for TTY/TDD users) or write to the Taxpayer Advocate at the IRS office that last contacted you.

VII. Appeals and judicial review. If you disagree with us about the amount of your tax liability or certain collection actions, you have the right to ask the IRS Appeals Office to review your case. You may also ask a court to review your case.

VIII. Relief from certain penalties. The IRS will waive penalties when allowed by law if you can show you acted reasonably and in good faith or relied on the incorrect advice of an IRS employee.

Examinations, Appeals, Collections, and Refunds

Examinations (Audits)

We accept most taxpayer's returns as filed. If we inquire about your return or select it for examination, it does not suggest that you are dishonest. The inquiry or examination may or may not result in more tax. We may close your case without change; or, you may receive a refund.

By mail. We handle many examinations and inquiries by mail. We will send you a letter with either a request for more information or a reason why we believe a change to your return may be needed. If you give us the requested information or provide an explanation, we may or may not agree with you, and we will explain the reasons for any changes. Please do not hesitate to write to us about anything you do not understand. If you cannot resolve a question through the mail, you can request a personal interview with an examiner.

By interview. If we notify you that we will conduct your examination through a personal interview, or you request such an interview, you have the right to ask that the examination take place at a reasonable time and place that is convenient for both you and the IRS. At the end of your examination, the examiner will give you a report if there are any proposed changes to your tax return. If you do not agree with the report, you may meet with the examiner's supervisor.

Repeat examinations. If we examined your tax return for the same items in either of the 2 previous years and proposed no change to your tax liability, please contact us as soon as possible so we can determine if we should discontinue the repeat examination. Publication 556, *Examination of Returns, Appeal Rights, and Claims for Refund,* will give you more information about the rules and procedures of an IRS examination.

Appeals

If you do not agree with the examiner's findings, you can appeal them to our Appeals Office. Most differences can be settled without expensive and time-consuming court trials. Your appeal rights are explained in detail in Publication 5, *Appeal Rights and Preparation of Protests for Unagreed Cases.*

If you do not wish to use our Appeals Office or disagree with its findings, you can take your case to the U.S. Tax Court, U.S. Court of Federal Claims, or the U.S. District Court where you live. If the court agrees with you on most issues in your case, and finds that our position was largely unjustified, you may be able to recover some of your administrative and litigation costs. You will not be eligible to recover these costs unless you tried to resolve your case administratively, including going through our appeals system, and you gave us all the information necessary to resolve the case.

Collections

Publication 594, *Understanding The Collection Process,* explains your rights and responsibilities regarding payment of federal taxes. It is divided into several sections that explain the procedures in plain language. The sections include:

1) *When you have not paid enough tax.* This section describes tax bills and explains what to do if you think your bill is wrong.

2) *Making arrangements to pay your bill.* This covers making installment payments, delaying collection action, and submitting an offer in compromise.

3) *What happens when you take no action to pay.* This covers liens, releasing a lien, levies, releasing a levy, seizures and sales, and release of property. Your appeal rights are explained in detail in Publication 1660, *Collection Appeal Rights for Liens, Levies, Seizures & Installment Agreement Terminations.*

Innocent spouse relief. Generally, both you and your spouse are responsible, jointly and individually, for paying any tax, interest, or penalties due on your joint return. However, you may not have to pay the tax, interest, and penalties you believe should be paid only by your spouse (or former spouse).

For more information, see Publication 971 and Form 8857.

Refunds

You may file a claim for refund if you think you paid too much tax. You must generally file the claim within 3 years from the date you filed your return or 2 years from the date you paid the tax, whichever is later. The law generally provides for interest on your refund if it is not paid within 45 days of the date you filed your return or claim for refund. Publication 556, *Examination of Returns, Appeals Rights, and Claims for Refund,* has more information on refunds.

How To Get More Information

You can order free publications and forms, ask tax questions, and get more information from the IRS in several ways. By selecting the method that is best for you, you will have quick and easy access to tax help.

This section describes several ways you can get free tax help from the IRS and from community volunteers (during the regular filing season).

Free tax services. To find out what services are available, get Publication 910, *Guide to Free Tax Services*. It contains a list of free tax publications and an index of tax topics. It also describes other free tax information services, including tax education and assistance programs and a list of TeleTax topics.

 Personal computer. With your personal computer and modem, you can access the IRS on the Internet at **www.irs.ustreas.gov**. While visiting our Web Site, you can select:

- *Frequently Asked Tax Questions* to find answers to questions you may have.
- *Fill-in Forms* to complete tax forms on-line.
- *Forms and Publications* to download forms and publications or search publications by topic or keyword.
- *Comments & Help* to e-mail us with comments about the site or with tax questions.
- *Digital Dispatch* and *IRS Local News Net* to receive our electronic newsletters on hot tax issues and news.

You can also reach us with your computer using any of the following.

- Telnet at **iris.irs.ustreas.gov**
- File Transfer Protocol at **ftp.irs.ustreas.gov**
- Direct dial (by modem) **703–321–8020**

TaxFax Service. Using the phone attached to your fax machine, you can receive forms, instructions, and tax information by calling **703–368–9694**. Follow the directions from the prompts. When you order forms, enter the catalog number for the form you need. The items you request will be faxed to you.

Page 262

 Phone. Many services are available by phone.

- *Ordering forms, instructions, and publications.* Call 1–800–TAX–FORM (**1–800–829–3676**) to order current and prior year forms, instructions, and publications.
- *Asking tax questions.* Call the IRS with your tax questions at **1–800–829–1040**.
- *TTY/TDD equipment.* If you have access to TTY/TDD equipment, call **1–800–829–4059** to ask tax questions or to order forms and publications.
- *TeleTax topics.* Call **1–800–829–4477** to listen to pre-recorded messages covering various tax topics. You can also check on the status of your 1998 refund using TeleTax's Refund Information service.

Evaluating the quality of our telephone services. To ensure that IRS representatives give accurate, courteous, and professional answers, we evaluate the quality of our telephone services in several ways.

- A second IRS representative sometimes monitors live telephone calls. That person only evaluates the IRS assistor and does not keep a record of any taxpayer's name or tax identification number.
- We sometimes record telephone calls to evaluate IRS assistors objectively. We hold these recordings no longer than one week and use them only to measure the quality of assistance.
- We value our customers' opinions. Throughout this year, we will be surveying our customers for their opinions on our service.

 Walk-in. You can pick up certain forms, instructions, and publications at many post offices, libraries, and IRS offices. Some libraries and IRS offices have an extensive collection of products available to print from a CD-ROM or photocopy from reproducible proofs.

Mail. You can send your order for forms, instructions, and publications to the Distribution Center nearest to you and receive a response 7 to 15 workdays after your request is received. Find the address that applies to your part of the country.

- **Western part of U.S.:**
  Western Area Distribution Center
  Rancho Cordova, CA 95743–0001
- **Central part of U.S.:**
  Central Area Distribution Center
  P.O. Box 8903
  Bloomington, IL 61702–8903
- **Eastern part of U.S. and foreign addresses:**
  Eastern Area Distribution Center
  P.O. Box 85074
  Richmond, VA 23261–5074

CD-ROM. You can order IRS Publication 1796, *Federal Tax Products on CD-ROM*, and obtain:

- Current tax forms, instructions, and publications.
- Prior-year tax forms, instructions, and publications.
- Popular tax forms which may be filled-in electronically, printed out for submission, and saved for recordkeeping.
- Internal Revenue Bulletins.

The CD-ROM can be purchased from National Technical Information Service (NTIS) for $25.00 by calling 1–877–233–6767 or for $18.00 on the Internet at **www.irs.ustreas.gov/cdorders**. The first release is available in mid-December and the final release is available in late January.

Written tax questions. You can send your written tax questions to your IRS District Director. You should get an answer in about 30 days. If you do not have the address, you can get it by calling 1–800–829–1040. (Do not send tax questions with your return.)

Braille tax materials. Braille tax materials are available for review from Regional Libraries for the Visually Impaired in conjunction with the National Library Service for the Blind and Physically Handicapped. To locate your nearest library, write to:

National Library Service for the Blind and Physically Handicapped
Library of Congress
1291 Taylor St., NW
Washington, DC 20542

Braille materials currently available for review include this publication, Publication 334, *Tax Guide for Small Business*, and Forms 1040, 1040A, and 1040EZ and their instructions.

Assistance with your return. Assistors are available in many IRS offices throughout the country to help you prepare your own return. To find the location of the IRS office nearest you, look in the phone book under "United States Government, Internal Revenue Service" or call 1–800–829–1040. If you want help with your tax return, you should bring in your tax package, Forms W–2 and 1099, and any other information (such as a copy of last year's return) that will help the assistor to help you.

At all IRS offices you can also get tax forms, publications, and help with questions about IRS notices or bills.

Volunteer Income Tax Assistance (VITA) and Tax Counseling for the Elderly (TCE). Free help from volunteers is available in most communities. After completing IRS training, these volunteers help prepare basic tax returns for taxpayers with special needs, including low-income people, persons with disabilities, the elderly, and non-English-speaking people. At some of these offices, you can file your tax return electronically. See *IRS e-file* in chapter 1 for information on electronic filing.

Call the IRS for the location of the volunteer assistance site near you. Or, for the location of an American Association of Retired Persons (AARP) Tax-Aide site in your community, call 1–888–AARPNOW or visit Internet Web Site at www.aarp.org/taxaide/home.htm.

Help with unresolved tax issues. Most problems can be solved with one contact by calling, writing, or visiting an IRS office. But if you have tried unsuccessfully to resolve a problem with the IRS, you should contact the Taxpayer Advocate's Problem Resolution Program (PRP). Someone at PRP will assign you a personal advocate who is in the best position to try to resolve your problem. The Taxpayer Advocate can also offer you

Publication 17, Your Federal Income Tax

special help if you have a significant hardship as a result of a tax problem.

You should contact the Taxpayer Advocate if:

- You have tried unsuccessfully to resolve your problem with the IRS and have not been contacted by the date promised, or

- You are on your second attempt to resolve a problem.

You may contact a Taxpayer Advocate by calling a new assistance number, 1–877–777–4778. Persons who have access to TTY/TDD equipment can call 1–800–829–4059 and ask for the Taxpayer Advocate. If you prefer, you can write to the Taxpayer Advocate at the office that last contacted you.

While Taxpayer Advocates cannot change the tax law or make a technical tax decision, they can clear up problems that resulted from previous contacts and ensure that your case is given a complete and impartial review. Taxpayer Advocates are working to put service first. For more information about PRP, get Publication 1546, *The Problem Resolution Program of the Internal Revenue Service.*

The Problem Resolution Program of the Internal Revenue Service

A Guide for Taxpayers Who have Unresolved Tax Problems With IRS

If you are unable to resolve a tax problem, after attempting to do so through normal channels, then this guide is for you.

PRP and The Taxpayer Advocate

The Internal Revenue Service (IRS) began its Problem Resolution Program (PRP) to provide an independent system to assure that taxpayers' unresolved problems are promptly and properly handled. The program is headed by the National Taxpayer Advocate. Each state and service center has a Taxpayer Advocate or Associate Taxpayer Advocate (formerly Problem Resolution Officers).

The goal of PRP is to protect taxpayer rights, to serve as an advocate for the taxpayer within IRS, and to represent the interests and concerns of taxpayers. This is accomplished in two ways:

- Ensuring that taxpayer problems, which have not been resolved through normal channels, are promptly and properly handled.
- Identifying issues that increase burden or create problems for taxpayers: bringing those issues to the attention of IRS management.

Who may Use PRP?

If you have a problem that has not been resolved through normal processes, you may contact a PRP office. The following criteria have been developed to determine if a problem should be referred to PRP:

- Second Contact - Same Issue
- No Response by Date Promised
- System Failed or Best Interest of the taxpayer or the Service

PRP is not a substitute for established procedure or the formal Appeals process. PRP cannot reverse legal or technical tax determinations.

 IRS

Department of the Treasury
Internal Revenue Service
Publication 1546 (Rev. 10-97)
Catalog Number 13266S

How do I reach the Problem Resolution Office?

  Write or FAX - The addresses and FAX numbers for PRP offices are listed (by state) at the end of this brochure.

- OR -

Call 1-800-829-1040 and ask for PRP assistance.

TTY/TTD help is available by calling 1-800-829-4059.

If you want to authorize another person to discuss the matter or to receive information about your case, send us Form 2848, Power of Attorney and Declaration of Representative, or Form 8821, Tax Information Authorization. You can get these forms at most local IRS offices or by calling the forms-only number, 1-800-829-3676.

What information should I provide to PRP?

- Your name and social security number or employer identification number,
- Your address and ZIP code,
- Your daytime telephone number and the hours you can be reached,
- The time, place, and kind of problem,
- Your previous attempts to solve the problem, and the office you contacted, and
- The type of tax return and year(s) involved.

What can I expect from Problem Resolution?

- Courtesy
- Acknowledgment within seven days
- The name and phone number of caseworker assigned
- Updates on progress
- Time frames for actions
- Speedy resolution

If I need assistance due to a hardship, what can I do?

Request a Taxpayer Assistance Order (TAO).

What does a TAO do?

- Requires the Taxpayer Advocate to determine if significant hardship exists
- Requires the Taxpayer Advocate to review the case to determine what action should be taken to relieve the hardship.

The majority of TAOs are resolved administratively by the Taxpayer Advocate (or Associate). Even in situations in which significant hardship is not deemed to be a factor, the Advocate is often able to help resolve the taxpayer's problem.

How do I apply for a TAO?

- File Form 911, Application for a Taxpayer Assistance Order; if available,
- Written request explaining hardship if no Form 911,
- FAX to Advocate in state where you reside or the service center where the return was filed, or
- Request that an IRS employee complete a Form 911 on your behalf.

To contact the Taxpayer Advocate for your local area, address your correspondence to: Taxpayer Advocate, Internal Revenue Service. Street addresses are provided if you wish to send correspondence by courier. FAX numbers are also listed if you prefer to send information by facsimile transmission.

Service Centers

Andover
310 Lowell St, Stop 120
Andover, MA 05501
FAX (978)474-5640

Atlanta
Box 48-549, Stop 29A
Doraville, GA 30362
or
4800 Buford Hwy
Stop 29-A
Chamblee, GA 30341
FAX (770)455-2527

Austin
Box 934, Stop 1005
Austin, TX 78767
or
3651 S Interregional Hwy
Stop 1005 AUSC
Austin, TX 78741
FAX (512)460-1930

Brookhaven
Box 960, Stop 102
Holtsville, NY 11742
or
1040 Waverly Ave.
Stop 102
Holtsville, NY 11742
FAX (516) 447-4879

Cincinnati
333 Scott St., Stop 11
Covington, KY 41019
FAX (606)292-5405

Fresno
Box 12161
Fresno, CA 93776
or
5045 East Butler Ave.,
Fresno, CA 93888
FAX (209)456-5272

Kansas City
Box 24551, Stop 1005KSC
Kansas City, MO 64131
or
2306 E. Bannister Rd.
Stop 1005
Kansas City, MO 64131
FAX (816)823-1932

Memphis
5333 Getwell Rd.
Stop 13
Memphis, TN 38118
FAX (901)546-2181

Ogden
Box 9941, Stop 1005
Ogden, UT 84409

or
1160 W 1200 South St,
Stop 1005
Ogden, UT 84201
FAX (801)620-6319

Philadelphia
Box 16053, DP 111
Philadelphia, PA 19114
FAX (215)516-2677

District & Local Offices

Alabama
(Birmingham Office)
801 Tom Martin Dr.
RM-268-PR
Birmingham, AL 35211
FAX (205)912-5632

Alaska
(Anchorage Office)
949 East 36th Ave.
Stop A-405
Anchorage, AK 99508
FAX (907)271-6824

Arizona
(Phoenix Office)
210 E. Earll Drive
Stop 1005 PX
Phoenix, AZ 85012
FAX (602)207-8250

Arkansas
(Little Rock Office)
700 West Capitol St.
Stop 1005 LIT
Little Rock, AR 72201
FAX (501)324-5183

California
(Laguna Niguel Office)
PO Box 30207
Laguna Niguel, CA 92607
or
24000 Avila Road
Laguna Niguel, CA 92656
FAX (714)360-2463

(Los Angeles Office)
PO Box 531791
Los Angeles, CA 90053
or
300 N Los Angeles St.
Rm. 4352
Los Angeles, CA 90012
FAX (213)894-6365

(Sacramento Office)
Box 2900, Stop SA 5043
Sacramento, CA 95812
or

300 N Los Angeles St.
Rm. 4352
Los Angeles, CA 90012
FAX (213)894-6365

(Sacramento Office)
Box 2900, Stop SA 5043
Sacramento, CA 95812
or
4330 Watt Ave
N. Highlands, CA 95660
FAX (916)974-5902

(San Francisco Office)
1301 Clay St., # 1540S
Oakland, CA 94612
FAX (510)637-2715

(San Jose Office)
Box 100, Stop HQ0004
San Jose, CA 95103
or
55 S Market St, # 900
San Jose, CA 95113
FAX (408)494-8065

Colorado
(Denver Office)
600 17th St, Stop 1005
Denver, CO 80202
FAX (303)446-1011

Connecticut
(Hartford Office)
135 High St, Stop 219
Hartford, CT 06103
FAX (860)240-4023

Delaware
(Wilmington Office)
409 Silverside Rd.,
Wilmington, DE 19809
FAX (302)791-4511

District Of Columbia
(Baltimore Office)
Box 1553, Rm. 620A
Baltimore, MD 21203
or
31 Hopkins Plaza, Rm 620
Baltimore, MD 21201
FAX (410)962-9340

Florida
(Ft. Lauderdale Office)
Box 17167
Plantation, FL 33318
or
One N University Dr.
Rm A-312
Plantation, FL 33324
FAX (954)423-7685

(Jacksonville Office)
Box 35045, Stop D:PRO
Jacksonville, FL 32202
or
400 West Bay St., Rm 116
Jacksonville, FL 32202
FAX (904)232-2266

Georgia
(Atlanta Office)
Box 1065
Stop 202-D Rm 1520
Atlanta, GA 30370
or
401 W Peachtree St, NW
Summit Bldg, Stop 202-D,
Room 1520
Atlanta, GA 30365
FAX (404)730-3438

Hawaii
(Honolulu Office)
300 Ala Moana Blvd.,
Stop H-405 Rm. 2104
Honolulu, HI 96850
FAX (808)541-3379

Idaho
(Boise Office)
550 West Fort St.,
Box 041
Boise, ID 83724
FAX (208)334-9663

Illinois
(Chicago Office)
230 S Dearborn St.,
Rm. 3214, Stop 1005-CHI
Chicago, IL 60604
FAX (312)886-1564

(Springfield Office)
320 W Washington St.
Stop 1005SPD
Springfield, IL 62701
FAX (217)527-6332

Indiana
(Indianapolis Office)
Box 44687, Stop 11
Indianapolis, IN 46244
or
575 N Pennsylvania St,
Stop 11
Indianapolis, IN 46204
FAX (317)226-6222

Iowa
(Des Moines Office)
210 Walnut St, Stop 1005
Des Moines, IA 50309
FAX (515)284-6645

Kansas
(Wichita Office)
271 W. 3rd St., North,
Stop 1005-WIC
Wichita, KS 67202
FAX (316)352-7212

Kentucky
(Louisville Office)
600 Dr MLK Jr Pl.
Federal Bldg, Room 363
Louisville, KY 40202
FAX (502)582-6463

Louisiana
(New Orleans Office)
600 South Maestri Place,
Stop 12
New Orleans, LA 70130
FAX (504)558-3250

Maine
(Augusta Office)
68 Sewall St., Stop 1010
Augusta, ME 04330
FAX (207)622-8458

Maryland
(Baltimore Office)
Box 1553, Rm 620A
Baltimore, MD 21203
or
31 Hopkins Plaza, Rm 620A
Baltimore, MD 21201
FAX (410)962-9340

Massachusetts
(Boston Office)
JFK Box 9112
Boston, MA 02203
FAX (617)565-4959

Michigan
(Detroit Office)
Box 330500, Stop 7
Detroit, MI 48232
or
McNamara Federal Bldg
477 Michigan Ave.
Rm 2492
Detroit, MI 48226
FAX (313)226-3502

Minnesota
(St. Paul Office)
316 North Robert St.
Stop 1005
St. Paul, MN 55101
FAX (612)290-4236

Mississippi
(Jackson Office)
100 W. Capitol St., Stop 31
Jackson, MS 39269
FAX (601)965-5251

Missouri
(St. Louis Office)
Box 66776, Stop 1005-STL
St. Louis, MO 63166
or
Robert A. Young Bldg
1222 Spruce Street
Stop 1005-STL
St. Louis, MO 63103
FAX (314)539-2362

Montana
(Helena Office)
Federal Bldg,
301 S. Park
Helena, MT 59626
FAX (406)441-1035

Nebraska
(Omaha Office)
106 S 15th St.
Stop 1005-OMA
Omaha, NE 68102
FAX (402)221-3051

Nevada
(Las Vegas Office)
4750 West Oakey Blvd, Rm 303
Las Vegas, NV 89102
FAX (702)455-1216

New Hampshire
(Portsmouth Office)
Box 720
Portsmouth, NH 03802
or
Federal Office Bldg,
80 Daniel St
Portsmouth, NH 03801
FAX (603)433-0739

New Jersey
(Newark Office)
Box 1143
Newark, NJ 07102
or
970 Broad St.,
Newark, NJ 07102
FAX (973)645-3323

New Mexico
(Albuquerque Office)
5338 Montgomery Blvd.,
NE, Stop 1005 ALB
Albuquerque, NM 87109
FAX (505)837-5519

New Jersey
(Newark Office)
Box 1143
Newark, NJ 07102
or
970 Broad St.,
Newark, NJ 07102
FAX (973)645-3323

New Mexico
(Albuquerque Office)
5338 Montgomery Blvd.,
NE, Stop 1005 ALB
Albuquerque, NM 87109
FAX (505)837-5519

New York
(Albany Office)
Leo O'Brien Federal Bldg,
Rm 617
Clinton Ave. & N. Pearl St.
Albany, NY 12207
FAX (518)431-4697

(Brooklyn Office)
GPO Box R
Brooklyn, NY 11202
or
10 Metro Tech Center
625 Fulton St.,
Brooklyn, NY 11201
FAX (718)488-3100

(Buffalo Office)
Box 500, Niagara Square Station
Buffalo, NY 14201
or
Thaddeus J. Dulski FOB,
111 W. Huron St.,
Buffalo, NY 14202
FAX (716)551-5473

(Manhattan Office)
Box 408
Church St Station
New York, NY 10008
or
290 Broadway, 7th Floor
New York, NY 10007
FAX (212)436-1900

North Carolina
(Greensboro Office)
320 Federal Place, Rm 125
Greensboro, NC 27401
FAX (910)378-2495

North Dakota
(Fargo Office)
Box 8
Fargo, ND 58107
or
657 2nd Ave, N.
Stop 1005-FAR
Fargo, ND 58102
FAX (701)239-5104

Ohio
(Cincinnati Office)
550 Main St, Rm 7010
Cincinnati, OH 45202
FAX (513)684-6417

Ohio
(Cincinnati Office)
550 Main St, Rm 7010
Cincinnati, OH 45202
FAX (513)684-6417

(Cleveland Office)
Box 99709
Cleveland, OH 44199
or
1240 E Ninth St.,
Cleveland, OH 44199
FAX (216)522-2947

Oklahoma
(Oklahoma City Office)
55 N. Robinson, Stop 1005OKC
Oklahoma City, OK 73102
FAX (405)297-4056

Oregon
(Portland Office)
1220 SW 3rd, Stop O-405
Portland, OR 97204
FAX (503)326-5453

Pennsylvania
(Philadelphia Office)
Box 12010
Philadelphia, PA 19106
or
600 Arch St, Rm 7214
Philadelphia, PA 19106
FAX (215)597-7341

(Pittsburgh Office)
Box 705
Pittsburgh, PA 15230
or
1000 Liberty Ave., Rm 1102
Pittsburgh, PA 15222
FAX (412)395-4769

Rhode Island
(Providence Office)
380 Westminster St.,
Providence, RI 02903
FAX (401)528-4312

South Carolina
(Columbia Office)
1835 Assembly St, Rm 571,
MDP 03
Columbia, SC 29201
FAX (803)253-3910

South Dakota
(Aberdeen Office)
115 4th Ave. Southeast,
Stop 1005-ABE
Aberdeen SD 57401
FAX (605)226-7270

Tennessee
(Nashville Office)
Box 1107 (Stop 22)
Nashville, TN 37202
or
801 Broadway, Stop 22
Nashville, TN 37203
FAX (615)736-7489

Texas
(Austin Office)
300 E 8th St., Stop 1005-AUS
Austin, TX 78701
FAX (512)499-5687

(Dallas Office)
1100 Commerce St.,
MC1005DAL
Dallas, TX 75242
FAX (214)767-0040

(Houston Office)
1919 Smith St.
Stop 1005-HOU
Houston, TX 77002
FAX (713)209-3708

Utah
(Salt Lake City Office)
50 South 200 East,
MS1005
Salt Lake City, UT 84111
FAX (801)779-6957

Vermont
(Burlington Office)
Courthouse Plaza
199 Main St.,
Burlington, VT 05401
FAX (802)860-2006

Virginia
(Richmond Office)
Box 10113, Rm 5502
Richmond, VA 23240
or
400 North 8th St
Richmond, VA 23240
FAX (804)771-2008

Washington
(Seattle Office)
915 2nd Ave Stop W-405
Seattle, WA 98174
FAX (206)220-6047

West Virginia
(Parkersburg Office)
Box 1040, Rm 1004
Parkersburg, WV 26102
or
425 Juliana St.
Parkersburg, WV 26101
FAX (304)420-6682

Wisconsin
(Milwaukee Office)
310 West Wisconsin Ave.
Rm M-28, Stop 1005-MIL
Milwaukee, WI 53203
FAX (414)297-3362

Wyoming
(Cheyenne Office)
5353 Yellowstone Rd., Rm 206A
Cheyenne, WY 82009
FAX (307)633-0811

Taxpayers Living Abroad or in US Territories

(A/C International)
Box 4817, L'Enfant Plaza Station
Washington, DC 20224
or
950 L'Enfant Plaza, SW
Washington, DC 20224
FAX (202)874-1752

UNITED STATES COURT

(FIRST)	(MIDDLE)	(LAST)

PLEASE TYPE OR PRINT)   Petitioner(s)

V.

COMMISSIONER OF INTERNAL REVENUE
                    Respondent   Docket No.

PETITION

1. Petitioner(s) disagree(s) with the tax deficiency(ies) for the year(s)_____
as set forth in the NOTICE OF DEFICIENCY dated , _____ A COPY OF WHICH
IS ATTACHED. The notice was issued by the Office of the Internal Revenue Service at

_____
                    (CITY AND STATE)

2. Petitioner(s) taxpayer identification (e.g. social security) number(s) is (are)

_____

3. Petitioner(s) disputes(s) the following:

Year	Amount of Deficiency Disputed	Addition to Tax (Penalty) if any, Disputed	Amount Over- payment Claimed
_____	_____	_____	_____
_____	_____	_____	_____
_____	_____	_____	_____

4. Set forth those adjustments, i.e. changes, in NOTICE OF DEFICIENCY with which you disagree and why you disagree.

_____
_____
_____
_____
_____
_____
_____
_____

Petitioner(s) request(s) that this case be conducted under the "small tax case" procedures to provide the taxpayer(s) with an informal, prompt and inexpensive hearing. A decision in a "small tax case" is final and cannot be appealed to a Court of Appeals by the Internal Revenue Service or the Petitioner(s). If you do not want this case conducted as a "small tax case" place an "X" in the following box.

SIGNATURE OF PETITIONER	DATE	(PRINT) PRESENT ADDRESS-STREET
		CITY STATE ZIP CODE ( ) AREA CODE TELEPHONE NO.

SIGNATURE OF PETITIONER (SPOUSE)	DATE	(PRINT) PRESENT ADDRESS-STREET
		CITY STATE ZIP CODE ( ) AREA CODE TELEPHONE NO.

SIGNATURE, NAME ADDRESS, TELEPHONE NO., AND TAX COURT BAR NUMBER OF COUNSEL, IF RETAINED BY PETITIONER(S)

T.C. FORM 2 (REV 4/92)

UNITED STATES TAX COURT

. . . .)
                             Petitioner(s))
)
)
) Docket No.
                       v.)
)
)
Commissioner of Internal Revenue,)
                               Respondent)
)

DESIGNATION OF PLACE OF TRIAL

Petitioner(s) hereby designate(s) . . . .

                                              City and State

as the place of trial of this case.

. . . .
Signature of Petitioner or Counsel

Date: . . . . 19 . . . . . .

ELECTION OF SMALL TAX CASE PROCEDURE AND PREPARATION OF PETITIONS

ADDRESS ALL MAIL TO:

United States Tax Court
400 Second Street, NW
Washington, DC 20217

Introduction

Congress has provided for a simple and informal procedure in the United States Tax Court where taxpayers may dispute a deficiency in taxes claimed by the Commissioner of Internal Revenue in his *Notice of Deficiency*. This simplified procedure is limited to those cases where the amount in dispute is $10,000 or less and provides for their early trial in the United States Tax Court.

The United States Tax Court is a court of record and is not connected in any way with the Internal Revenue Service. The Tax Court decides whether a tax deficiency claimed by the Commissioner of Internal Revenue is correct.

If a *Notice of Deficiency* has been issued in which the amount of the deficiency, and additions to tax, if any, or the part of it you wish to dispute, is $10,000 or less (and you are not claiming an overpayment of more than $10,000) for any one year, you may use the simplified procedure for small tax cases described in this pamphlet.

The following instructions tell you how to proceed and how to complete the required forms. Use the Quick Checklist on page 8 to be sure you have been given all the needed information.

You may file a petition with the Tax Court only after the Commissioner of Internal Revenue has sent you a *Notice of Deficiency*, sometimes called a "90-day letter." The *Notice of Deficiency* shows the year and the amount of any deficiency determined by him and states that it is a *Notice of Deficiency*. It will tell you that the deficiency determined by the Commissioner of Internal Revenue will be assessed against you after 90 days from the date of *mailing* of the letter unless within that period of time you file a petition with the United States Tax Court. The date shown on the *Notice of Deficiency* is the date the notice was mailed to you.

Bringing a Case in the Tax Court

You may begin a case in the United States Tax Court by paying a filing fee and filing a proper petition with the Court in Washington, D.C. You must file your petition not later than 90 days after the *Notice of Deficiency* was mailed to you. (150 days if the notice is addressed to a person outside the United States.) Saturdays, Sundays, or local holidays in the District of Columbia are not counted as the last day. The date shown on the *Notice of Deficiency* is the date the notice was mailed to you.

To be timely filed, your petition must actually be received by the Court within the 90-day period, or received in an envelope addressed to the United States Tax Court, 400 Second Street, NW, Washington, DC 20217 with a United States postmark showing a legible date within the 90-day period. If your petition is even 1 day late, your case must be dismissed for late filing because the law allows the Court to hear only those cases for which a petition is filed within the 90-day period. Please note that the period is 90 days and not 3 months.

For example, for a *Notice of Deficiency* mailed on April 10, 1990, the last day for delivering or mailing a petition would be July 9, 1990—90 days later. It would not be July 10, 1990—3 months later. By filing your petition early, you will ensure your right to dispute in the Tax Court the claim made against you by the Commissioner of Internal Revenue.

Small Tax Case Petition Form

A simple printed form—Petition, Form 2—is supplied by the Clerk of the Court, United States Tax Court, 400 Second Street, NW, Washington, DC 20217. When completing the form, fill in all the information asked for. The information you must give (though not in this order) is: (1) the years for which the Commissioner of Internal Revenue claims a tax deficiency, (2) the disputed dollar amount of the deficiency for each year, (3) the dollar amount of any tax overpayment you are claiming for each deficiency year, (4) the city and state where the office of Internal Revenue is located, (5) your social security number (or other taxpayer identification number, if any), (6) a short statement of any change the Internal Revenue Service wants to make in your tax return that you do not agree with, and (7) why you do not agree with the change . Only the person or persons to whom the *Notice of Deficiency* is addressed may properly begin a case. If the *Notice of Deficiency* is addressed to only one person, only that person should enter his or her name in the blank space above the word "Petitioner[s]"; and sign and date the form. If the *Notice of Deficiency* is addressed to more than one person and both wish to dispute the deficiency then both names should be entered in the blank space above the word "Petitioner[s]"; and both should sign and date the form. Also show your present address and telephone number in the places indicated, and be sure to attach a complete copy of your *Notice of Deficiency* to the original and each copy of the petition you file. You should not attach anything else to the petition.

Electing the Small Tax Case Procedure

If your case meets the $10,000 test, you may elect to have your case handled as a small tax case under the simple, informal procedure. To do this leave blank the box at the end of your Petition, Form 2.

Filing Fee and Case Identification

The fee for filing a petition is $60. If you are unable to pay the filing fee you may request the Court waive the fee. You must give reason as to why you are unable to pay the fee. The fee is payable when you file your petition. When you file your petition, the Clerk of the Court will assign to your case a special number, called a docket number . That number will be followed by the letter "S" if you select the special procedure. (For example: Docket Number 1627-85S.) Once you know your case's docket number you should put it on all documents or letters that you send to the Court.

Choosing the Place of Trial

You may select from the list below a place of trial in the city nearest you. The cities marked by asterisks (*) are those in which only small tax case trials are heard. In the other cities, both regular and small tax cases are heard. At the top of Form 4 (Designation of Place of Trial) that was sent to you, fill in your name (names of both husband and wife for a joint petition) above the word

"[Petitioner[s]]". Choose the city nearest you in which you would like your trial held and enter it in the space provided on the form. Then, date and sign it and forward it *with your petition* to the clerk of the United States Tax Court.

Places for Hearing Small Tax Cases

Alabama	Louisiana	Oklahoma
Birmingham	New Orleans	Oklahoma City
Mobile	*Shreveport	Oregon
Alaska	Maine	Portland
Anchorage	*Portland	Mississippi
Arizona	Maryland	Jackson
Phoenix	Baltimore	Biloxi
Arkansas	Massachusetts	Pennsylvania
Little Rock	Boston	Philadelphia
California	Michigan	Pittsburgh
*Fresno	Detroit	South Carolina
Los Angeles	Minnesota	Columbia
San Diego	St. Paul	South Dakota
San Francisco	Missouri	*Aberdeen
Colorado	Kansas City	Tennessee
Denver	St. Louis	Knoxville
Connecticut	Montana	Memphis
Hartford	*Billings	Nashville
District of	Helena	Texas
Columbia	Nebraska	Dallas
Washington	Omaha	El Paso
Florida	Nevada	Houston
Jacksonville	Las Vegas	Lubbock
Miami	Reno	San Antonio
*Tallahassee	New Jersey	Utah
Tampa	Newark	Salt Lake

Places for Hearing Small Tax Cases (cont.)

Georgia	New Mexico	City
Atlanta	Albuquerque	Vermont
Hawaii	New York	*Burlington
Honolulu	*Albany	Virginia
Idaho	Buffalo	Richmond
Boise	New York City	*Roanoke
*Pocatello	*Syracuse	Washington
Illinois	Westbury	Seattle
Chicago	North Carolina	Spokane
*Peoria	Winston-Salem	West Virginia
Indiana	North Dakota	Charleston
Indianapolis	*Bismarck	Huntington
Iowa	Ohio	Wisconsin
Des Moines	Cincinnati	Milwaukee
Kansas	Cleveland	Wyoming
*Wichita	Columbus	*Cheyenne
Kentucky		
Louisville		

Mailing Petition and Other Papers

The petition (Form 2) is a four-part form. You must submit to the Court the original and two copies of the petition. You should keep the last copy of the petition for your records. Remember to attach to each copy of the petition submitted to the Court a complete copy of your *Notice of Deficiency.*

You have also received with this booklet a Designation of Place of Trial (Form 4). You should submit an original and two copies to the Court.

You should also enclose a check or money order for your filing fee. Make your check or money order payable to the "Clerk, United States Tax Court."

You have been given an envelope for your use in mailing these various papers to the Court.

After your petition is filed, the Court will send a copy to the lawyer for the Commissioner of Internal Revenue.

Trial Calendar Assignment

Your case will be listed for trial at the next trial session regularly scheduled for the city you chose. Trial sessions will be announced and a notice of trial will be sent to you about 60 days before the trial date. The trial date will be set to give you a hearing as quickly as possible.

Removal of Small Tax Case Designation

At any time before trial the Court, on its own motion or on a motion filed by you or by the Commissioner of Internal Revenue, may revoke the small tax case designation from your case and direct that it be handled as a regular case. After trial but before final decision, the Court may order proceedings as a small tax case discontinued if the disputed deficiency or claimed overpayment will exceed $10,000 and justice requires discontinuance, taking into account the inconvenience and expense for both parties that would result from taking such action.

Informal Trial Procedure

You may represent yourself or you may be represented by anyone you choose who is admitted to practice before the Tax Court. Most petitioners in small tax cases represent themselves. The trial will be conducted in an orderly manner, as simply as possible. Any evidence you offer which the Court thinks will have value as proof of your claim will be admissible.

If you have receipts or other papers or documents which support your claim, you should bring them with you when you come to Court for trial. The Court will try to help you develop the facts in your case through your testimony and that of other witnesses, and any receipts, papers, or documents which you bring with you to the trial.

Any information or documents which you have previously supplied to the Internal Revenue Service are not available to the Court and thus you must be prepared to present your oral information as testimony and to have available any necessary documents to be received in evidence at the trial. If you need documents which you have given to the Internal Revenue Service to support your claim, you should ask the Government lawyer to bring them to court for the trial of your case so that you can offer them in evidence as proof of your claim. Where original documents are lost or destroyed you may offer copies, if you have them.

Your testimony and that of any other witness will be recorded and you may order and pay for a transcript of the testimony if you wish. After you and any other witnesses have testified, you may argue your case orally.

Finality of Decision

If you elect to have your case tried as a small tax case under the provisions of section 7463 of the Internal Revenue

Code, the decision of the Tax Court is final and cannot be appealed. Thus, if the decision is in your favor, in whole or in part, the Government cannot appeal to a higher court to change the decision. On the other hand, if the Tax Court decides the deficiency claimed by the Commissioner of Internal Revenue is correct, in whole or in part, you cannot appeal.

Quick Checklist

(When you file your petition, be sure to include all the following information and attachments required.)

(1) Your full name (both names if the *Notice of Deficiency* was addressed to both and both wish to dispute the deficiency).

(2) The years of the claimed deficiencies.

(3) The name of the city and state from which the Internal Revenue Service sent your *Notice of Deficiency*

(4) Your social security or other taxpayer identification number .

(5) (a) The year; (b) amount of the disputed deficiency; (c) amount of any disputed addition to tax (additional amount or penalty); and (d) for an overpayment, the amount claimed.

(6) A statement of the Internal Revenue Service's proposed changes with which you do not agree.

(7) Your reasons for disagreement with the proposed changes.

(8) Your signature, date, present address, and telephone number at the bottom of the petition.

(9) Your spouse's signature, date, present address, and telephone number if you are filing a joint petition.

(10) In your mailing to the Clerk of the Court include: (a) The original and two copies of your petition with a complete copy of your *Notice of Deficiency* attached to the original and each copy; (b) your filing fee in the form of a check or money order, payable to "Clerk, United States Tax Court"; and (c) your designation, Form 4, showing in which city you wish your case to be tried.

Index

CATALOG

...more from nolo.com

PRICE   CODE

BUSINESS

▣ Book with disk
⊙ Book with CD-ROM

CALL 800-992-6656 OR USE THE ORDER FORM IN THE BACK OF THE BOOK

	PRICE	CODE
Nolo's California Quick Corp (Quick & Legal Series)	$19.95	QINC
⊙ Open Your California Business in 24 Hours (Book w/CD-ROM)	$24.95	OPEN
▣ The Partnership Book: How to Write a Partnership Agreement (Book w/Disk—PC)	$34.95	PART
Sexual Harassment on the Job	$18.95	HARS
Starting & Running a Successful Newsletter or Magazine	$24.95	MAG
Take Charge of Your Workers' Compensation Claim (California Edition)	$29.95	WORK
Tax Savvy for Small Business	$29.95	SAVVY
Trademark: Legal Care for Your Business and Product Name	$34.95	TRD
Wage Slave No More: Law & Taxes for the Self-Employed	$24.95	WAGE
Your Rights in the Workplace	$21.95	YRW

CONSUMER

	PRICE	CODE
Fed Up with the Legal System: What's Wrong & How to Fix It	$9.95	LEG
How to Win Your Personal Injury Claim	$26.95	PICL
Nolo's Everyday Law Book	$24.95	EVL
Nolo's Pocket Guide to California Law	$12.95	CLAW
Trouble-Free Travel...And What to Do When Things Go Wrong	$14.95	TRAV

ESTATE PLANNING & PROBATE

	PRICE	CODE
8 Ways to Avoid Probate (Quick & Legal Series)	$15.95	PRO8
9 Ways to Avoid Estate Taxes (Quick & Legal Series)	$22.95	ESTX
How to Probate an Estate (California Edition)	$39.95	PAE
Make Your Own Living Trust	$24.95	LITR
Nolo's Law Form Kit: Wills	$14.95	KWL
▣ Nolo's Will Book (Book w/Disk—PC)	$29.95	SWIL
Plan Your Estate	$24.95	NEST
Quick & Legal Will Book (Quick & Legal Series)	$15.95	QUIC

FAMILY MATTERS

	PRICE	CODE
Child Custody: Building Parenting Agreements That Work	$26.95	CUST
The Complete IEP Guide	$24.95	IEP
Divorce & Money: How to Make the Best Financial Decisions During Divorce	$26.95	DIMO
Do Your Own Divorce in Oregon	$19.95	ODIV
Get a Life: You Don't Need a Million to Retire Well	$18.95	LIFE

▣ Book with disk

⊙ Book with CD-ROM

CALL 800-992-6656 OR USE THE ORDER FORM IN THE BACK OF THE BOOK

	PRICE	CODE
The Guardianship Book (California Edition)	$39.95	GB
How to Adopt Your Stepchild in California	$34.95	ADOP
How to Raise or Lower Child Support in California (Quick & Legal Series)	$19.95	CHLD
A Legal Guide for Lesbian and Gay Couples	$25.95	LG
The Living Together Kit	$29.95	LTK
Nolo's Pocket Guide to Family Law	$14.95	FLD
Using Divorce Mediation: Save Your Money & Your Sanity	$21.95	UDMD

GOING TO COURT

	PRICE	CODE
Beta Your Ticket: Go To Court and Win! (National Edition)	$19.95	BEYT
Collect Your Court Judgment (California Edition)	$29.95	JUDG
The Criminal Law Handbook: Know Your Rights, Survive the System	$24.95	KYR
Everybody's Guide to Small Claims Court (National Edition)	$18.95	NSCC
Everybody's Guide to Small Claims Court in California	$18.95	CSCC
Fight Your Ticket ... and Win! (California Edition)	$19.95	FYT
How to Change Your Name in California	$34.95	NAME
How to Mediate Your Dispute	$18.95	MEDI
How to Seal Your Juvenile & Criminal Records (California Edition)	$24.95	CRIM
How to Sue For Up to $25,000...and Win!	$29.95	MUNI
Mad at Your Lawyer	$21.95	MAD
Represent Yourself in Court: How to Prepare & Try a Winning Case	$29.95	RYC

HOMEOWNERS, LANDLORDS & TENANTS

		PRICE	CODE
▣	Contractors' and Homeowners' Guide to Mechanics' Liens (Book w/Disk—PC)	$39.95	MIEN
	The Deeds Book (California Edition)	$24.95	DEED
	Dog Law	$14.95	DOG
▣	Every Landlord's Legal Guide (National Edition, Book w/Disk—PC)	$34.95	ELLI
	Every Tenant's Legal Guide	$26.95	EVTEN
	For Sale by Owner in California	$24.95	FSBO
	How to Buy a House in California	$24.95	BHCA
	The Landlord's Law Book, Vol. 1: Rights & Responsibilities (California Edition)	$34.95	LBRT
	The Landlord's Law Book, Vol. 2: Evictions (California Edition)	$34.95	LBEV
	Leases & Rental Agreements (Quick & Legal Series)	$18.95	LEAR
	Neighbor Law: Fences, Trees, Boundaries & Noise	$17.95	NEI

▣ Book with disk
◉ Book with CD-ROM

	PRICE	CODE
Renters' Rights (National Edition—Quick & Legal Series))	$15.95	RENT
Stop Foreclosure Now in California	$29.95	CLOS
Tenants' Rights (California Edition)	$21.95	CTEN

HUMOR

	PRICE	CODE
29 Reasons Not to Go to Law School	$9.95	29R
Poetic Justice	$9.95	PJ

IMMIGRATION

	PRICE	CODE
How to Get a Green Card: Legal Ways to Stay in the U.S.A.	$24.95	GRN
U.S. Immigration Made Easy	$44.95	IMEZ

MONEY MATTERS

		PRICE	CODE
▣	101 Law Forms for Personal Use (Quick & Legal Series, Book w/disk—PC)	$24.95	SPOT
	Bankruptcy: Is It the Right Solution to Your Debt Problems? (Quick & Legal Series)	$15.95	BRS
	Chapter 13 Bankruptcy: Repay Your Debts	$29.95	CH13
	Credit Repair (Quick & Legal Series)	$15.95	CREP
▣	The Financial Power of Attorney Workbook (Book w/disk—PC)	$24.95	FINPOA
	How to File for Chapter 7 Bankruptcy	$26.95	HFB
	IRAs, 401(k)s & Other Retirement Plans: Taking Your Money Out	$21.95	RET
	Money Troubles: Legal Strategies to Cope With Your Debts	$19.95	MT
	Nolo's Law Form Kit: Personal Bankruptcy	$16.95	KBNK
	Stand Up to the IRS	$24.95	SIRS
	Take Control of Your Student Loans	$19.95	SLOAN

PATENTS AND COPYRIGHTS

		PRICE	CODE
▣	The Copyright Handbook: How to Protect and Use Written Works (Book w/disk—PC)	$29.95	COHA
	Copyright Your Software	$24.95	CYS
	How to Make Patent Drawings Yourself	$29.95	DRAW
	The Inventor's Notebook	$19.95	INOT
▣	License Your Invention (Book w/Disk—PC)	$39.95	LICE
	Patent, Copyright & Trademark	$24.95	PCTM
	Patent It Yourself	$46.95	PAT

▣ Book with disk

◉ Book with CD-ROM

	PRICE	CODE
Patent Searching Made Easy	$24.95	PATSE
Software Development: A Legal Guide (Book with CD-ROM)	$44.95	SFT

RESEARCH & REFERENCE

	PRICE	CODE
⊙ Government on the Net (Book w/CD-ROM—Windows/Macintosh)	$39.95	GONE
⊙ Law on the Net (Book w/CD-ROM—Windows/Macintosh)	$39.95	LAWN
Legal Research: How to Find & Understand the Law	$24.95	LRES
Legal Research Made Easy (Video)	$89.95	LRME
⊙ Legal Research Online & in the Library (Book w/CD-ROM—Windows/Macintosh)........	$39.95	LRO

SENIORS

	PRICE	CODE
Beat the Nursing Home Trap	$21.95	ELD
The Conservatorship Book (California Edition)...	$44.95	CNSV
Social Security, Medicare & Pensions	$21.95	SOA

SOFTWARE

Call or check our website at www.nolo.com for special discounts on Software!

	PRICE	CODE
⊙ LeaseWriter CD—Windows/Macintosh	$99.95	LWD1
⊙ Living Trust Maker CD—Windows/Macintosh	$79.95	LTD2
⊙ Small Business Legal Pro 3 CD—Windows/Macintosh	$79.95	SBCD3
⊙ Personal RecordKeeper 5.0 CD—Windows/Macintosh	$59.95	RKD5
⊙ Patent It Yourself CD—Windows	$229.95	PPC12
⊙ WillMaker 7.0 CD—Windows/Macintosh	$69.95	WMD7

Special Upgrade Offer

Get 35% off the latest edition off your Nolo book

It's important to have the most current legal information. Because laws and legal procedures change often, we update our books regularly. To help keep you up-to-date we are extending this special upgrade offer. Cut out and mail the title portion of the cover of your old Nolo book and we'll give you 35% off the retail price of the NEW EDITION of that book when you purchase directly from us. For more information call us at 1-800-992-6656. This offer is to individuals only.

▣ Book with disk
⊙ Book with CD-ROM

ORDER FORM

Code	Quantity	Title	Unit price	Total
		Subtotal		
		California residents add Sales Tax		
		Basic Shipping ($3.95)		
		UPS RUSH delivery $8.00–any size order*		
		TOTAL		

Name

Address

(UPS to street address, Priority Mail to P.O. boxes)

* Delivered in 3 business days from receipt of S.F. Bay Area use regular shipping. order.

FOR FASTER SERVICE, USE YOUR CREDIT CARD & OUR TOLL-FREE NUMBERS

Order 24 hours a day   1-800-992-6656
Fax your order   1-800-645-0895
Online   www.nolo.com

METHOD OF PAYMENT

☐ Check enclosed

☐ VISA   ☐ MasterCard   ☐ Discover Card   ☐ American Express

Account #   Expiration Date

Authorizing Signature

Daytime Phone

PRICES SUBJECT TO CHANGE.

VISIT OUR STORE   VISIT US ONLINE

You'll find our complete line of books and software, all at a discount.

950 Parker Street
Berkeley, CA 94710
1-510-704-2248

on the Internet

www.nolo.com

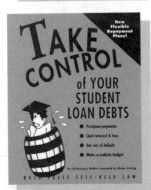

Take 2 minutes & Give us your 2 cents

Your comments make a big difference in the development and revision of Nolo books and software. Please take a few minutes and register your Nolo product—and your comments—with us. Not only will your input make a difference, you'll receive special offers available only to registered owners of Nolo products on our newest books and software. Register now by:

PHONE
1-800-992-6656

FAX
1-800-645-0895

EMAIL
cs@nolo.com

or **MAIL** us
this registration card

REMEMBER:
Little publishers have big ears. We really listen to you.

- fold here -

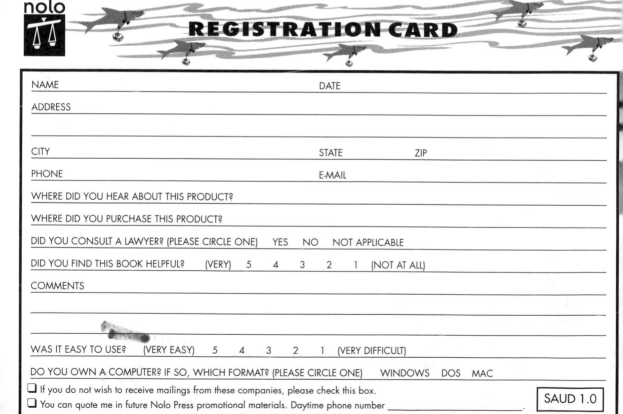

nolo

REGISTRATION CARD

NAME _____ DATE _____

ADDRESS _____

_____

CITY _____ STATE _____ ZIP _____

PHONE _____ E-MAIL _____

WHERE DID YOU HEAR ABOUT THIS PRODUCT? _____

WHERE DID YOU PURCHASE THIS PRODUCT? _____

DID YOU CONSULT A LAWYER? (PLEASE CIRCLE ONE)   YES   NO   NOT APPLICABLE

DID YOU FIND THIS BOOK HELPFUL?   (VERY)   5   4   3   2   1   (NOT AT ALL)

COMMENTS _____

_____

_____

WAS IT EASY TO USE?   (VERY EASY)   5   4   3   2   1   (VERY DIFFICULT)

DO YOU OWN A COMPUTER? IF SO, WHICH FORMAT? (PLEASE CIRCLE ONE)   WINDOWS   DOS   MAC

☐ If you do not wish to receive mailings from these companies, please check this box.

☐ You can quote me in future Nolo Press promotional materials. Daytime phone number _____

SAUD 1.0

NOLO IN THE NEWS

"Nolo helps lay people perform legal tasks without the aid—or fees—of lawyers."

—USA TODAY

Nolo books are ..."written in plain language, free of legal mumbo jumbo, and spiced with witty personal observations."

—ASSOCIATED PRESS

"...Nolo publications...guide people simply through the how, when, where and why of law."

—WASHINGTON POST

"Increasingly, people who are not lawyers are performing tasks usually regarded as legal work... And consumers, using books like Nolo's, do routine legal work themselves."

—NEW YORK TIMES

"...All of [Nolo's] books are easy-to-understand, are updated regularly, provide pull-out forms...and are often quite moving in their sense of compassion for the struggles of the lay reader."

—SAN FRANCISCO CHRONICLE

fold here

- -

nolo.com
950 Parker Street
Berkeley, CA 94710-9867

Attn: | **SAUD 1.0**